KT-439-161

THE TIMES
HIGHER
EDUCATION SUPPLEMENT

2000 TIPS
for Lecturers

edited by PHIL RACE

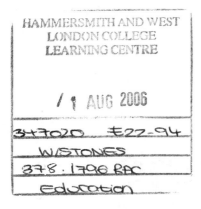
First published in 1999
Reprinted in 2001

Kogan Page Limited
120 Pentonville Road
London
N1 9JN
UK

Stylus Publishing Limited
22883 Quicksilver Drive
Sterling
VA 20166
USA

The views expressed in this book are those of the author and are not necessarily the same as those of *The Times Higher Education Supplement*.

British Library Cataloguing in Publication Data

A CIP record for this book is available from the British Library.

ISBN 0 7494 3046 X

Typeset by Kogan Page
Printed and bound by Bell and Bain Limited, Glasgow

Contents

Chapter 4 Designing and using learning resources   63

Chapter 5 Assessment   111

Chapter 6 Feedback, evaluation and external scrutiny 178

Chapter 7 Looking after yourself 201

Chapter 8 Getting published 221

Foreword

The Times Higher Education Supplement is delighted to be associated with this essential handbook.

Lecturers are the lifeblood of universities, without whom research would remain locked away in rarely read papers and lab results, and students would be unenlightened. Lately, government policy – prompted by public pressure – has appeared more ready to recognize the true importance of teaching in higher education, but this has brought new emphasis on training, assessment and professionalism, which are each adding to the increasing pressure on academics' time.

With students ever more numerous and more demanding as their courses cost them more; as new technologies require new skills; and as quality assessments take up ever more time and administrative effort, teachers in further and higher education need all the help they can get. We hope this handbook for lecturers will help save time and will prove a useful source of advice, inspiration and practical suggestions. Many will adapt and add to the ideas in *2000 Tips for Lecturers* acccording to their personal experience. At *The Times Higher Education Supplement* we hope new ideas will be shared with our readers. For so complex and demanding a job, even 2000 tips can only be a start.

Auriol Stevens
Editor, **The Times Higher Education Supplement**

Preface

It has been both pleasurable, and salutary, to revisit the content of several volumes of the Kogan Page '500 Tips' series, looking for the most important 2,000 practical suggestions to offer to lecturers at the turn of the millennium.

This book is for lecturers. That includes lecturers, new and experienced, in universities. Equally, this selection of suggestions is designed to embrace most parts of the work of lecturers in other parts of tertiary education systems, such as Further Education institutions in the UK, Polytechnics in New Zealand and elsewhere, and Community Colleges in North America.

Teaching is one of the most complex processes known to humankind, and there is a vast body of research on the theories and models that underpin successful teaching, learning and assessment. A 'hints and tips' approach should not replace the need for good practice to be informed by the findings from such research. It remains the case that the majority of practitioners in tertiary education are extremely busy people, and often find it difficult to give the time and the energy to immerse themselves fully into studying at first hand this body of research. Therefore, it can be argued that practical suggestions have their place in:

- supporting busy lecturers in balancing the various demands made on them;
- helping them to benefit from some of the experience around them;
- assisting them in their continuing professional development and reflective practice aspirations;
- helping them to carry out their work without reinventing too many wheels.

Each reader of this book will bring his or her own particular strengths and weaknesses. Do not expect, therefore, that all 2,000 of the suggestions in this book will be directly relevant to your own work! You may well be implementing, or exceeding, many of the suggestions in this book. It is in those areas of your work where the suggestions here can give you some positive ideas that you can act on straightaway that the real value of this collection should emerge.

The present collection contains a large number of new tips, and a thorough reworking and reprioritizing of what have been found to be the most useful parts of many of the separate '500s'. All of the '500s' authors and co-authors have given their support to the design and production of this volume. In particular, the work of the following people is represented in this book:

- Brenda Smith (co-author with Sally Brown and myself of *500 Tips on Assessment* and *500 Tips on Quality Enhancement*);
- David Anderson (co-author of *500 Tips for Further and Continuing Education Lecturers*), who also provided valuable help in updating several of the sections;
- Abby Day (co-author with Sally Brown, Dolores Black and myself of *500 Tips on Getting Published* and with John Peters and myself of *500 Tips for Learning Organisations*); and
- Steve McDowell (co-author with myself of *500 Computing Tips for Trainers*).

Sally Brown is co-author of most of the source materials, and some of the new material. The collection also contains significant extracts from my own *500 Tips on Open and Flexible Learning*.

At the end of the day, however, someone had to take the decision on what could be included in this '2000 Tips' collection, where there was a tight word-limit to make it possible for the book to be published at an affordable price. The blame for decisions about content and balance must rest firmly on my shoulders!

My earnest hope is that all lecturers who see this book will find in it some useful things they can try out straightaway, and some more that they can start to think about for the future.

Phil Race
April 1999

Chapter 1

Towards student-centred learning

Teaching-learning situations and processes
1. *Different teaching-learning situations*
2. *Exploring learning processes*
3. *Helping students to learn how they learn*
4. *Designing a new programme*
5. *Developing students' key skills*

Making the most of learning outcomes
6. *Why use learning outcomes?*
7. *Where can learning outcomes be useful to students?*
8. *Designing and using learning outcomes*

Communications and information technologies
9. *Using communications and information technologies*

This chapter introduces very briefly some of the themes that pervade most of the rest of this collection of suggestions for lecturers.

The range of **teaching-learning processes** practised by lecturers extends far beyond standing up and giving lectures. We start by exploring some of the most common **teaching-learning situations**, and linking these to the learning processes we wish our students to engage in. Some immediate suggestions are then offered regarding curriculum design, and ways in which students' key skills can be deliberately developed through the curriculum.

The next section in this brief chapter is on **learning outcomes**. These too are mentioned throughout the book. There is now increased emphasis that learning outcomes are appropriate, that teaching is designed to help students to achieve them, and that assessment instruments and processes really set out to measure students' achievement of such outcomes. It has never been more important to express learning outcomes well right from the outset.

The intended learning outcomes are the most important starting-point for any teaching-learning programme. Learning outcomes give details of syllabus content. They can be expressed in terms of the objectives that students should be able to *show* they have achieved, in terms of knowledge, understanding, skills and even attitudes. They are written as descriptors of ways that students will be expected to demonstrate the results of their learning. The links between learning outcomes and assessment criteria need to be clear and direct. Learning outcomes indicate the standards of courses and modules, and are spotlighted in quality review procedures.

This chapter ends with a short overview of the use, in student-centred ways, of **communications and information technologies**. This overview is intended to provide headlines only, and introduces a theme that recurs in much more detail in several parts of this book.

1. Different teaching-learning situations

You won't always be able to choose how best to deliver a particular part of the curriculum. When you do have such an opportunity (for example, when planning a new course or curriculum element, or when revalidating existing provision), you may find it useful to think about a range of possibilities. Ideally, you should seek to explore several different methodologies for the delivery of any element of the curriculum, but each alternative will have its own advantages and drawbacks, both economically and pedagogically:

- **Full-time taught courses, lecture based.** These remain the most usual provision in most higher education institutions, and have potential benefits associated with social interaction between students, and between lecturers and students. Several parts of this book offer advice, for example, on preparing lectures and designing assessment to match such course delivery.

- **Part-time taught courses.** Here there may be limited opportunity for social interaction among students, but teaching may be similar or common to that in full-time provision.

- **Work-based training programmes.** These are essentially teaching-learning situations that involve students having placements arranged in a suitable employment location for a given period of time. The relevance of the content of the training to the students' overall needs is more easily guaranteed.

- **Open, flexible and distance learning programmes.** These cover situations where students work through specifically designed self-study materials (often print-based) on their own. This may be alongside conventional college-based delivery, or at a distance from the institution, at times and places of their own choosing, and at their own pace. The institution provides tutorial support, counselling and assessment.

- **Resource-based learning.** This includes learning workshops, open access and drop-in centres where the institution offers tuition, counselling and learning support plus access to materials and equipment. The materials may be print-based, computer-based or multimedia in nature, and there may be opportunities for group and individual contact with lecturers, as well as access to college-based assessment provision.

- **Online learning.** This methodology includes computer-based learning, which may be college-based or done at networked computer facilities at the students' home or workplace locations. Tutorial support and learning materials are networked to the computer terminals where students study, and their study times can be varied to suit their individual requirements. Virtual or real-time group working is also possible along with one-to-one lecturer contact.

- **Collaborative learning.** This methodology is used when it is intended that students work together in small groups for significant parts of their learning. It can be arranged as a college-based process, or for students to undertake in the actual situations they are learning about.

- **Independent study pathways.** These are particular elements of the curriculum which individual students are able to choose or adapt to their particular needs or requirements. They may involve using print-based or computer-based learning resource materials, on or off the college campus. By definition they are individualized but will normally involve lecturer contact and support.

2. Exploring learning processes

One of the most important factors that predetermines students' success in learning is confidence. We need to give our students every chance to develop this confidence, and one of the best ways of us helping them to do this is to assist them to gain greater ownership of, and control over, the processes they apply during their learning:

- **Help students to want to learn.** They may need to be helped to increase their motivation by showing them the benefits they will gain from the achievement of their intended learning outcomes. When possible, enhance their motivation by making learning fun, interesting and rewarding. Don't mistake lack of confidence for lack of motivation.

- **Needing to learn something can be almost as productive as wanting to learn it.** When students know *why* something will be useful to them, even if they find it difficult, they are more likely to maintain their efforts till they have succeeded.

■ **Provide students with learning-by-doing opportunities.** Most learning happens when students practise things, have a go, and learn by making mistakes and finding out why. Care needs to be taken to ensure that learning-by-doing is focused on practising useful, important things, and not just anything to keep students busy!

■ **Look for ways of giving students as much feedback as is reasonably possible.** Students need to find out how their learning is actually going. Feedback from lecturers is very useful, but lecturers can also facilitate students getting feedback from each other, and from various kinds of learning resource materials. It follows too that feedback must be timely for it to be of optimum use to students.

■ **Help students to set out to make sense of what they are learning.** It is of little value learning things by rote, or becoming able to do things without knowing why or how. Getting students to think about how their learning is happening is one step towards helping them to develop a sense of ownership of their progress. Learning is not just a matter of storing up further knowledge; it is about being able to apply what has been learned, not just to familiar situations but also to new contexts.

■ **Provide students with cues about how they are expected to learn from the ways in which we teach them.** If we simply concentrate on supplying them with information, they are likely simply to try to store this. If we structure our teaching so that they are practising, applying, extending, comparing, contrasting, evaluating, and engaging in other higher-level processes, they are likely to see these processes as central to the ways they should be using for their learning.

■ **Use assessment to drive learning productively.** Students are often quite strategic in structuring their learning to be able to do the best they can in the contexts in which their learning is to be assessed. Assessment formats and instruments can be used to help students to structure their learning effectively, as well as to give them appropriate timescales within which to organize their learning.

■ **Encourage students to learn from each other.** While much can be learned by students working on their own, with handouts, books and learning resource materials, they can also learn a great deal by talking to each other, and attempting tasks and activities jointly.

3. Helping students to learn how they learn

This is the most important thing that human beings ever learn. In an educational institution, it is vital that everyone is fully aware of the natural processes underpinning human learning, so that they can take control of these consciously, and develop them systematically. The following suggestions may help you to keep learning-to-learn uppermost in your teaching, and in your students' approaches to learning:

- **Remind students how long they've been learning to learn.** Ask them to reflect on just how much they actually learned during the first two or three years of life. Remind them that most of this learning they did more or less under their own steam, without any conscious thought about teaching, or even learning. Remind them that they still own the brain that did all of this, and can still use it to learn vast amounts of new knowledge, skills and competences.

- **Ask students about their learning in school.** They will have learned large amounts of information, and will have forgotten most of this! Also, however, they will have learned a great deal about *how* to take in knowledge and information, and will still have this skill.

- **Remind students that they will never stop learning to learn.** Get them to talk about learning to senior people they know, and retired ones too. Ask them what they have learned only recently. Ask them *how* they learned it. Ask them what they found out about themselves while learning it. Then ask them which of these was the most important and most interesting to them.

- **Provide programmes for students to learn about learning.** Training programmes can help students to tune in to the power of their own minds. A good learning facilitator can help students to gain control of the processes by which they learn most efficiently. Many students find it useful to explore how their minds work in the company of other students, and learn from each other's experiences.

- **Provide resources to help students to learn about their own learning.** Not everyone is comfortable attending a training programme about learning to learn. Some students fear that inadequacies or deficiencies may be exposed. Computer-based or print-based packages that help students explore their own learning in the comfort of privacy may be more attractive to such students.

- **Get students asking themselves: 'What did I learn about *myself* when I learned this?'** Learning to learn is closely connected with understanding one's own mind, and one's own preferences and choices.

- **Get students asking: 'What really worked when I learned this?'** The chances are that the factors that made one element of learning successful will be transferable to their next element of learning. There are long words for this, such as 'metacognitive processing', but it's simply about helping students to be looking inwards at what works for them when they learn, and what doesn't.

- **Get students teasing out what slows their learning down.** The more we all know about how the brakes work, the better we can use them only when we need them.

4. Designing a new programme

Designing a new area of curriculum is an exciting but complex task, requiring the integration of a whole range of interdependent elements. The following set of tips is designed to help you do so in a systematic way in sequence. These are most likely to be of use to you if you are (or will be) in the role of course leader for the new programme. Further suggestions about many of the steps listed below are given throughout this book; this list is just a start-up menu:

■ **Identify the market for your programme.** Few new programmes these days are offered to a captive, pre-determined market of potential students. You will need therefore to have good evidence of a real demand for your proposed programme. It will be useful to identify the competition – other institutions offering a similar programme. Can you show that either the market is sufficiently large or that you can offer something very different to attract a sufficient number of students? Your institution will require you to show how your programme will sit within the existing course portfolio.

■ **Clarify the rationale for the new programme.** You need to be sure of your reasons for its particular flavour and its ultimate viability. Can you run it with the human and physical resources you can get? Can you provide for a sufficiently large number of students? Specifically consider: the unique characteristics of the group it is aimed at; the programme's aims, intended learning outcomes, and the qualification or accreditation that it will lead to.

■ **Clarify how it will be costed and funded.** This is a daunting process if it's your first time, and we advise you to gather know-how from other colleagues in your institution who have already planned and implemented a new programme. There may well be formal institutional checklists and guidelines for you to follow.

■ **Decide upon a time frame.** Curriculum design is a complex and time-consuming process. Mistakes are made if the process is rushed. If a programme is to be designed from scratch, sufficient time should be allowed to negotiate and incorporate internal as well as external quality assurance processes. Time is also needed to market the course effectively. Be realistic about a start date!

■ **Expect to become involved in the recruitment of students.** It is often found that, particularly with new programmes, students receive inappropriate guidance and advice, and can end up taking a course for which they are not suited. Retention statistics are increasingly under the spotlight in institutional review procedures. A useful part of planning a new programme is to look at how students will be guided before they enrol, and the kinds of follow-up support they are most likely to need after enrolment. Such guidance has been found to be an essential factor in ensuring that students don't drop out of new programmes.

■ **Map out the intended learning outcomes.** You will need to design these carefully, based on the programme rationale and its target student group, so that they are specific, measurable, achievable, realistic and time-specified, and in parallel with the standards and benchmarks that may already exist in the subject area concerned.

- **Decide on how the outcomes are to be addressed.** It can often be useful in planning the delivery of learning outcomes to use the terminology of the UK's vocational qualification framework: performance criteria, evidence indicators and range statements. If these are translated into simple, jargon-free language, you will find that both your students and colleagues will be really clear about what is required of them.

- **Consider appropriate teaching and learning strategies.** You will need to decide to what extent you will use traditional teaching methods, resource-based learning, flexible learning pathways and communications technologies in the delivery of your programme.

- **Think about who will deliver it.** You will most likely need to assemble a course team to deliver the programme. It is not a good idea to design a programme that is dependent on the particular qualifications or expertise of individual staff members. Typically they will leave or drop out in due course. This requires you to identify a pool of appropriate staff to whom you can turn. It's a good idea therefore to assemble a collection of CVs of staff who are likely to contribute.

- **Think carefully about the resources you will need to run the programme effectively.** These will include teaching staff, support staff, and library and information technology resources. You may also need to budget for laboratory, workshop or studio facilities, specialized equipment, printing and photocopying. Do not assume that institutional resources and facilities will be automatically available to you just because the programme is approved.

- **Consider the staff development the team may need to deliver the programme effectively.** There will be training needs associated with any new programme, be it in using unfamiliar delivery methods, standardizing assessment procedures, content updating or simply team-building.

- **Decide how the learning outcomes will be assessed.** It is common to express the content of a programme in terms of what students will be able to do or know. Good decisions on how best to assess whether the specified learning outcomes have been achieved are crucial. There is a real danger of assessing only some of the learning outcomes and then only partially. For this reason, put assessment (and quality assurance) at the top of your list of things to get right.

- **Plan carefully for the internal and external validation processes that will be required.** If you have yet to experience a validation event, talk to someone who has. If practical, involve such a person in your own preparations for the event, perhaps even to do a dry run with you. Scrutinize your own institution's internal validation processes and ensure that you complete all the required paperwork in good time. If you are working with a professional body you will also need to be fully acquainted with their processes.

■ **Think about the values that underpin your programme.** For example, your underpinning philosophies about how students learn need to be explicit, agreed and shared by the course team.

■ **Plan into the structure of the programme a process of continuous quality review and improvement.** It is critical that you look at how you will monitor the success of your programme. This will include student satisfaction, peer review, retention and completion rates, and assessment reliability.

5. Developing students' key skills

The development and accreditation, for all students, of a core of transferable skills (referred to by UK institutions as 'key skills') is now a major concern both for educational providers and for employers. Many institutions are working on the use of the subject-based curriculum as a vehicle for this development. In the UK, government policy has been to set targets for the achievement of key skills at minimum levels for school children, students in further and higher education, and apprentices and trainees at work. At the time of writing, detailed specifications and requirements have been produced for the following key skills areas:

> communication (including written and oral skills);
> application of number;
> information technology;
> improving learning and performance;
> working with others.

The development of students' problem solving skills is also increasingly being addressed in higher education. The following suggestions may help you think about your own ways to implement students' development of these skills:

■ **Try wherever possible to build into your course provision the assessment of students' key skills.** Whilst stand-alone key skills assessment and accreditation is now available to UK students, the evidence suggests that a subject-based, integrated approach works better for most students.

■ **Use assignments as the vehicle for testing students' key skills.** When designing assignments, angle the activities and tasks that you set towards meeting specific key skills criteria. For example, look at how an assignment might involve 'working with others' elements. Be careful, however, not to pack in too many key skills requirements, or to allow assignments to become too unwieldy for students to undertake, or for you to assess.

■ **Use local expertise.** Work with colleagues in your institution who may have key skills responsibilities, or specific expertise in productive partnerships. It's tempting to leave key skills development to the specialists if they are available. By bringing them into your teaching programmes as equal partners, your own confidence in addressing key skills will develop, and your students will see more clearly the relevance of key skills support to their specific learning programmes.

■ **Link key skills to each other.** For instance, the task of undertaking a survey can address many of the key skills, particularly communication, application of number and information technology elements.

■ **Liaise with colleagues to ensure that students are not required to cover the same key skills areas too often.** If different areas of the curriculum require students to demonstrate similar evidence, you should ensure that they are not doing the same sort of activity repeatedly. It is useful to establish which key skills are most directly associated with each individual subject or topic, and then to look for ways of addressing any of the key skills that are still 'missed' in the overall picture of students' work.

■ **Consider using learning agreements to address key skills evidence.** This can have the benefit of giving students a sense of ownership of the ways that they individually go about accumulating their evidence of key skills development, and can help to provide an 'added value' ethos, rather than a 'minimum competencies' scenario. The evidence derived from learning agreements can be vital in allowing students to demonstrate key skills relating to managing their own learning.

■ **Consider using student peer-assessment.** This helps students to increase their understanding of subject material, and at the same time develop communication skills. Ways of implementing peer-assessment are suggested in Chapter 5.

■ **Explore the uses of student self-assessment.** This can help students to develop skills in managing their own learning, and show them useful detail about the assessment culture in which they will need to survive. Suggestions on implementing student self-assessment are offered in Chapter 5.

■ **Highlight effective communication.** Getting evidence relating to written communication skills is relatively straightforward, and can be incorporated into most areas of the curriculum. Evidence of oral communication skills can be built into many parts of the curriculum in most subject areas, such as those associated with student individual or group presentations. Such evidence often arises from activities that represent good opportunities for learning, and enable students to gain feedback not only from their lecturers but from each other.

■ **Make good use of information technology.** The growth in the use of computer-based learning resource materials lends itself to helping students gather evidence of their use of information technology, and to do so in the context of their subject-based studies, rather than having to undertake additional tasks to accumulate evidence of this kind. When students are also using information technology for communication, such as e-mail, they can also use such evidence to add to evidence of their communications skills.

■ **Promote the benefits of students becoming better at managing their learning.** The important step is to ensure that students collect evidence that relates to them reflecting about *how* they learn things, and *how* they think about their own performance in the various tasks and activities that they undertake in the course of their studies. The use of learning agreements is a productive source for this kind of development.

■ **Help students to value working with each other.** This key skill is highly valued by employers, yet too often education programmes tend to measure students' individual work rather than their collaborative work. While it is sometimes difficult to establish how to assess collaborative work fairly, it remains very useful to set students collaborative tasks. It is productive to build into the assessment arising from such tasks, elements that involve students themselves reflecting on how well (or how badly) the collaboration worked in practice. Chapter 3 of this book contains many new suggestions on helping students to work well in groups.

6. Why use learning outcomes?

■ **Well-expressed statements of intended learning outcomes** help students to identify their own targets, and work systematically towards demonstrating their achievement of these targets.

■ **Learning outcomes are now required,** in the higher education sector in the UK, for subject review by the Quality Assurance Agency, and will be increasingly cross-referenced by Academic Reviewers against assessment processes, instruments and standards.

■ **In the context of benchmarking,** learning outcomes can provide one of the most direct indicators of the intended level and depth of any programme of learning.

7. Where can learning outcomes be useful to students?

Learning outcomes should not just reside in course validation documentation (though they need to be there in any case). They should also underpin everyday teaching-learning situations. They can be put to good use in the following places and occasions:

■ **In student handbooks,** so that students can see the way that the whole course or module is broken down into manageable elements of intended achievement, and set their own targets accordingly.

- **At the start of each lecture,** for example on a slide or transparency, so that students are informed of the particular purposes of the occasion.

- **At the end of each lecture,** so that students can estimate the extent to which they have travelled towards being able to achieve the intended outcomes associated with the lecture.

- **At suitable points in the briefing of students for longer elements of their learning,** including projects, group tasks, practical work and fieldwork.

- **On each element of handout material** issued before, during or after lectures, to reinforce the links between the content of the handout and students' intended learning.

- **On tasks and exercises, and briefings to further reading,** so that students can see the purpose of the work they are intended to do.

- **On the first few screens of each computer-based learning programme** that students study independently (or in groups).

- **At the beginning of self-study or flexible learning packages,** so that students can estimate their own achievement as they work through the materials.

8. Designing and using learning outcomes

- **Work out exactly what you want students to be able to do by the end of each defined learning element.** Even when you're working with syllabus content that is already expressed in terms of learning outcomes, it is often worth thinking again about your exact intentions, and working out how these connect together for different parts of students' learning.

- **Don't use the word 'students' in your outcomes** – except in dry course documentation. It is much better to use the word 'you' when addressing students. 'When we've completed this lecture, you should be able to compare and contrast particle and wave models of radiation' is better than stating 'The expected learning outcome of this lecture is that students will …'. Similarly, use the word 'you' when expressing learning outcomes in student handbooks, handouts, laboratory briefing sheets, and so on. Students need to feel that learning outcomes belong to them, not just to other people.

- **Work imaginatively with existing learning outcomes.** There may already be externally defined learning outcomes, or they may have been prescribed some time ago when the course or programme was validated. These may, however, be written in language that is not user-friendly or clear to students, and which is more connected with the teaching of the subject than the learning process. You should be able to translate these outcomes, so that they will be more useful to your students.

■ **Match your wording to your students.** The learning outcomes as expressed in course documentation may be off-putting and jargonistic, and may not match the intellectual or language skills of your students. By developing the skills to translate learning outcomes precisely into plain English, you will help the outcomes to be more useful to them, and at the same time it will be easier for you to design your teaching strategy.

■ **Your intended learning outcomes should serve as a map to your teaching programme.** Students and others will look at the outcomes to see if the programme is going to be relevant to their needs or intentions. The level and standards associated with your course will be judged by reference to the stated learning outcomes.

■ **Remember that many students will have achieved at least some of your intended outcomes already.** When introducing the intended learning outcomes, give credit for existing experience, and confirm that it is useful if some members of the group already have some experience and expertise which they can share with others.

■ **Be ready for the question 'Why?'** It is only natural for students to want to know why a particular learning outcome is being addressed. Be prepared to illustrate each outcome with some words about the purpose of including it.

■ **Be ready for the reaction 'So what?'** When students, colleagues, or external reviewers still can't see the point of a learning outcome, they are likely to need some further explanation before they will be ready to take it seriously.

■ **Work out your answers to 'What's in this for me?'** When students can see the short-term and long-term benefits of gaining a particular skill or competence, they are much more likely to try to achieve it.

■ **Don't promise what you can't deliver.** It is tempting to design learning outcomes that seem to be the answers to everyone's dreams. However, the real test for your teaching will be whether it is seen to enable students to achieve the outcomes. It's important to be able to link each learning outcome to an assessable activity or assignment.

■ **Don't use words such as 'understand' or 'know'.** While it is easy to write (or say) 'When you have completed this module successfully, you will understand the third Law of Thermodynamics', it is much more helpful to step back and address the questions: 'How will we know that they have understood it?', 'How will they themselves know they have understood it?', and 'What will they be able to do to *show* that they have understood it?'. Replies to the last of these questions lead to much more useful ways of expressing the relevant learning outcomes.

■ **Don't start at the beginning.** It is often much harder to write the outcomes that will be associated with the beginning of a course, and it is best to leave attempting this until you have got into your stride regarding writing outcomes. In addition, it is often much easier to work out what the 'early' outcomes actually should be once you have established where these outcomes are leading.

■ **Think ahead to assessment.** A well-designed set of learning outcomes should automatically become the framework for the design of assessed tasks. It is worth asking yourself 'How can I measure this?' for each draft learning outcome. If it is easy to think of how it will be measured, you can normally go ahead and design the outcome. If it is much harder to think of how it could be measured, it is usually a signal that you may need to think further about the outcome, and try to relate it more firmly to tangible evidence that could be assessed.

■ **Keep sentences short.** It is important that your students will be able to get the gist of each learning outcome without having to reread them several times, or ponder on what they really mean.

■ **Consider illustrating your outcomes with 'for example …' descriptions.** If necessary, such extra details could be added in smaller print, or in brackets. Such additional detail can be invaluable to students in giving them a better idea about what their achievement of the outcomes may actually amount to in practice.

■ **Test-run your learning outcome statements.** Ask target-audience students 'What do your think this really means?', to check that your intentions are being communicated clearly. Also test your outcomes statements out on colleagues, and ask them whether you have missed anything important, or whether they can suggest any changes to your wording.

■ **Aim to provide students with the whole picture.** Put the student-centred language descriptions of learning outcomes and assessment criteria into student handbooks, or turn them into a short self-contained leaflet to give to students at the beginning of the course. Ensure that students don't feel swamped by the enormity of the whole picture! Students need to be guided carefully through the picture in ways that allow them to feel confident that they will be able to succeed a step at a time.

■ **Don't get hung up too much on performance, standards and conditions** when expressing learning outcomes. For example, don't feel that such phrases as 'on your own', or 'without recourse to a calculator or computer' or 'under exam conditions' or 'with the aid of a list of standard integrals' need to be included in every well-expressed learning outcome. Such clarifications are extremely valuable elsewhere, in published assessment criteria. Don't dilute the primary purpose of a learning outcome with administrative detail.

■ **Don't be trivial!** Trivial learning outcomes support criticisms of reductionism. One of the main objections to the use of learning outcomes is that there can be far too many of them, only some of which are really important.

■ **Don't try to teach something if you can't think of any intended learning outcome associated with it.** This seems obvious, but it can be surprising how often a teaching agenda can be streamlined and focused by checking that there is some important learning content associated with each element in it, and removing or shortening the rest.

■ **Don't confuse learning outcomes and assessment criteria.** It is best not to cloud the learning outcomes with the detail of performance criteria and standards until students know enough about the subject to understand the language of such criteria. In other words, the assessment criteria are best read by students *after* they have started to learn the topic, rather than at the outset (but make sure that the links will be clear in due course).

■ **Don't write any learning outcomes that can't (or won't) be assessed.** If it's important enough to propose as an intended learning outcome, it should be worthy of being measured in some way, and it should be *possible* to measure.

■ **Don't design any assessment task or question that is not related to the stated learning outcomes.** If it's important enough to measure, it is only fair to let students know that it is on their learning agenda.

■ **Don't state learning outcomes at the beginning, and fail to return to them.** It's important to come back to them at the end of each teaching-learning element, such as lecture, self-study package, element of practical work, and so on. Turn them into checklists for students, for example along the lines 'Check now that you feel able to …' or 'Now you should be in a position to …'.

9. Using communications and information technologies

These technologies are now widely used in many aspects of teaching, learning and assessment. The acronyms 'ICTs' and 'CITs' are used almost equally, referring to the same combinations of technologies. Detailed suggestions on getting the most from them are given in several parts of this book, and in particular in Chapter 4. The suggestions below are just intended to be headlines:

■ **Don't just make traditional material available electronically.** Putting straight lecture notes onto an intranet or (worse!) on the Internet is of very limited value. Such media are just not appropriate for large amounts of text. Handouts and lecture notes rarely lend themselves to being seen on monitor screens, where only a small part of the whole may be visible at a time. If the only way for students to handle the materials is to print them off, and then learn from them in traditional ways, it is worth thinking twice before making the material available electronically.

■ **Be wary about overwhelming your students with information.** The amount of material available to students through their computer screens grows exponentially. The quantity of information that students can be exposed to in a 'sitting' is vastly more than might have been covered by a lecturer in a lecture.

■ **Be clear about the intended learning outcomes.** When students are working with electronically delivered materials, it is more important than ever that they know what they are looking for. They need to be able to make sensible decisions regarding what to scan, what to keep, and what to ignore. Carefully formulated learning outcomes can alert students to the agenda for their usage of electronic sources.

- **Help students to develop 'search and select' skills.** Whether working from an electronic database or from the Internet, it is vital that students know how to find the *relevant* material for their purposes. Searching for relevant and useful information within a reasonable time period is an advanced skill. You must be prepared to give your students plenty of support and guidance on this.

- **Help students to develop a critical perspective.** Electronic sources are no different from traditional print-based ones in that the authors' biases, inaccuracies or lack of currency can affect the reliability with which the resource may be used. The authenticity and quality of textbooks and journal articles may be guaranteed by the editorial and review processes prior to publication. Because of the immediacy and democracy of the Internet, there may not be such guarantees.

- **Build in plenty of activity.** Students will soon become bored when all they are doing is pointing and clicking. Build in small tasks, tests and quizzes, and opportunities to reflect upon what they have learned. Look for ways in which each electronic medium provides students with genuinely interactive learning experiences.

- **Look ahead to what you're going to assess.** Start by working out what it is *possible* to assess! It is of limited value simply getting students to use electronic sources, unless you have decided how you can measure the quality of their usage. Work out the kinds of *evidence* from which the quality and effectiveness of students' usage of electronic sources can be quantified.

- **Use each medium to do the things that it does well.** Use electronic media to avoid replicating effort, to save multiple postal mailings, to deliver volumes of material that would be expensive to copy onto paper, and to communicate with a number of people at once, or where speed is crucial.

- **When developing your own materials, write to match the medium.** The best Web-based materials are essentially visual, and use short sentences, lots of bullet points, and user-friendly language. They use a letterbox format, rather than the A4 page.

- **Think how you will make your own screen-based materials visually interesting.** Explore your capacity to use graphics, video-clips, colour and images to help students to feel excited about their learning materials. Design your material to the lowest common denominator of computer specification that you can reasonably assume your students will be using.

- **Be aware of copyright problems.** This is still a minefield, so don't do anything you would hesitate, for copyright reasons, to do on paper. This particularly includes cutting and pasting extracts from other third-party electronic sources.

■ **Be aware that effective computer-based learning material takes time to develop.** Estimates of 100 developer-hours per hour of student learning are not unusual. Allow for this in your development plans.

■ **Look at what is already available.** A wealth of useful material has already been developed, and it important to seek every opportunity to adapt or adopt them (with permission) where they are relevant. Monitor Web listings and guides for sources of potential materials. These are extensive, and growing and changing continuously.

■ **Remember that computer-based learning materials need updating.** Just as with any other curriculum delivery mechanism, computer-based learning materials need to be reviewed regularly, and revised as situations and contexts change. It is often much less expensive, and quicker, to edit computer-based materials than print-based ones.

■ **Get your students to help you make the materials better.** Many of our younger students learnt information technology skills soon after they learnt to walk, so they are likely to be very familiar with what works and what does not work on-screen. Ask students to evaluate your computer-based learning packages, and note carefully both their criticisms and their praise.

■ **Help students to use electronic communication effectively.** The main problems are information overload and time management. Be prepared to give students guidance about how to put their messages across effectively. Help them to keep messages concise and clear, and set an example with your own electronic messages. However, do not patronize or undervalue those students who are already skilled at electronic communication.

■ **Look for ways of using electronic communication to save you time and energy.** For example, consider using computer-conferences to give general feedback to a large class on your marking of their reports or essays. Personal e-mail to individual students can then give them additional direct feedback about the strengths and weaknesses of their work.

■ **Consider using computer conferencing methods as a means of course delivery.** Online learning can be very effective with large groups, and can make up for limited opportunities of face-to-face sessions. The evidence suggests that the more reserved students find it less daunting to ask questions by e-mail, and find it easier to participate in 'virtual' group activities.

■ **Ensure that students have adequate access to electronic sources.** If progress or assessment depends upon such access, make sure that such access is generous. There is already evidence that student appeals against assessment decisions are being based on claims that access to particular resources was not sufficiently possible.

■ **Don't expect to do away with face-to-face time altogether.** Human interaction is often one of the key elements that students report as helping them to learn. The virtual tutor should not totally replace the human one in most overall learning contexts.

Chapter 2

Lectures

Giving lectures
1. *Preparing your first lectures*
2. *Giving lectures*
3. *Handouts for lectures*

Technology in lectures
4. *Working with overhead projectors*
5. *Why use computer-aided presentations?*
6. *Some don'ts for presentation managers!*
7. *Helping students to learn from computer-aided presentations*

Observing others
8. *Observing other lecturers, and being observed yourself*
9. *Some qualities to observe in lectures*

Giving lectures is the most public side of the work of most higher education lecturers. Attending lectures is part of the life of most higher education students. Although some parts of this chapter are specifically about lecturing, most of the suggestions apply to working with large groups of students whether in higher or further education. Suggestions in this chapter include ways to help large-group sessions deliver increased learning payoff to students. In effect, we explore many of the ways in which the principles of active, interactive learning can be brought into the lecture room or large-group classroom.

Next, attention is turned to some of the **technology in lectures** used by most lecturers, starting with overhead projectors, and leading into suggestions for using computer-managed presentation systems well.

The chapter concludes with some suggestions about ways to make the most of the benefits of **observing others** at work in the lecture room or classroom, and to learn from feedback when your own work is observed. Familiarity with teaching observation pays dividends when subject review or other forms of external scrutiny come your way.

1. Preparing your first lectures

The suggestions below are for *new* lecturers, about to step onto the rostrum for the first time! Please skip these if you're already practised:

- **Find out where your topics fit into the syllabus.** The more you know about what students will have learned already, the easier it is to avoid boring them by repeating things they already know. Look at the syllabus and see where your bit fits in. Borrow copies of the most central undergraduate texts on the topics. Make brief notes of the most important parts, and remember to keep references to the sections you will ask students to consult.

- **Find out more about the students.** Talk to colleagues who are already working with them. Ask them what sort of class it seems to be. Ask about any aspects of teaching which seem to be working particularly well with them.

- **Get yourself used to the lecture room.** Go in some evening when it's empty, and find out where the lighting controls are, how the overhead projector works, and how it feels to 'talk to the seats' for a while.

- **Decide not to imitate the lecturers who taught you.** It's worth trying to emulate the good things you remember, but there's no need to do some of the more boring things you'll also remember! Your students will think more of you if you simply are yourself.

- **Build in plenty of lead-in time.** Preparing and giving lectures at the last minute is not a good idea – even for experienced lecturers! It can easily take ten hours or much more to prepare a new one-hour lecture. It may take even longer if you're planning to prepare handouts and overheads to support your lecture.

- **Go to some more lectures!** Most of the lectures you will have been to will have been occasions when you were trying to capture the gist of the lecture. It's worth going to a few more just to observe the good (and bad) ways that different lecturers approach the task of working with a group of students. Make notes of how they do it.

- **Remember what it was like when you were a student.** You will probably have learned a great deal about your subject since you were lectured on it. And even then, you were probably a 'high flier' – that's why you're lecturing yourself now. Think of the average student, and plan to pitch your lecture to such students.

- **Do a dry run before your first lecture.** If possible, get some friends in to role-play the audience. Even better, try to get someone to make a video of you doing your dry run. You can learn a great deal about how you're coming across from watching yourself perform.

- **Think about your pace.** Some of the worst disasters that happen in lectures are associated with either going far too fast, or (more commonly) devastatingly slowly. The most difficult job of all when starting to teach is to gauge how long a new lecture will take; this remains problematic even for very experienced lecturers, but you won't notice it when you watch them, as they will have developed coping strategies. Try to build in some flexibility so you can say more or less, depending on how fast you are covering the material.

- **Think about your delivery.** Find out more about how you can project your voice. If the room is very large, you may need a microphone (and should ask for one). Otherwise you can help your voice to carry by standing up, breathing slightly more deeply than normal, using the walls of the room to help your audibility, addressing the student most distant from you, and just relaxing. Never shout.

- **You may not need to start with the 'first' lecture.** If you're going to do a series of lectures, it may be preferable to start with a topic you feel confident to lecture on, or where you've got interesting visual backup to support your talk. Getting off to a good start with your students helps you (and them) to feel better about the rest of your series.

- **Prepare some handout material to support your lecture.** Handout materials are particularly useful if you're feeling nervous, as you can refer students to things in the materials when you need all eyes to be off you for a moment or two!

- **Think about making your handouts 'interactive'.** For example, include in your handouts tasks for students to do (individually or in twos and threes) during the lecture, with space for them to write down their ideas.

- **Prepare overhead transparencies or presentation-manager slides to support your lecture.** Don't put too much on any transparency – bullet point lists of main headings are usually enough.

- **Build up your store of 'interesting things'.** Students often remember the anecdotes better than the main points of a lecture! Try to collect several points which are amusing or memorable, and which will also help to capture students' attention at key points in your lectures.

- **Don't over-prepare.** Everyone seems to prepare far more for their first few lectures than they can ever get through. Be modest in your expectations of how much you will cover.

2. Giving lectures

Lectures remain a fact of life for the majority of students, despite often being described as a relatively inefficient way of promoting student learning, motivation and involvement. Large-group lectures can indeed be turned into memorable learning experiences for students. Also, lectures constitute one of the most 'public' forms of teaching, and therefore are high on the quality assurance agenda. These tips are designed to optimize the learning potential of lectures, and to remind you of ways that large-group sessions can pay real dividends to students.

- **Make the most of opportunities when you have the whole group together.** There are useful benefits of whole-group shared experiences, especially for setting the scene in a new subject, and talking students through known problem areas. Use these as sessions to develop whole-group cohesion, as well as to give briefings, provide introductions, introduce keynote speakers, and hold practical demonstrations.

- **Make sure that lectures are not just 'transmit–receive' occasions.** Little is learned by students just writing down what the lecturer says, or copying down information from screens or boards. There are more efficient ways of providing students with the information they need for their learning, including the use of handout materials, textbooks and other learning resource materials.

- **Be punctual, even if some of your students are late.** Chat to the nearest students while people are settling in. Ask them 'How's the course going for you so far?', for example. Ask them 'What's your favourite topic so far?' or 'What are the trickiest bits so far?'

- **When you're ready to start, capture students' attention.** It's often easier to do this by dimming the lights and showing your first overhead, than by trying to quieten down the pre-lecture chatter by talking loudly. Do your best to ignore latecomers. Respect the courtesy of punctuality of those already present, and talk to them.

- **Make good use of your specific intended learning outcomes for each lecture.** Find out how many students think they can already achieve some of these – and adjust your approach accordingly! Explaining the outcomes at the start of the session, or including them in handout materials given out to students, can help them to know exactly what they should be getting out of the lecture, serving as an agenda against which they can track their individual progress during the minutes that follow.

- **Help students to place the lecture in context**. Refer back to previous material (ideally with a short summary of the previous lecture at the beginning) and give them forewarning of how this will relate to material they will cover later.

- **Use handout material to spare students from copying down lots of information.** It's better to spend time discussing and elaborating on information that students can already read for themselves.

■ **Face the class when using an overhead projector.** Practise in a lecture room using transparencies as an agenda, and talking to each point listed on them. By placing a pen on the transparency you can draw attention to the particular point on which you are elaborating, maintaining vital eye contact with your students.

■ **Work out some questions that the session will address.** Showing these questions as an overhead at the beginning of the session is a way of helping students to see the nature and scope of the specific learning outcomes they should be able to address progressively as the session proceeds.

■ **Give your students some practice at note-making (rather than just note-taking).** Students learn very little just from copying out bits of what they see or hear, and may need quite a lot of help towards summarizing, prioritizing, and making their notes their own individual learning tools.

■ **Get students learning-by-doing, even during lectures.** Just about all students get bored listening for a full hour, so break the session up with small tasks, such as problems for students to work out themselves, applying what you've told them, reading extracts from their handout material, or discussing a question or issue with the students nearest to them. Even in a crowded, tiered lecture theatre, students can be given things to do independently for a few minutes at a time, followed by a suitable debriefing, so that they can compare views and find out whether they were on the right track.

■ **Variety is the spice of lectures.** Make sure that you build into large-group lectures a variety of activities for students, which might include writing, listening, looking, making notes, copying diagrams, undertaking small discussion tasks, asking questions, answering questions, giving feedback to you, solving problems, doing calculations, putting things in order of importance, and so on.

■ **Ask the students how you are doing.** From time to time ask 'How many of you can hear me clearly enough?', 'Am I going too fast?', 'Is this making sense to you?' Listen to the answers and try to respond accordingly.

■ **Use lectures to start students learning from each other.** Getting students to work in small groups in a lecture environment can allow them to discuss and debate the relative merits of different options in multiple-choice tasks, or put things in order of importance, or brainstorm possible solutions to problems. After they have engaged with each other on such tasks, the lecturer can draw conclusions from some of the groups, and give expert-witness feedback when needed.

■ **Use lectures to help students make sense of things they have already learned.** It is valuable to make full use of the times when all students are together to give them things to do to allow them to check out whether they can still do the things they covered in previous sessions.

- **Use lectures to help shape students' attitudes.** The elements of tone of voice, facial expression, body language and so on can be used by lecturers to bring greater clarity and direction to the attitude-forming shared experiences which help students set their own scene for a topic or theme in a subject.

- **Genuinely solicit students' questions.** Don't just ask 'Any questions?' as you are picking up your papers at the end of a class. Treat students' questions with courtesy even if they seem very basic to you. Repeat the question so all students can hear, and then answer in a way that doesn't make the questioner feel stupid.

- **Don't waffle when stuck!** Don't try to bluff your way out of it when you don't know the answers to some of the questions students may ask. Tell the questioners that you'll find out the answers to their questions before your next lecture with them – they'll respect you more for this than for trying to invent an answer.

- **Use some lecture time to draw feedback from students.** Large-group sessions can be used to provide a useful barometer of how their learning is going. Students can be asked to write on slips of paper (or post-its) questions that they would like you to address at a future session.

- **Use whole-class time to explain carefully the briefings for assessment tasks.** It is essential that all students have a full, shared knowledge of exactly what is expected of them in such tasks, so that no one is disadvantaged by any differentials in their understanding of the performance criteria or assessment schemes associated with the tasks.

- **Show students how the assessor's mind works.** This can be done by devising class sessions around the analysis of how past examples of students' work were assessed, as well as by going through in detail the way that assessment criteria were applied to work that the class members themselves have done.

- **Record yourself on video every now and then.** Review the video to help you see your own strengths and weaknesses, and look for ways to improve your performance. Your keenest critic is likely to be yourself, so don't try to resolve every little habit or mannerism at once, just tackle the ones that you think are most important, little by little. It may also be useful for a group of colleagues together to look at each other's videos, and offer each other constructive comments. This is excellent practice for inspection or other quality assessment procedures.

- **Use all opportunities to observe other people's lectures.** You can do this not only in your own department, but also at external conferences and seminars. Watching other people helps you to learn both from what others do well, which you might wish to emulate, and from awful sessions where you resolve never to do anything similar in your own classes.

- **Put energy and effort into making your lectures interesting and stimulating.** A well-paced lecture which has visual impact and in which ideas are clearly communicated can be a motivating shared experience for students. Become comfortable using overhead projectors and audio-visual equipment in imaginative ways.

■ **Watch the body language of your audience.** You'll soon learn to recognize the symptoms of 'eyes glazing over' when students are becoming passive recipients rather than active participants. That may signal the time for one of your prepared anecdotes, or better, for a task for students to tackle.

■ **Don't tolerate poor behaviour.** You don't have to put up with students talking, eating or fooling around in your lectures. Ask them firmly but courteously to desist, and as a last resort, ask them to leave. If they do not do so, you should leave yourself for a short period to give them a cooling-down period.

■ **Don't feel you've got to keep going for the full hour.** Sometimes you will have said all you need to say, and still have 10 or 15 minutes in hand. Don't feel you have to waffle on. It may come as a surprise to you, but your students may be quite pleased to finish early occasionally!

■ **Don't feel that you have to get through all of your material.** Even very experienced lecturers, when preparing a new lecture, often overestimate what they can cover in an hour. It is better to cover part of your material well, than to try to rush through all of it. You can adjust future sessions to balance out the content.

■ **Use large-group sessions to identify and answer students' questions.** This can be much more effective, and fairer, than just attempting to answer their questions individually and privately. When one student asks a question in a large-group session, there are often many other students who only then realize that they too need to hear the answer.

■ **Help the shy or retiring students to have equal opportunity to contribute.** Asking students in large groups to write questions, or ideas, on post-its helps to ensure that the contributions you receive are not just from those students who aren't afraid to ask in public. It can be comforting for students to preserve their anonymity in asking questions, as they are often afraid that their questions may be regarded as silly or trivial.

■ **Come to a timely conclusion.** A large-group session must not just fizzle out, but should come to a definite and robust ending. It is also important not to over-run. It is better to come to a good stopping place a few minutes early, than to end up rushing through something important right at the end of the session.

3. Handouts for lectures

With modern developments in desktop publishing, coupled to the ready availability of photocopiers and offset litho printing, the use of handout materials has escalated dramatically. There is still, however, the danger that handout material is simply filed by students, and not used for active learning. Some ways round this are suggested below:

■ **Make handouts look attractive.** Gone are the days when a plain handwritten or typed summary of a lecture was enough. The quality of the message is now inextricably associated with the quality of the medium; scrappy handouts tend not to be valued.

■ **Use the start of a handout to remind students what its purposes are.** It can be useful to state on each handout the intended learning outcomes of the particular element of work involved.

■ **Use plenty of headings.** There's little more off-putting than a solid page of unbroken text. Where possible, make headings stand out, by using bold print, or large-size print. When a glance at a handout gives information about the structure of its contents, it has already started to help people learn.

■ **Use white space.** For students to develop a sense of ownership of handouts, they need to have room to write their own notes on them. Space between paragraphs, space at the top and bottom of pages, or a wide margin on one side are all ways of giving them this possibility of ownership.

■ **Make handouts interactive.** In other words, include tasks and activities for students to do, either in the group session where the handout was issued, or as later follow-up activities.

■ **Include 'committed space' for students to do things in handouts.** Structured tasks are best, such as 'Think of six reasons why the economy is in recession and list them below.' The fact that space has been provided for students' answers helps persuade them (often subconsciously) to have a try at the tasks rather than simply skip them.

■ **Use tasks as chances for students to learn by doing, and to learn by getting things wrong.** Multiple-choice questions are useful for this. The handout can serve as a useful reminder of 'wrong' options chosen, as well as a pleasant reminder of 'correct' choices.

■ **Use handouts to get students making notes, not just taking notes.** Use handouts to avoid the wasteful process of students simply writing down things you say, or transcribing things they see on the screen or board. Copying things down is a low-level learning activity. Having such information already in handout form allows you to spend face-to-face time getting your students probing into the meaning of the information, interpreting it, questioning it, extrapolating from it, analyzing it and so on.

■ **Work out what you intend students to add to the handout during your session.** For example, leave spaces for individual 'brainstorms' (eg 'List five symptoms of anaemia'), and for the products of buzz-group discussions (eg putting some factors in order of importance). The aim should be that the handout students take away at the end of the session is much more valuable than the blank one they were given at the start.

■ **Include annotated bibliographies in handout materials.** A few words about what to look for in each particular source can make a big difference to the ways in which students follow up references.

■ | **Where possible, store your handout materials on disk.** Go for small print runs. It is then easy to make considerable adjustments and additions to handouts each successive time you use them. Avoid the waste associated with piles of handouts that you've subsequently replaced with updated, improved versions.

4. Working with overhead projectors

The overhead projector is one of the most common ways of displaying visual information to students, particularly in large-group situations. Two major advantages of overhead projection are that you can face your audience as you speak, and you do not need to darken the room. The following guidelines may help your students get the most from your use of the overhead projector:

■ | **Know your machine.** Most machines have a focus control, but this is located differently on different types of projector. Most machines also have a red–blue adjustment lever (or fringe control). It's well worth your time to take steps to become familiar with the particular machine you're going to work with. Don't be afraid to move it to get it into good focus, across the whole of the screen area. When you can, adjust the height and positioning of the projector to avoid 'keystoning' (the top of the image being a different width from the bottom).

■ | **Ensure that your transparencies will fit any projector**. Many projectors have a plate of approximately A4 size (and can usually be arranged for vertical or lateral display). Some projectors have square screens, wider but less deep vertically than A4 size.

■ | **Get the machine position right.** The aim is to ensure that all your students can see the screen without anything obstructing their vision (particularly *you!*). Put on a slide, and sit in various seats in the room (before the students are there) so that you know that the screen is clearly visible, and that the average overhead will be easily seen.

■ | **Be ready for problems!** If the bulb should suddenly go, is there a 'switchable' spare? If there is, check in any case that this works. Alternatively, have a spare projector (which you know works) sitting inconspicuously in a corner of the room.

■ | **When all else fails ….** Have one or two exercises up your sleeve which do not depend at all on the availability of an overhead projector. Plan these so that while your students are engaged on them you give yourself the time to arrange a new projector.

■ | **'The medium is the message.'** Good-quality overheads can add credibility to your messages. It's worth using desktop publishing programs to make your principal overhead transparencies look professional and believable. With inkjet and laser colour printers, it's nowadays relatively easy to produce coloured transparencies with graphics.

■ **Be careful with coloured print or writing.** Some colours, especially red, are harder than you might imagine to see from the back of a large room. Throw away any orange or yellow ones from your set of overhead pens – unless you're using them for colouring in blocks on diagrams or flowcharts, for example.

■ **Don't use typewritten overheads.** To be clearly visible, most fonts need to be at sizes '18', '24' or larger – considerably bigger and bolder than typical typewritten materials. Make sure that each transparency you prepare will be visible from the back of the largest room you are likely to use, even by someone without perfect eyesight.

■ **Keep the number of words down.** A good overhead transparency only needs to contain the main ideas, not the details. You can add the details as you discuss the main points on the transparencies. Your own 'crib' notes can then be written onto a paper copy of each transparency.

■ **Use landscape rather than portrait orientation.** This helps you to make the best use of the top half of the screen, which is usually more easily visible to most of your audience.

■ **Watch students' eyes.** As soon as you notice students having to move their head positions to see something on one of your transparencies, it's worth trying to move that part up so that they can see it without moving their gaze.

■ **Get your transparencies into the right order before your lecture.** There's nothing worse than watching a lecturer sifting and sorting to try to find the right overhead. It's sometimes worth arranging them into two sets: ones you will *definitely* use, and ones you *might* wish to use if time permits, or if anticipated questions arise.

■ **Use the top half of the screen.** By sliding your transparencies 'up', you can normally make the most important pieces of information appear towards the top of the screen – more easily visible by students at your sessions.

■ **Try not to read out your overheads!** Your students can read much faster than you can speak. People don't like having things read out to them that they can read for themselves.

■ **Give people time to take notes if they wish.** Sometimes, you may have copies of your transparencies in handout materials you issue to students. Otherwise, expect that at least some students will want to jot down the main points they see on the screen, and make sure that they've done this before you move on to another transparency.

■ **Minimize passive transcribing by students.** Copying down words from transparencies is not the most productive of learning activities. Where possible, issue handout materials that already contain the wording from your principal overhead transparencies.

■ **Don't point at the screen itself.** This would mean losing eye contact with your students. Use a pen or pencil to rest on the transparency, indicating the part you're talking about.

■ **Be prepared to add things to your transparencies during discussions.** This ability to edit slides 'live' is an advantage of overhead projectors over computer-based presentation managers, and can help your students to feel that their comments are important and valued. With transparencies produced from ink-jet printers, however, don't write on your original; put a blank sheet of acetate over it!

■ **Don't over-use 'progressive reveal' techniques** (showing transparencies a bit at a time by gradually moving a masking sheet of paper). Some students feel manipulated if they are continually 'controlled' in this way. It can be better to build up a complex overhead using multiple overlays.

■ **Make your own masking sheet.** Tape a pen or short ruler to what will be the top edge, or stick a piece of Blu-tack there. The extra weight will help to ensure that the sheet does not slip off your transparencies, prematurely revealing your last line or two (which may be punch lines!).

■ **Remember to switch the projector off!** Most overhead projectors make at least some noise. When you're not actually showing something, it's important that you are not distracting your students both visibly and audibly.

5. Why use computer-aided presentations?

The package most commonly used is Microsoft PowerPoint. The suggestions that follow relate to this program, but apply to most other presentation managers. Lecturers choose to use computer-aided presentations for different reasons. Interrogate your own reasons against those listed below:

■ **Because you want to make a good impression on your audience.** Some people may think that if you are just using old-fashioned ways of giving presentations in your teaching, your message itself may be outdated. However, the quality of your use of the medium is actually more important than simply choosing an up-to-date medium.

■ **Because you want to be able to edit your presentation easily and frequently.** Computer-generated presentations are very easy (and very inexpensive) to edit, even to restructure completely. It is much easier to adjust a computer-delivered presentation after every experience of giving it, than it would be to prepare a new set of overhead transparencies each time.

■ **Because you want your handout material to relate directly to your presentation.** In PowerPoint presentations, for example, you can print off handout pages containing multiple slides. You can also annotate individual slides to make handouts with additional notes and background information. The strongest advantage of printing out your slides as handout materials is that your students then don't need to do menial tasks such as simply copying your slides into their own notes, but can do more active things such as writing their own notes onto their print-outs of your slides.

■ **Because you want to show things that can't be shown using traditional methods.** For example, if you want to show your students pictures, moving images or graphics, which would be difficult or impossible to do using overhead transparencies, you can be fairly sure that you are justified in making your presentations computer-aided.

■ **Because you want to be able to have *all* of your teaching presentations available.** A single floppy disk can carry hundreds of slides of presentation material. If your teaching repertoire is wide and varied, it might be impossible to carry it all around with you on overheads or handouts. Carrying a few disks is much more feasible, and you can customize a new presentation from your repertoire quite easily once you have had some practice at editing, and print off those handouts you need locally.

■ **Because you want your students to be able to have another look at your presentation later.** You can give students your computer-managed presentation on disk, to work through at a machine in the resources centre, or at home. You can e-mail the presentation to students at a distance, or place it in a virtual library or conference area on your computer network.

6. Some *don'ts* for presentation managers!

Any presentation medium can be used well or badly. The following suggestions should help you to avoid some of the most common pitfalls with presentation managers:

■ **Don't just use computer-aided presentations because everyone else seems to be using them.** This may be a reason for making at least some of your presentation computer-aided, but it is worth thinking hard about whether computers provide the best medium for the exact purposes of each element of your presentation. It is better to mix and match, rather than to switch blindly to a different way of supporting your presentation.

■ **Don't just use computer-aided presentations because the equipment happens to be there.** Some institutions lay on computer-delivered presentation systems as a matter of routine. It is still possible to use overhead projectors, markerboards and flipcharts too! Sometimes, these may be pushed out of sight to make room for the computer and projector, but they are usually not far away.

■ **Don't cause 'death by bullet point'!** Even though computer-aided presentation packages can introduce bullet points to slides in a variety of ways (fly from left, dissolve, and so on), bullet points can quickly become tiresome to an audience. It is worth having a good reason for building any slide step by step.

■ **Don't underestimate the problems that can arise.** You may not be able to get the room dark enough for students to see your presentation properly. There may be compatibility problems between the software version you have used to create your presentation, and the version on the computer through which you wish to show it. The image size on your laptop may not be compatible with that required by the data projector. The resolution of the projection equipment may not be sufficient to show fine details of images that you carefully placed into your presentation.

■ **Don't overdo the special effects.** Doing the whole presentation in a single format becomes boring for your audience, but programming a random sequence of slide builds tends to be irritating for you as presenter, as you don't know what build sequence will be produced when you move to your next slide. Similarly, don't go overboard on the snazzy changes from one slide to the next.

■ **Don't use it just like an overhead projector substitute!** Simply transferring the contents of your overhead transparencies into a computer-delivered presentation does not make full use of the medium. Try to do *other* things with computer-aided presentations, for example making good use of the possibilities of moving images, graphics and so on.

■ **Don't forget that it's not that bright!** Most computer-aided presentation packages rely on projection equipment that is not nearly as bright as a good overhead projector. This means that you may need to take particular care with room lighting, daylight from windows, and (worst of all) direct sunlight. If you use a liquid crystal display tablet, it isn't a good idea to place it on top of an ordinary overhead projector; you need a high-powered one (1000 W or more) for reasonable visibility.

■ **Don't forget to check the focus before you start.** Some projection systems are fine for video projection, but turn out to be too fuzzy for computer-managed presentation projection. Modern systems have easy ways of adjusting the focus, but older systems may need to be set up in considerable detail before an acceptable image quality is produced, or may just not be capable of producing clear still images. Looking for any length of time at fuzzy images can give some members of your audience headaches, as their eyes try in vain to compensate for the fuzziness.

■ **Don't forget the conditions appropriate for human sleep!** Turning down the lights, sitting comfortably in the same place for more than a few minutes, and listening to the sound of your voice may be just the right conditions for your audience to drop off, particularly if the images are unclear.

■ **Don't forget that sunlight moves.** If you're setting up a teaching room first thing in the morning, you may need to plan ahead for where any sunlight may be later in the day.

■ **Don't put too much on any slide.** There still seem to be few computer-aided presentations where *all* of the slides are perfectly readable from the back of the room. It is better to have twice as many slides, rather than to cram lots of information onto each slide. It usually takes two or more slides to project the same amount of information that would have taken one overhead transparency.

■ **Don't put important text in the lower half of slides.** Unless all members of your audience have an uninterrupted view of the screen, people sitting at the back may have to peer around their nearer neighbours to read any text at the bottom of the screen. Unlike overhead projection, you can't simply move a transparency up the plate to make the final points visible to people at the back.

■ **Don't use 'portrait' layout.** You will usually have the choice between landscape and portrait, so use landscape to make the most of the top part of the screen. You may already have found that the same applies to overhead transparencies.

■ **Don't import tables or text files.** The fact that you *can* import such files into a computer-managed presentation package leads many into temptation. These are very often the slides which can't be read from the back (or even from the front). It is normally better to give students such information as handouts, rather than to try to show them it on screen.

■ **Don't use the wrong colours.** Colours that look good on a computer screen don't always show up so well when they are projected. If most of your presentations will be in rooms with natural daylight, it is usually best to stick to dark colours for text, and light (or even white) backgrounds. If you know you're going to be working in a lecture theatre where you have full control of the lighting, you can then be more adventurous, and use light lettering against dark backgrounds (not forgetting that you may be lulling your audience to sleep when you turn down the lights).

■ **Don't use the same slide format for all of your slides.** Computer-managed presentation packages may allow you to switch your whole presentation into different pre-prepared styles, but the result can be that your slides all look too similar to have an optimum learning payoff for your viewers. Vary the layout, colours and backgrounds, so that each new slide makes its own impact.

■ **Don't leave a slide on when you've moved on to talk about something else.** It is better to switch the projection off, rather than to leave up information that people have already thought about. If you're within reach of the computer keyboard, pressing 'B' on some systems causes the display to go black, and pressing 'B' again brings the display back. This is far simpler and safer than switching the projector to standby, and risking having to wait for it to warm up again when you want to project your next slide. An alternative is to insert a 'black' slide, where you wish to stop your audience from looking at the screen. Don't, however, forget where you've placed these, and panic about where your display has gone!

■ **Don't talk to the screen!** With overhead projectors, it's easy to develop good habits, including looking at the transparency rather than at the screen, and avoiding turning your back on your audience. With projected images, you may have no alternative but to watch the screen, but you need to make sure that you talk to your audience. If you can arrange things so that you can look at a computer screen rather than the projection screen, the problem can be partly solved.

- **Don't go backwards for too long!** If you need to return to a slide you showed much earlier, it is better to switch the display off, and find the slide you want without your audience seeing every step. The same applies to returning to your original place in your presentation.

- **Don't forget to rehearse your presentation.** With overhead transparencies you always know what is coming next; with presentation managers it is all too possible to forget. If *you* look surprised when your next slide appears, it does not do much for your credibility with your audience.

- **Don't underestimate the potential of remote controls surprising you!** Many systems allow you to change slides with a remote control connected to your computer, or to the projection equipment. Pressing the wrong button on this can switch the system to something quite different (for example, video input), and can mean that you can find yourself unable to get back to your presentation without losing your cool. It is best to find out in advance which buttons *not* to press, and possibly to place some adhesive tape over them to reduce the possibility of pressing them.

- **Don't forget to check your spelling.** PowerPoint, for example, can do this for you, but you have to instruct the software appropriately. Be careful not to let the software replace words automatically, or you will get some strange slides if you are using unfamiliar words.

- **Don't fail to get feedback on your presentation before you run it.** It is really useful to get someone else to watch your slides, and to ask about anything that isn't clear, or point out anything that could irritate an audience. It's also useful to check your timing, and the overall length of your presentation in practice.

- **Don't miss out on seeing your presentation on paper.** Consider printing out your slides, for example six per page. This helps you to get an overview of your presentation, and can sometimes alert you to where to insert an additional slide or two. It is also useful to have such pages in front of you as you present, so that you can easily remind yourself of what's on the next slide.

- **Don't neglect to adjust and improve your slides.** It is so easy to alter a set of slides that there's no real excuse for not editing your presentation frequently so that it is always finely tuned to the particular audience and context. The most beneficial additions are often new slides inserted to address frequently asked questions in advance.

- **Don't stop watching other people's technique.** This is one of the fastest ways of improving your own presentations. Look for things that work well for other people, and find out how the effects were achieved, then emulate them. More importantly, look for things that don't work, and make sure that you avoid them.

- **Don't forget your overheads!** It is still useful to have at least some of your computer slides on traditional acetate. Computers can go down. More likely, you can still press the wrong button on a remote control, and switch your projector onto video or off altogether. At such times, it can seem life-saving to be able to go to an overhead projector, at least temporarily.

7. Helping students to learn from computer-aided presentations

- **Remember that people don't actually remember a great deal of what they see.** Keep your computer-aided presentations down to relatively small, self-contained episodes, and intersperse them with activities that involve your students in learning-by-doing, or other activities such as discussing, prioritizing, or summarizing.

- **Get your students to formulate some questions before you start your computer-aided presentation.** For example, ask groups of students to decide what they want to find out about the topic you're going to cover, and to write down some questions that they hope will be covered. When they have already got questions in their minds, they are much more receptive to the answers when your presentation addresses the questions.

- **Help your students to *make* notes.** This is much more productive than merely *taking* notes, such as when they copy down things they see on the screen, or write down verbatim things that you say. When you give your students copies of your computer-projected slides, you can encourage them to annotate their copies, adding in thoughts of their own, and questions that arise in group discussion.

- **Build tasks into your computer-aided presentation.** Get your students to *do* things with the information that is presented on-screen, rather than just watch it. Use your computer slides to pose questions and then answer them, rather than just present the answers alone. Get your students to work out which are the most important points from an on-screen list, or to work out the consequences of changing the conditions in a scenario.

- **Include questions to students in your presentations.** For example, pose a question on-screen, then pick a student at random to try to answer it. Don't make the student too uncomfortable if an answer is not immediately forthcoming, however. When students become accustomed to being put in the position of having to try to answer a question at short notice, they naturally become more attentive, as no one likes to be found lacking an answer.

- **Consider making your presentation available to students, to consult individually, after the group has seen it.** It is normally straightforward to install your presentation onto a computer, where your students can have the chance to refresh their memories of it when they choose to. Alternatively, if your students have their own computers, or regular access to computer provision, you could consider giving them copies of your presentation on disk. You may be wise to make such copies 'read-only', and have your name clearly as a footer on each slide, to prevent anyone from pirating your expertise.

- **Stop and switch the presentation off every now and then.** Design tasks to get your students recalling and consolidating what they have just seen and heard. Think about short tasks that they can do in twos or threes where they are sitting, so that they can be reminded of the main things that you wish them to remember from the episode of presentation that they have just seen.

- **Consider turning a presentation into a question and answer session.** You can brief students with the questions on-screen, then turn off the presentation while they try to work out (or guess) answers to the questions. When you resume the presentation they will be more receptive to the answers that your presentation already contains, than if they had not been trying to answer the questions themselves for a while.

8. Observing other lecturers, and being observed yourself

Many institutions build teaching observation into quality assurance procedures as a matter of routine. In some, however, a stranger in the classroom or lecture theatre is less common. The following suggestions aim to help you to get the most out of seeing others teach, and getting feedback from colleagues on your own teaching. Since the most significant arena of observation is likely to be in the context of one or other variety of inspection (such as subject review visits in universities in the UK), many of the suggestions below relate to using teaching observation as preparation for such events:

- **Value feedback from your colleagues.** It is useful to get used to taking critical feedback from someone you know, as preparation to taking it well from someone you don't know. It is useful to encourage actively staff from other parts of the institution, who already have some experience regarding quality visits, to make this experience available to you.

- **Don't allow practising to go wrong.** Sometimes it is harder to take critical feedback from someone you know than from someone vested with authority from outside. The criticism may be just as valid, however! Make sure that everyone involved in mock visits feels that the visitors are allowed to role-play rather than make enemies.

- **Accept observation as normal.** This means that when the practice is really needed, prior to a real visit for example, it is much easier to find the time for it to happen. It also means that many of the potential problems will have already been recognized and dealt with.

- **Make use of opportunities to be observed, in staff development programmes.** The sooner that you become accustomed to the experience of other people watching your teaching performance, the greater becomes your confidence at handling such situations.

- **Make appropriate use of existing checklists.** Your institution may well have specific checklists relating to key features of lectures or classroom work, on aspects such as 'planning and preparation', 'use of resources', 'involving students', 'responding to individual needs', and so on.

- **Lead in new colleagues gently.** Avoid the situation of the performances of new staff being observed against a framework of detailed criteria intended for practised and experienced teachers.

- **Make sure that not too much emphasis is placed on presentation skills.** Include room for the quality of handouts, overheads, media elements, and class exercises to be covered in the observation criteria. This can help spread the load, so that colleagues are not overly anxious about their presentation skills.

- **Remind yourself that in real teaching you are not being observed every second.** While it is possible that some students will notice slips you may make, you are unlikely to have the undivided attention of the whole class at any such time (or any other time!).

- **Beware of the possibility of getting into a rut.** When anyone has been teaching a particular topic for a considerable time, it is natural to tend to go on autopilot, and be less aware of what is actually happening during teaching sessions. Teaching observation can act as a powerful aid to refreshing your approach.

- **Take advantage of team teaching opportunities.** When you are regularly in the position of observing parts of your colleagues' teaching, and vice versa, a considerable amount of automatic staff development occurs as you learn from each other's triumphs and disasters.

- **It doesn't take long.** Suppose an observer gives you (say) three tips at the end of an hour; this can be very good value compared to just reading a book on teaching practices, where you may not happen to read the things you may most need to find out.

- **Involve students.** Give students practice in giving feedback to visitors, by getting them to give you the same sorts of feedback as visitors may ask them for. Explain why you welcome their comments, and then tell them what you intend to do differently as a result of their feedback.

- **Make case studies out of existing feedback.** Use published feedback to other institutions as a means of developing the skills of interpreting feedback comments, and role-playing responses to such feedback and the decision making that would have been appropriate on the basis of such feedback. All this paves the way to being better able to deal with the real feedback your institution will derive from quality visits.

- **When you've observed someone else teach, always give positive feedback first.** Help to put the colleague you are observing at ease by giving the good news first (and indeed making sure there is always some good news!). We are all much more likely to take on board the 'could do betters' if we have received the positive statements first.

- **Try to give three positives for every one 'could do better'.** Even when there is much to comment adversely on, it is important to give sufficient good news. If people are given too much adverse comment, they may lose track of which are the most important parts of the agenda that they need to address.

■ **When you've been observed, treat it as free consultancy.** 'Isn't is wonderful to have a colleague or friend who finds time to engage in an educational conversation with me?' is a much better approach than 'I haven't time for all this practising, let's just hope it goes alright on the day!'

■ **Take the attitude that all feedback is potentially useful.** Feedback is an important part of everyday learning, and it is constructive to regard quality visits not so much in terms of the verdicts that may be reached, but in terms of the availability of valuable feedback that they may bring.

■ **Be prepared to receive positive feedback.** In many cultures, there is a sense of embarrassment when receiving praise. This leads people to shrug it off, and to fail to really take on board the value of finding out more about what is regarded as successful. It is worth practising *receiving* positive feedback, verbally acknowledging it, and thanking the people who deliver it.

■ **Get practising for receiving negative feedback.** Regard criticism as useful feedback. Avoid the temptations to become hostile, or to justify one's position, or to make excuses for things that were found to be lacking. When critical feedback is felt to have been openly received and taken note of, the people giving such feedback are much more satisfied that their job has been done effectively, than when they are not at all sure that the feedback has been listened to and heeded.

■ **Practise eliciting feedback.** Gain skills in drawing out feedback, and getting the people giving it to clarify it and expand on it when necessary. 'What do you consider the *best* thing about the way we are handling so-and-so?' and 'What is the first thing about this that you would suggest we try to change?' are the sort of questions that help in this process.

■ **Share feedback on your teaching with your students.** They like to feel involved. Ask them what they think of feedback you've received. Ask them what actions they might suggest that you consider. Explain why you might be doing something different; this could lead to more feedback.

9. Some qualities to observe in lectures

It would be boring for students if all lectures were conducted to a standard specification. However, there are many factors which can contribute to successful and productive lectures, and the following questions may offer a starting point for your own observation checklists for large-group sessions:

■ **How well were the intended learning outcomes of the session communicated?** Did the lecturer make it clear to students what they should gain from the lecture, and where the topic fits into the overall course?

- **Was the lecturer clearly audible?** Was the voice quality such that students learning in English as a second language could keep up with the wording? Was it possible for students in the most distant parts of the room to hear clearly?

- **Was the lecture relevant to the stated learning outcomes?** It is worth checking that lectures make good use of the face-to-face contact with students, and avoid going off on tangents away from the central agenda of the syllabus.

- **Did the lecture hold students' attention well?** It is easy for an observer to notice from students' expressions and body language when their attention is straying. It is not so easy for lecturers themselves to be aware of this, as the students nearest them are more likely to be attentive (or at least looking attentive!).

- **Was the lecture sufficiently interactive?** The sorts of interaction which may be desirable include making sure that students have the opportunity to ask questions or seek clarification, and activities where students learn by doing tasks or solving problems, then gain feedback from the lecturer and from each other on how successfully they did such tasks.

- **Was the lecture well structured?** In a coherent lecture, it is possible to follow how the agenda set at the beginning unfolds and develops, and to remain aware of the purposes of the whole lecture as each part occurs. Was the structure outlined in ways that helped students to make useful notes? Were there cues to distinguish key points from elaboration? Were visual devices used to emphasize key words, phrases and definitions? Were explanations and relationships developed through the use of diagrams?

- **Did the lecture remind students of what they should already have understood from previous work?** One of the useful dividends of a well-structured lecture is that students can gain reminders about the things they are expected to have mastered already from previous lectures.

- **Did the lecturer have a suitable range of techniques for dealing with students' questions?** For example, it's useful to be able to respond to some questions straightaway. When this is not possible, ways round the problem include agreeing to report back on a future occasion, perhaps asking the rest of the group to research the answer to a question as well meanwhile.

- **Did the session come to a robust conclusion?** A danger is that some lectures just seem to peter out, without coming to a definite and hopefully memorable conclusion. One way of signifying the end of a lecture is to go back and check whether students feel they have now achieved the intended learning outcomes.

- **Did the lecturer seek feedback from students?** It's too late to leave such feedback to the end of a whole series of lectures, or the end of a course. When lecturers gain student feedback intermittently during a series, they are able to fine-tune the progression in line with students' reactions and comments. It is, however, important to avoid boring the students by using the same feedback device (however well it may work) repeatedly.

Chapter 3

Small-group teaching and learning

Working with students

This chapter starts with some suggestions about **working with students** and some of the particular needs of various categories of students. Most of the suggestions in this book are about dealing with students. There is, of course, no such person as an 'average' student. Students range widely in their ambition, personality and nature. However, this first section is intended to remind you of some special constituencies of students, and of some of the additional care you may need to take, especially in one-to-one and small-group situations, to help them get the most out of their educational experience.

The main part of this chapter is about getting **student group work** going effectively. This includes helping students work together effectively in small-group situations, including seminars, tutorials and other group-work scenarios. It is widely realized that students learn a great deal from each other, and that group work is a useful arena in which students can develop valued transferable skills, so this chapter is intended to help colleagues maximize the benefits of peer-group learning.

1. Mature students

It is important that we treat mature students appropriately, and that they feel comfortable even when in groups or classes where they are working alongside much younger students. The following suggestions may alert you to some of the principal issues that arise when working with mature students:

- **Consider designing a self-profiling questionnaire for all of your students.** This can give you an accurate picture of where the skills and competences of your mature students and their younger classmates overlap or diverge.

- **Check out the expectations of your mature students.** Ask them why they have chosen to study your subject, and how they believe it will fit into their future careers, or how it may feed into their plans for further studying. They will often have more definite answers to these questions than younger students who are simply taking your subject because it's part of their whole course.

- **Be aware of the anxieties that mature students often have when first returning to studying.** They may have negative memories of their last experiences in education, and things may have changed a great deal since they were last students. Try not to allow them to feel vulnerable or exposed until they have had sufficient time to gain confidence.

- **Remember that mature students may know a lot!** Their work experience could well have equipped them with knowledge of how some of the topics they are studying relate to the real world, and it's worth giving them the chance to share this experience. This can do a lot to increase their confidence in the group, especially in contexts where their younger counterparts are ahead of them in other ways, such as a familiarity with computers and electronic communication.

- **Some mature students tend to be demanding.** This can be a serious problem with students on assessed credit-rated programmes of study. Such students often take their studying a lot more seriously than some of their younger counterparts, one reason being that they are often footing the bill themselves, or are being invested in by their employers.

■ **Remember that mature students don't know everything – or may be 'rusty'.** Just because mature students look older doesn't automatically mean that they have picked up some of the things that their younger counterparts have learnt. There will be gaps, so ensure that mature students find out about these gaps with minimum embarrassment. Specifically designed study-support, or learning-skills induction programmes, for mature students can be most valuable to them, and much appreciated by them.

■ **Take care about assumptions.** Some mature students will have covered ground you might never have expected them to have done, and others won't have experienced things you would have expected them to have covered. It's well worth spending a little time finding out a bit more about mature students' views of their own strengths and weaknesses.

■ **Treat mature students appropriately!** They do not like being treated like children – but of course neither do younger students – or children themselves! It is worth reminding yourself that at least some mature students who are just learners in your classroom are likely to be experienced professionals like yourself in other places. Be sensitive about the different focus that mature students need regarding their first week or two on a course.

■ **Help mature students to save face.** Mature people often don't like to be seen to get things wrong, especially when seen by younger people. Watch out for occasions when feedback from assessments may raise this issue. Be sensitive to mature students' feelings when they make contributions in class; if their comments or questions are shown to be 'silly' or inappropriate, such students can take this as a serious blow to their confidence.

■ **Give mature students the chance to interact well with the rest of the group.** When choosing groups for tasks or projects, it is often worth trying to get a good mix regarding age and background, in order to allow exchange of knowledge and experience in as many directions as possible.

■ **Be realistic about other demands on mature students' time and energy.** They normally have abundant motivation and drive, but sometimes other pressures in their lives can affect the possibility of them meeting deadlines or targets.

■ **Be a mature student yourself!** It is always useful to put yourself in a position similar to that of your students. Even if the course or topic you're studying is a minor part of your life, being a learner again will alert you to ways of refreshing your own teaching practice. It can be particularly helpful to take an assessed course yourself, as this will remind you what it feels like to prepare yourself for a tutor to look critically at your work. This can help you remain sensitive to the feelings of your students.

2. Part-time students

Universities and colleges have experienced a major shift towards the provision of part-time courses for students, and this trend is certain to continue, with greater numbers of people requiring professional updating programmes and mid-career retraining. Part-time students are often mature ones, but here we look at the characteristics that arise principally because of their part-time studying. It is becoming more common to run courses and classes concurrently for both part-time and full-time students, and the following suggestions should help to ensure that the quality of provision for part-timers is enhanced even when they are studying alongside full-time students:

- **Remember that part-time students aren't full-time students!** In particular, they have not got the time to spend on unproductive activities such as waiting around, queuing, sorting out administrative details, and other things that can be done easily by full-time students in between classes and lectures. As part-time students have less chance to solve problems with course documentation by talking to each other, ensure that all written guides and instructions that they use are particularly clear and unambiguous.

- **Part-time students usually have cars!** Make provision for part-timers to have the chance to apply for restricted parking permits, such as Wednesday only. Lack of equal treatment regarding car parking often makes part-time students feel like second-class citizens even before they get to their classes.

- **Part-time students usually have family responsibilities.** Even when part-time students have high motivation and ability, those with such responsibilities may be quite unable to guarantee to attend any session if needed urgently elsewhere. It is therefore particularly important that when such students miss important sessions for good reasons, every effort needs to be made to help them catch up.

- **Think carefully about the starting time for daytime part-time sessions.** When classes for part-timers start at 10.00, it may be impossible for them to find anywhere to park their cars, as everywhere will already be full. Coming in at 08.20 to park means wasting a lot of their precious time, or if they call in at their workplace before coming to college they may well be delayed or prevented from coming altogether by pressing demands. Consider timing the start of part-time sessions early, and even *before* normal full-time classes commence.

- **Think about when to start evening part-time sessions.** Most part-time students attend on an evening-only basis. For many, starting at 17.00 poses more problems than starting at 18.00.

- **Have special library arrangements to suit part-timers.** This can include arranging priority status for short loans on selected key texts for part-time students, and library hours that allow them to come in after work or at weekends.

- **Make face-to-face time as relevant as possible for part-time students.** In particular, make sure that they are not sitting passively listening to things they already know. Check at the beginning of each topic to find out what the existing knowledge base is in the group, and prioritize your agenda accordingly. Use face-to-face time for things where part-timers really need a shared experience. Part-time students have less opportunity to talk to each other than full-timers, and we need to make sure that they get as much feedback from each other as we can arrange, during the times the group is together.

- **Choose the topics well for class sessions.** Use valuable contact time to address subjects where part-timers are likely to need your expertise. This means choosing to spotlight important parts of the syllabus, and deal with these in depth, rather than trying to run through the whole syllabus during limited contact time.

- **Make it easy for part-timers to work on their own through appropriate parts of the syllabus.** Turn notes, handouts and other learning resources into effective self-study materials, so that part-timers can make their own way through topics that don't normally cause problems. Consider the potential benefits of making study materials and tutor comment available to part-time students by e-mail, or through computer conferences, 'virtual colleges' or online learning.

- **Making video recordings of key lectures, seminars or tutorials can be a real benefit to part-time students.** When they miss a crucial session unavoidably, they can catch up very significantly if it is possible for them to see exactly what they missed.

- **Don't assume that part-time students have out-of-hours access to facilities.** Most of their in-college time is likely to be timetabled in classes. If they will require information technology facilities for work to be handed in for assessment, they may need a longer lead-in time to allow them to arrange access to such facilities.

- **Lack of refreshment provision can be a real problem.** Many part-timers arrive on campus after a busy time at their workplace, and without having had the chance to get anything to eat or drink. When campus facilities offer only limited provision, part-timers can end up hungry and dehydrated – not the best state to learn effectively. Moreover, good catering provision helps part-timers to congregate together and talk before or after sessions, and the learning pay-off of such interaction is highly significant.

- **Part-time students may need the same sorts of help as full-time students.** Support services such as counselling and personal tutoring can be just as crucial for part-time as for full-time students. Problems can remain unsolved if the support provision does not extend to times when part-timers can make use of it.

- **Take particular care regarding referred reading and set coursework.** Part-timers may not have the time to read widely, and it helps them a lot if you make references quite specific, indicating to them exactly what you intend them to derive from their work with each source.

Because of the other demands on their time, part-time students need plenty of notice of deadlines for assessed coursework, and additional leeway if they are finding it hard to meet particular deadlines.

■ **Use alternative means of communication for part-timers.** Use internal mail for question-and-answer communication between yourself and part-time students, and (for those students with access to appropriate facilities) make the most of e-mail and computer conferencing possibilities.

■ **Keep part-time students informed.** Find systems for letting them know about changes to timetables, or other changes that are often last-minute ones. They hate travelling in only to find that their lecture that day has been rearranged or cancelled!

3. International students

The suggestions we offer below aim to alert you to some of the particular help that may be needed by this particular cross-section of your student population. Students from other countries, or from a different ethnic background to the majority of your students, may need additional support in various ways, and at different stages of their studying. The suggestions below aim to help you minimize the disadvantages that such students can experience, when they are studying on programmes where they may be minority groups:

■ **Arrange specialist induction provision for international students.** Pre-sessional courses addressing aspects of cultural acclimatization, and study-skills good practice, can be of enormous benefit in helping such students start off their academic studies without being disadvantaged.

■ **Produce clear information for international students.** Try to ensure that they receive this information before they arrive at college. Ideally we should be producing clear information for all students, such as by using course handbooks, but it is particularly important that international students should receive good documentation about their courses, as well as about the institution and its environs. International students are more likely to need to revisit such information again and again until they have tuned in to their new situation, and they can often do this more successfully when the information is in print rather than in easy-to-forget face-to-face formats.

■ **Help students from other countries or cultures to understand what is expected of them in assessment.** Assessment cultures vary widely round the world, and what is regarded as normal practice in some places is seen as cheating or plagiarism in others. It is important that all students are aware of the ways they are expected to behave in preparing for and undertaking any kind of assessment. It can be particularly important to help students adjust to those parts of their courses involving independent study, and about how to prepare for the assessment associated with such studies.

■ **Help them to understand what is expected of them in seminars.** Many international students come from cultures with particularly formal methods of education, and find it hard to cope with the more interactive modes of teaching. Students from some cultures can find it a shock to encounter the full and frank debates between students and tutors that are regarded as healthy indicators of a seminar. This may explain their own reluctance to become involved, and they will need patient encouragement to adopt the roles that they are expected to play in their new setting.

■ **Search for ways of lessening the isolation of international students.** Encourage them out of the institution, so they can absorb more of the local culture, and make new contacts and friends, without putting them under any pressure to break their normal links with fellow students from the same background.

■ **Be sensitive on issues of religion.** Some religions require followers to pray at specific times and in particular settings. This can be a problem for students required to fit in with tight timetabling, and sensitive flexibility needs to be shown regarding their needs and rights.

■ **Help students with special food requirements.** Coping with a new culture is enough of a hurdle for students from different backgrounds and cultures, without imposing the additional burden of having to cope with 'majority' food habits. Gather feedback on what would be acceptable alternatives that could be built into menus and catering provision. Advise those arranging catering at induction events to be especially sensitive about labelling food, so that international students don't become anxious about what they can and cannot eat.

■ **Consider getting previous students from each country to write an introductory guide to the idiosyncrasies of the British!** It can be useful for new students from overseas, and for staff and students not from abroad, to get the chance to see themselves through the eyes of people from other cultures or countries.

■ **Recognize cultural differences regarding attitudes to alcohol.** Even if mainstream attitudes are alcohol-tolerant, significant groups of staff and students come from cultures where alcohol may be forbidden on religious grounds. Sensitivity regarding attitudes to alcohol does not just mean expecting groups of students, whatever their background, to go on field trips or visits which include a stop on the way back at a suitable pub! Class discussions of alcohol marketing strategies or pub social behaviours will be offensive or alien to students (or staff) whose culture forbids alcohol.

■ **Consider the special facilities needed by students from other countries.** For example, toilet and washing facilities need to accommodate the different practices that are involved in some cultures or religions. When such students attempt to make use of 'normal' facilities, their actions are in danger of being misunderstood.

■ **Consider the accommodation needs of students from other cultures.** Students from some countries, when booking their place at an institution in the UK, may not know what is meant by 'hall of residence', 'single-study-bedroom' or 'shared student apartment'. Accommodation literature needs to be written or supplemented so that all students know what each category of accommodation entails.

■ **Offer language support at appropriate levels.** Students studying in English as a second or other language will need different kinds of language support as they continue their studies. At first, they may need help in getting started in English, but later the help they need may be more connected to how they should use written language in assessed work, and spoken English in interviews with tutors or in oral examinations.

■ **Help them to communicate with home, especially in emergencies.** International telephone or fax charges are high, and students may not have access to locations where they can use such communications in relative privacy. The costs, both financial and academic, of students having to make emergency visits home are more serious, and ways need to be found of helping students sort out some of the problems that could lead them into such costs.

■ **Make arrangements to celebrate success.** Students who come to study from other countries are often unable to celebrate their achievements at the times when their results are available, by which time they may have gone home. Consider having end-of-teaching-session events as well as, or instead of, end of course events.

4. Students with special needs

Colleges have a responsibility to provide the best possible educational opportunities within their remit for all students. Open-access policies, together with statutory requirements, mean that we need to take into account the requirements of students with special needs when planning our programmes of learning. These suggestions are designed to help you think about how best to approach this:

■ **Adopt a positive action approach.** Students with special needs should not be regarded as a problem to be dealt with, rather as a constituency of users whose needs must be taken into account.

■ **Involve the students in managing the support you offer.** The people who are most affected are usually the best to advise you on appropriate support strategies. They should be consulted alongside specialist external advisers when designing your provision.

■ **Think carefully about the language you use.** The term 'handicapped' can cause offence, since it is derived from those who came 'cap in hand' to ask for help. 'Disability' can also be seen as a derogatory term, suggesting something of less value than ability. People with special needs usually prefer to be regarded as people first and last, rather than being categorized by what they can't do.

- **Don't assume that people with mobility problems are wheelchair-bound.** Most people entitled to use the UK orange badge on their vehicles are not, in fact, users of wheelchairs. They may, however, experience difficulties in walking long distances, climbing stairs, or undertaking other strenuous activities. Be aware of hidden disabilities, such as asthma and heart problems.

- **Don't use difficult buildings as an excuse to exclude people with special needs.** It can be expensive and difficult to install lifts, automatic doors and ramps, especially into old buildings, but lateral thinking can work miracles. Careful timetabling can permit the teaching of classes including someone with mobility problems, in ground-floor or easy-access rooms. In the UK, government funds are often available to improve access when a need has been clearly identified.

- **Help people with visual impairments.** Colleges can do much to help students who don't see well, to study effectively. Allowing students access to tape-record classes, and making available on loan recording equipment from the college, can help considerably. Visual impairment is frequently not total, and lecturers can do their bit by using large font sizes on overhead transparencies, and making material available to students who find it difficult to copy from the board or screen in class. The mobility of people with visual impairments can be improved moderately easily by such means as Braille signing, tactile strips on corridor floors, and 'talking' lifts.

- **Help students with hearing difficulties.** Many colleges now have audio loop systems, which enable students to amplify sound in classrooms. These can be supplemented by individual lecturers ensuring that students who don't hear well can have their choice of seats in class. Lecturers can facilitate audibility by speaking clearly, and providing backup material on request.

- **Make provision for students with learning difficulties.** These students cope well in colleges, especially when given additional targeted support as required in the classroom and around the college, and can fully contribute to the life of the institution. Learning resources centres can be especially helpful in providing a range of resources to support the learning of these students.

- **Provide support for students with, and recovering from, mental illness.** Individual counselling and guidance can be enormously beneficial in enabling these students to use college study as part of a programme of personal recovery and development.

- **Keep in mind health and safety requirements for students with special needs.** Procedures for fire or bomb-threat evacuation need to take account of those people who cannot move fast, who may not hear or see warnings, or who may be unduly alarmed by emergency situations.

Ensure that your strategies for coping with emergencies of all kinds take account of the special needs of all of your students.

5. Preparing students for group work

Students often feel that they are competing with each other, and need considerable encouragement to relax such feelings and begin to work collaboratively effectively. The following suggestions should help to get your students started in productive group activities:

- **Help students to understand the benefits of being able to work together in groups.** Explain to students that there are real skills to be gained from group-work tasks, and that the ability to contribute effectively to teams that they will develop is important to employers.

- **Think about the different ways of forming groups.** These include forming groups randomly, using alphabetical lists, or forming groups on the basis of background, interest or ability, or allowing students to choose their own group compositions. Each method has its own advantages and drawbacks. The best compromise is to rotate group membership and ensure that students are not 'stuck' in the same group for too long, especially if it does not have a successful dynamic.

- **Think about the optimum group size for the group tasks you have in mind for students.** The most suitable group size will differ according to the nature of the task. Pairs are ideal for some tasks, while for other kinds of group work, threes, fours or fives are better. If the group is larger than about six, individuals tend to opt out or feel unable to make useful contributions to the group.

- **Give students some training in group processes.** It can be useful to use an icebreaker with the whole class, during which students work for a short while in groups, and are then briefed to analyse exactly what went well and what didn't work in the group episode, and to identify reasons for good and bad processes.

- **Structure students' early attempts at group work.** It can be helpful to provide quite detailed lists of briefing instructions, and ask each group to allocate the tasks among the members. This can be useful towards helping groups to work out their own directions, and then allocate them fairly in future group work.

- **Help students to understand the reasons why group work can go wrong.** The more students know about the things that work, and the hazards of interpersonal relationships and group dynamics, the better they can cope with the aspects of human nature that inevitably play their part in any kind of group situation.

- ■ **Ensure that there are suitable places for students to work in groups.** Arrange that there are places where students can talk, argue and discuss things, and not just in whispers in an area that is supposed to be kept quiet. It is also useful if the group-work venues are such that students are not being observed or overheard by their tutors, or by any other groups, at least for some of the time they work together.

- ■ **Give students support and guidance when things go wrong.** It is not enough just to criticize a group where processes have failed; students need advice on what to do to rectify the situation, and how to handle disagreements or conflicts successfully.

- ■ **Be fair and firm with assessment.** Always ensure that individuals' contributions are fairly measured and assessed. Don't allow students to think that they will all earn the same mark even if they have not all made equal contributions to the work of the group. Logs of meetings, breakdowns of who agreed to do what, and evidence of the contributions that each member brought to the group, can all be prepared by students, and can all lend themselves to assessment at the end of the group work.

- ■ **Get students to evaluate the effectiveness of their group work.** Including such an evaluation as an assessed element in each student's work can cause all of the members of a group to reflect on the processes involved in their working together, and to deepen their learning about the processes involved in effective team working.

6. Some dos and don'ts

Tutorials, seminars and other small-group situations can be highly productive learning experiences for students. Larger overall class sizes make it more difficult to provide such occasions for students, and it is therefore important that the quality of those sessions that are provided is as high as we can make it. The following suggestions may help you to enhance the quality of students' learning in small groups:

- ■ **Make sure that the goals of each tutorial are clearly communicated to students.** Sometimes the goals can be published in advance, while on other occasions they will depend on the questions and issues that the students bring to the occasion. In either case, the learning payoff is enhanced if the goals are established or reviewed at the start of the session concerned.

- ■ **Help students to know the purposes of small-group work.** Students often don't really know what the differences are between the different kinds of teaching-learning sessions on their timetables, in terms of the different sorts of behaviour expected of them, and the teaching-learning processes involved in each kind of small-group work. The more students know about why we are giving them each different episode of small-group work, the better they can benefit from such occasions.

- **Prepare for small group sessions!** There is a tendency (as noticed by teaching quality reviewers!) for tutors to prepare well for lectures but not for tutorials. This leads students to come to their own unfortunate conclusions about the relative importance of each of these teaching-learning environments.

- **Start each new group session with a short icebreaker.** This helps each group's members get to know each other, relax, and become confident to work with each other. There are dozens of icebreakers that take no more than five minutes to run. Experiment with them, find your own favourites, then invent better ones.

- **Keep the beginning of the main task short and simple.** To Einstein is attributed 'everything should be made as simple as possible, but no simpler'. Make sure that the first stage of each group task is something that does not cause argument, and does not take any time to interpret. Once a group is under way, it is possible to make tasks much more challenging.

- **Don't talk too much!** A problem with small-group sessions is that it is all too easy for the tutor to fill all of the available time. Even when answering students' questions, it is usually more productive to provide good short answers to several questions than an in-depth definitive answer to just one question.

- **Make good use of question-and-answer processes.** Come in to a small-group session with a list of questions you may or may not actually ask, and concentrate first on all the questions you can draw from the students. Towards the end of a tutorial, you can select from your 'unanswered' questions some for the students to prepare their own answers ready for a future session. It can be useful to give each member of the group a different question to go away with (but making sure that none of the questions are so difficult that the students will not return on the next occasion).

- **Ensure that student participation is high on the agenda.** Getting *all* the students to participate is quite an art. Just asking for verbal contributions can allow the confident, pushy student to dominate. Asking each of the students to write down their own immediate answers to a question, for example on post-its or small pieces of overhead film, can be a way of promoting equal participation opportunity, and can help the more retiring students to provide their contributions to the group. Vary the nature of students' activities, for example getting them to make flipchart lists, post-it replies to questions, mind-maps, pictorial metaphors, flowcharts, and so on.

- **Think about introducing student-managed small-group sessions.** These can be occasions where the students themselves are given freedom to prepare the content, and manage the processes by which they tackle the topic concerned.

- **Don't ask questions that just depend on recall.** It is much more useful to consider questions which help students to make sense of what they are learning than just to remind them about what they may have forgotten.

■ **Don't ask too many questions at once.** Learning in small groups happens best when the students know exactly which question or issue they are addressing at a given time. It can, however, be useful to write up the 'whole' list of questions on a flipchart or whiteboard, so students can see where each question fits into the whole picture.

■ **Don't put a student on the spot with a difficult question too early!** This can deter students from participation, and can even make them so uncomfortable that they may choose not to attend your next session with them. It is much more acceptable to put some of the students on the-spot with hard questions towards the end of the session, but to move away from them if they have not got ready answers, as these questions can then be the agenda for the next session, giving all the students involved some time to prepare their answers.

■ **Don't ask questions then answer them yourself.** Though it can be hard to wait for students to work towards the answer to a question, and you may be itching to provide the answer, students will learn a lot more by struggling if necessary. You can help them converge towards a good answer by giving feedback on those parts of their thinking that are along the lines required, and explaining to them why other ideas are not correct or appropriate.

■ **Don't ignore students' answers.** Even when students give incorrect or confused answers to a question you've asked them, they need some helpful feedback on *their* answers, and not just to be told what the right answers should have been. Where possible, build on students' own responses when leading towards the correct answers.

7. Keeping momentum

■ **Foster ownership of the task.** Wherever possible, try to arrange that the members of the whole group have thought of the issues to be addressed by small-group work. When possible, allow members to choose which group task they wish to engage in. When people have chosen to do a task, they are more likely to attempt it wholeheartedly.

■ **Don't rely only on oral briefings.** Oral briefings are useful, as they can add the emphasis of tone of voice, facial expression and body language. However, when *only* oral briefings are given for group learning tasks, it is often found that after a few minutes different groups are attempting quite different things.

■ **Prepare printed briefings.** It is useful to put the overall briefing up on an overhead transparency or PowerPoint slide, but if groups then move away into different syndicate rooms, they can lose sight (and mind) of the exact briefing. It is worth having slips of paper containing exactly the same words as in the original briefing, which groups can take away with them.

■ **Visit the groups in turn.** It can make a big difference to progress if you spend a couple of minutes just listening to what is happening in a group, then chipping in gently with one or two useful suggestions, then moving on. During such visits, you can also remind groups of the deadline for the next report-back stage.

■ | **Clarify the task when asked.** Sometimes, groups will ask you whether you mean one thing or another by the words in the briefing. It is often productive if you are able to reply 'either of these would be an interesting way of interpreting the task; you choose which interpretation you would prefer to address'. This legitimizes the group's discovery of ambiguity, and can increase the efforts they put into working out their chosen interpretation.

■ | **Have an early, brief, report-back from groups on the first stage of their task.** This can help to set expectations that everyone will be required to be ready for later report-back stages at the times scheduled in the task briefing. Any group that finds itself unprepared for the initial report-back is likely to try to make sure that this position does not repeat itself.

■ | **Break down extended tasks into manageable elements.** Often, if the whole task is presented to groups as a single briefing, group members will get bogged down by the most difficult part of the overall task. This element might turn out to be much more straightforward if they had already done the earlier parts of the whole task.

■ | **Try to control the amount of time that groups spend on successive stages of each task.** It can be useful to introduce a sense of closure of each stage in turn, by getting groups to write down decisions or conclusions before moving on to the next stage in the overall task.

8. Gender issues in group work

When problems occur in groups due to gender issues, they can be felt more deeply than problems arising from almost any other cause. The following suggestions may help you to avoid some problems of this sort from arising in the first place, or to alert group members themselves to the potential problems, so that they can work round them in their own approaches to group work:

■ | **Think about gender when forming groups.** There are advantages and disadvantages for single sex groups, depending on the balance of the sexes, and other issues including culturally sensitive ones. In some cultures, females may be much happier, for religious reasons, working in single sex groups.

■ | **Try to avoid gender domination of groups.** This can happen because of majority gender composition of groups. If this is inevitable because of the overall gender balance of the whole class, try to manage group composition so that minority participants don't feel isolated.

■ | **Decide when single gender groups might be more appropriate.** For group work on gender-sensitive issues, it can be best to set out to form single sex groups.

- **Require appropriate behaviour.** For group work to be effective, all participants need to behave in a professional way, with standards that would be expected in an effective working environment. Outlaw sexist or offensive behaviour.

- **Decide when to ring the changes.** Use random group formation processes to form different kinds of groups for respective tasks and activities. For example, form some groups on the basis of month of birthday, others by alphabetical processes, including 'last letter of first name', and so on. This can ensure that groups that develop problems don't continue for too long.

- **Decide when to stick with existing group compositions.** When a set of groups is working well, without any gender-related or other problems, don't just change the group composition without a good reason.

- **Set ground rules for talking and listening.** It can be useful to agree on ground rules that will ensure that all group participants (irrespective of gender) are heard, and not talked down by other participants.

- **Avoid setting up excessive competition between male groups and female groups.** When there are gender-specific groups, don't egg a group of one gender on, by saying words to the effect 'Come on, you can do better than them', referring to groups of the other gender.

- **Be sensitive about role assignment.** For example, try to raise awareness about the dangers of tasks being allocated within groups on the basis of gender stereotypes, such as typing or making arrangements being handled by females, and 'heavy' work by males.

- **Alert groups to be sensitive to leadership issues.** It is often the case that, for example, male members of groups may automatically see themselves as stronger contenders to lead the group than their female counterparts, and put themselves forward. When group members are aware that this is an issue, they are more likely to agree on a more democratic process for deciding who will lead an activity, or who will report back the outcomes.

- **Be alert to the pros and cons of putting couples in the same group.** Couples can result in productive partnerships in group work, but can easily become exclusive or dominating if there is only one other person in the group.

- **Avoid sexual preference oppression.** When it is known that group participants have different sexual preferences from the majority of the group, there is a tendency for them to be oppressed in one way or another by the rest of the group. It can be delicate to raise this issue in general briefings, and it may be best to respond to it as a facilitator when it is seen to be likely to occur.

- **Keep peer-assessment fair.** When peer-assessment is being used within group work, or between groups, watch out for the tendency for females to underrate and males to overrate.

9. Establishing ground rules for groups

Ground rules can be very useful indeed in group-work contexts. Below are some starting-points from which practical ground rules can be developed:

- **Create ownership of the ground rules.** The various ground rule agendas suggested below should only be regarded as starting-points for each group to adopt or adapt and prioritize.

- **Be truthful.** Successful group work relies on honesty. It is as dishonest to 'put up with' something you don't agree about, or can't live with, as to speak untruthfully.

- **You don't have to like people to work with them.** In group work, as in professional life, people work with the team they are in, and matters of personal conflict need to be managed so they don't get in the way of the progress of the group as a whole.

- **Affirm collective responsibility.** Once issues have been aired, and group decisions have been made as fully as possible, the convention of collective responsibility is applied, where everyone lives with the group decisions, and refrains from articulating their own personal reservations outside the group.

- **Develop and practise listening skills.** Every voice deserves to be heard, even if you don't initially agree with the point of view.

- **Participate fully.** Group work relies on multiple perspectives. Don't hold back from putting forward your view.

- **Everyone takes a fair share of the work.** This does not mean that everyone has to do the same thing. It is best when the members of the group have agreed how the tasks will be allocated among members.

- **Working to strengths can benefit the group.** The work of the group can be achieved efficiently when tasks are allocated according to the experience and expertise of each member of the group.

- **Don't always work to strengths, however!** Activities in groups can be developmental in purpose, so task allocation may be an ideal opportunity to allow group members to build on areas of weakness or inexperience.

- **Keep good records.** There needs to be an output to look back upon. This can take the form of planning notes, minutes, or other kinds of evidence of the progress of the work of the group. Rotate the responsibility for summing up the position of the group regarding the tasks in hand, and recording this.

- **Group deadlines are sacrosanct.** The principle: 'you can let yourself down, but it's not OK to let the group down' underpins successful group work.

- **Cultivate philanthropy.** Group work sometimes requires people to make personal needs and wishes subordinate to the goal of the group.

- **Value creativity and off-the-wall ideas.** Don't allow these to be quelled out of a desire to keep the group on task, and strike a fair balance between progress and creativity.

- **Work systematically.** Establishing a regular programme of meetings, task report-backs and task allocation is likely to lead to effective and productive group performance.

- **Regard ground rules as a continuing agenda.** It can be productive to review and renegotiate the ground rules from time to time, creating new ones as solutions to unanticipated problems that might have arisen. It is important, however, not to forget or abandon those ground rules which proved useful in practice, but which were not consciously applied.

10. Addressing conflict in group work

Much has been written about the stages that are quite normal in group work. For example, it is common for teams to progress through stages of 'forming, storming, norming and performing' – not necessarily in one particular order! Groups, however, need not be the same as teams. The following suggestions may help you to minimize the dangers associated with conflict in group work, and to maximize the benefits that can be drawn from people who sometimes disagree:

- **Legitimate disagreement.** It is important to acknowledge that people don't have to agree all of the time, and to open up agreed processes by which areas of disagreement can be explored and resolved (or be accepted to remain as known areas of disagreement).

- **Establish the causes of conflict.** When conflict has broken out in a group, it is easy for the root causes to become subsumed in an escalation of feeling. It can be productive to backtrack to the exact instance that initiated the conflict, and to analyse it further.

- **Encourage groups to put the conflict into written words.** Writing up the issues, problems or areas of disagreement on a flipchart or marker-board can help to get them out of people's systems. Conflict feelings are often much stronger when the conflict is still bottled up, and has not yet been clearly expressed or acknowledged. When something is 'up on the wall', it often looks less daunting, and a person who felt strongly about it may be more satisfied. The 'on the wall' issues can be returned to later when the group has had more time to think about them.

- **Establish the ownership of the conflict.** Who feels it? Who is being affected by it? Hesitate to probe 'whose fault is it?', however! Distinguish between individual issues and ones that affect the whole group.

■ | **Distinguish between people, actions and opinions.** When unpacking the causes of conflict in a group situation, it is useful to focus on actions and principles. Try to resolve any actions that proved to cause conflict. Try to agree principles. If the conflict is caused by different opinions, it can help to accept people's entitlement to their opinions, and leave it open to people to reconsider their opinions if and when they feel ready to do so.

■ | **Use conflict creatively.** It can be useful to use brainstorming to obtain a wider range of views, or a broader range of possible actions that can be considered by the group. Sometimes, the one or two strong views that may have caused conflict in a group look much more reasonable when the full range of possibilities is aired, and areas of agreement are found to be closer than they seemed to be.

■ | **Capture the learning from conflict.** When conflict has occurred, it can be beneficial to ask everyone to decide constructive things they have learned about themselves from the conflict, and to agree on principles which the whole group can apply to future activities to minimize the damage from similar causes of conflict arising again. Try to encourage 'win-win' approaches, rather than 'win-lose' ones.

■ | **Refuse to allow conflict to destroy group work.** You may wish sometimes to tell groups that achievement of consensus is an aim, or a norm, or alternatively you may wish to ask groups to establish only the extent of the consensus they achieve.

■ | **Consider arbitration processes.** When conflict is absolutely unresolvable, the facilitator may need to set up a 'court of appeal' for desperate situations. The fact that such a process is available often helps groups to sort out their own problems without having to resort to it.

■ | **Make it OK to escape.** When people know that they can get out of an impossible situation, they don't feel trapped, and in fact are more likely to work their own way out of the conflict. It can be useful to allow people to drop out of a group, and move into another one, but only as a last resort. Beware of the possible effects of someone who is seen as a conflict generator entering a group which has so far worked without conflict!

11. 'Followership' skills development

Leadership is often discussed in the context of teamwork, but it can be argued that 'followership' is just as important. The suggestions below may help you to ensure that leaders in your groups have skilled followers! They may also help to optimize the learning that can be achieved through well-thought-out following:

■ | **Brief groups about the concept of followership.** It can be important to legitimize followership as a vital factor to underpin the success of group work.

■ **Explain that followership should not be regarded as weakness.** When leadership is rotating between group members, they should regard their work when *not* leading as every bit as important as when they are directing the actions of the group.

■ **Accept that followership requires well-developed skills and attributes.** For example, patience may be needed. When it takes a little time for the purpose or wisdom of a leadership decision to become apparent, it is sometimes harder to wait for this to happen than to jump in and try to steer the group, or argue with the decision.

■ **More followers than leaders are needed!** It is virtually impossible to have a successful group where all members are adopting leading stances at the same time. Though the credit for successful group work is often attributed to the leader, it is often the followers who actually own the success. It is more than good sense to acknowledge this right from the start of any group-work situation.

■ **Followership is a valuable, transferable key skill.** In all walks of life, people need to be followers at least for some of the time. It can be useful to employ group-work situations to help people to develop skills that will make them good followers in other contexts of their lives and careers.

■ **Good followership is not the same as being 'easily led'.** Being 'easily led' usually is taken to imply that people are led into doing things against their better judgement. Good followership is closer to being easily led when the direction of the task in hand coincides quite closely to individuals' own judgement.

■ **Followership should not be blind obedience!** Encourage group members to think about how they are following, why they are following, for how long they are going to be content with following, and what they are learning through following.

■ **Suggest that group members experiment with a 'followership log'.** This could be private notes to themselves of their experiences of being led, but it is more important to make notes on their feelings as followers than to write down criticisms of the actions of the leaders. Whether the logs are treated as private or shared notes can be decided later by everyone involved in a group.

■ **Legitimize followership notes as authentic evidence of the operation of a group.** Such notes can tell their own stories regarding the relative contributions of members of the group, and the group processes that worked well and those that worked badly. When it is known that followership records will count towards the evidence of achievement of a group, leadership itself is often done more sensitively and effectively.

■ **Followership is vital training for leadership.** People who have been active, reflective followers can bring their experience of followership to bear on their future leadership activities. Having consciously reflected on the experience of following informs leadership approaches, and makes their own leadership easier for others to follow.

■ | **Good followership is partly about refraining from nit-picking.** When people have too strong a desire to promote their individuality, it often manifests itself in the form of expending energy in trying to achieve unimportant minor adjustments to the main processes going on in group work. Good followership involves adopting restraint about minor quibbles, and saving interventions for those occasions where it is important not to follow without question.

12. Using post-its and flipcharts in group work

Getting things down on paper is often a vital element in keeping group learning going. The largest common size of paper is the A1 flipchart, and the smallest the post-it (which come in various sizes, of course). The following suggestions may help you to decide which medium to use for which purposes:

■ | **Use post-its for private brainstorming.** When all members of the group are intended to think in parallel, before putting together their ideas, it is useful to give everyone one or more post-its, on which they can write their individual ideas, views or questions.

■ | **Use post-its to overcome 'blank sheet fright'.** Faced with a whole sheet of paper on which to jot down ideas, students often become inhibited and don't know quite where to start. A post-it is much smaller, and less challenging, and helps students to make that first step, getting at least one idea down in words.

■ | **Use post-its for individual named contributions.** Getting everyone in a group to write their names on each post-it along with their contribution makes it possible to keep track of ownership of ideas. This can, however, inhibit free brainstorming of ideas, so it is important to use names only when there is a good reason for doing so.

■ | **Use post-its as an equal opportunity medium.** One of the problems with oral brainstorming is that it can so easily become dominated by the most extrovert or confident members of the group. Writing ideas on post-its overcomes the inhibitions of the less forthcoming members of the group.

■ | **Use post-its to save time transcribing ideas to a flipchart.** It can be painfully slow for a facilitator or group scribe to write up all the ideas onto a flipchart. It is much faster to simply stick the post-its onto a flipchart, to present a visual display of all of the ideas generated. Also, transcription tends to be unfaithful, and people's meanings often become distorted by the words chosen by the transcriber, causing a loss in the sense of ownership individuals have regarding their ideas.

■ | **Use post-its for prioritization.** When everyone in a group has written some ideas onto post-its, it is much easier for the whole group to attempt to prioritize the ideas in order of importance (or practicability, or likely payoff, and so on). This can be done by rearranging and readjusting the post-it display on a flipchart, with the most crucial ideas at the top, and the less important ones further down. It can be very productive to get groups to choose and prioritize only the top nine ideas, using a 'diamond-9' formation on the flipchart.

■ **Use flipcharts to create something that can be shown to other groups.** A display of post-its adhered to a flipchart is fine for the group which created the ideas, but is less suitable for sharing with other groups, because of the size of handwriting. It is worth summarizing the ideas which may have been generated on post-its onto a freshly drawn flipchart, using broad marker pens, and colour to emphasize importance and links between ideas.

■ **Use flipcharts to exchange between groups.** A very productive way of exchanging ideas between groups, without tedious repetitive report-back stages, is for one member to cross over to another group, bearing the flipchart product from the previous group, and talk the new group through the thinking behind the flipchart. It is then useful to get the new groups to add further ideas to the flipchart, by asking them to extend the original task in specified directions.

■ **Use flipcharts for exhibitions.** This is especially useful when different groups have been tackling different issues relating to an overall theme. Pasting the flipcharts to a wall and allowing all group members to circulate round them can be more interesting than listening to a series of report-backs from each group. This can be further enhanced when one member of the group that created each flipchart stands by the exhibit to explain it as necessary to visitors.

■ **Details on flipcharts can be captured and circulated.** This is, of course, possible when electronic flipcharts are available, allowing a print-out of the contents of a 'chart' to be made and copied to all members of the group. However, it is becoming more attractive to have a digital camera, and snap each chart, loading the contents into a computer and printing them out, if necessary with editing or explanations added. Once such equipment is available, the running costs are almost negligible.

13. Ringing the changes

There are many different ways of enhancing the quality of learning in student groups. The following suggestions expand on the question-and-answer ideas for use in tutorial-type sessions given elsewhere in this book, and are among the processes which teaching quality reviewers are looking for in their observations of group work:

■ **Get individual students to prepare and present seminars.** This can include the student leading the seminar taking questions from the rest of the group, and maybe also from the tutor involved in the group. The attention of the student audience can be significantly increased by getting the students receiving the seminar to use processes of peer-assessment, with straightforward and well-expressed criteria which have preferably been formulated by the student group.

■ **Consider getting pairs or groups of students to prepare and present seminars.** This can be less intimidating than solo performances, and can involve the development of useful cooperation and collaboration skills. Again, peer-assessment can help *all* the students involved get more from such seminars.

■ **Use tutorless groups for appropriate learning activities.** These give students the freedom to contribute without the fear of being found lacking, or making mistakes in front of a tutor. For such groups to work well, it is useful to provide the students with carefully formulated briefings in print, and to require an appropriate report-back product.

■ **Use buzz-groups in large-group sessions.** These are particularly useful for generating in an informal way a lot of ideas or opinions, which can then be reported-back and explored in greater depth with the large group.

■ **Use brainstorming techniques to generate ideas.** This is useful in small groups, and still works well with groups of 20 or more students. It is important to formulate strict ground rules for brainstorming, such as 'give no comment on ideas already given', 'say "pass" if you've nothing to add when it's your turn', and 'think creatively and say anything that comes to mind'. After producing as many ideas as possible in a few minutes, the group can start prioritizing and clustering them.

■ **Use snowballing or pyramiding to refine ideas.** This can be a way of enhancing learning in quite large groups by getting students to work together in a structured way. For example, get students to think of ideas in pairs, then combine with another pair to take the ideas further, and then combine with another four to prepare a report-back to the whole class.

■ **Use crossovers to enhance students' communication in groups.** For example, divide a group of 16 into four groups of four. Set the small groups a first-stage task, then ask one member from each group to move to another group and report the findings. Set the second stage of the task to the revised groups, then ask a different member to move on and report, and continue doing this till everyone has worked with everyone else.

■ **Consider using fishbowls in medium-sized groups.** For example, from a group of 20 students, six could be drawn (or volunteer) to sit in a circle in the middle of the room. The inner circle could then be briefed to discuss a scenario, with everyone else observing, and with an exchange mechanism by which students from outside the group wanting to make contributions could replace someone in the group.

■ **Use role-plays to help students contribute more-easily.** Some students who are reluctant to contribute to group discussions or debates because of shyness, lose most of such inhibition if they are playing someone else. Printed handout sheets giving sufficient details of each role help students to adopt the role they are intended to play, and are useful for allowing each student to react to the other roles involved as they unfold in the role-play.

■ **Self-help groups can enhance students' learning.** It can be worthwhile to start such groups up with tutor support, and help the students in each group start out to generate their own ground rules and targets. Then the groups can be left to operate without further support, other than perhaps a mechanism to bring unresolved problems to a class meeting or to a tutor.

14. Helping students to write reflections on group learning

Many students who work in groups or teams are asked to write a reflective piece on the way in which their group worked. Students are asked to reflect on what happened and particularly their own role within it in order to consolidate what they have learnt and draw out lessons for the future. However, this activity can present a number of problems and you need to give some guidance on how to write in this way and how the writing will be assessed:

■ **Start with description.** Good reflection should be based on a clear account of who did what, when, what kinds of difficulties were encountered and so on. Reflection without description is usually far too vague, impressionistic and sloppy.

■ **Use a framework for analysis.** After the description, you will be expecting students to analyse group activities. You could provide a framework for this or help students to develop one. One possibility is a set of prompt questions such as: What was the group trying to achieve at this point? What were the different views? What was said and what was left unsaid? How was the decision made? How did you feel about this? How did other group members feel? What were the group energy levels and motivation like at this point? Did anything unexpected happen?

■ **Lead into action planning.** A key purpose of individual reflection is to gain a better understanding of what happened in group work and your personal role within it. Ask students to identify what they contributed to the group and what difficulties they experienced and then to use this to identify their own strengths and weaknesses and issues they would like to address in future.

■ **Encourage the linking of theory and experience.** Most students who are asked to work in groups have been introduced to some relevant theories about working collaboratively. Encourage them to draw on such theories and discuss how they might apply to their own experiences in relation to motivation, leadership, team roles, competitiveness and so on.

■ **Develop ground rules for writing about other group members (and the tutor).** All kinds of problems can arise if group members write about other students or the tutor in ways that are inappropriate. Some students may be reluctant to write anything about their peers if they know that the tutor will see it. Some ground rules might be: Don't make assumptions about the motives and feelings of other students – check by asking them or, if this is not possible, acknowledge that it is only your perception; for example, 'Stuart seemed to me to be upset'. Don't write anything about a fellow student that you would not want them to read (even if you don't expect them to read it). Such rules may seem unduly restrictive but in many professional contexts we need to be able to comment on and criticize the behaviour of others in a constructive way and students need to learn how to do this.

■ **Ask students to focus on critical incidents.** Where students have participated in a lengthy group task, their written reflections will, of necessity, be selective. Ask them to identify two or three 'critical incidents' which were turning points for the group, or which illustrate particular difficulties or successes, and concentrate on those.

■ **Help students to learn how to write reflectively.** Ask them to write a short piece on a small element of group working, for example about the first one-hour meeting of the group, on how the group divided tasks up, or how the group responded to feedback from the tutor. Give feedback on these early attempts. Encourage students to share what they have written within the group, so that they can see the different approaches and learn from each other. Show students examples of good pieces of writing that would score highly on your assessment criteria.

■ **Make the assessment requirements clear.** Students are often very unsure about what kinds of things it is acceptable to write in a reflective piece. Is it OK to admit to having made mistakes? Is it OK to talk about how you felt? Would it be OK to say that you stayed up until 3 am to write your section of the group report on the day before it was due to be handed in? Clear indications that you are looking for elements such as clear descriptions of what went on in the group, analysis of successes and difficulties, and acknowledgement of feelings and concerns, will help students to decide what to write.

■ **Decide whether you really want to assess reflective writing!** There are many problems with assessing it so perhaps you don't need to! The most useful purpose for reflective writing is for individual students to learn from their reflections and also acquire the habit of reflecting on experiences and learning from them. (Reflective writing is not actually a very good way of telling you, as tutor, what 'really' went on in the group!) If you need to assess something, perhaps it could be a list of action points, or strengths and weaknesses, supported by selected extracts from the students' reflections on the group.

■ **Make reflection a group activity.** Rather than individuals writing a reflective commentary, the group could discuss what went on, what they achieved, what problems were encountered and so on. They could then agree a written group statement covering the aspects required for assessment.

15. Virtual group work

Using computers is often thought of as a solitary activity. Computers can, however, be very useful for group activities. Group working can have many advantages, ranging from the interchange of ideas to providing social contact. Working together at a distance may sound paradoxical, but sometimes it is easier to arrange group activities in this way. Because of computer communications, some barriers of distance and timing can be removed. In order for your students to participate, they will need e-mail facilities as a bare minimum:

- **Think carefully about the number of people who should be in each group.** If groups are too small, the students may have to work too hard and they may not have all the skills needed for the task. If the groups are too large, they may be unwieldy and it might be difficult and time consuming for decisions to be made. In large groups, there is a risk that skills can be duplicated so that some people are under-utilized.

- **Decide whether you will choose who is in which group or whether the students will organize themselves.** If you choose, you have more control over the whole process of group working. If the students organize themselves, they will feel more empowered and will be taking more responsibility for their work.

- **Think about the task the groups will have to tackle and how it affects the composition of the 'ideal' group.** Some tasks require special skills and it may be necessary to distribute skill holders amongst the groups. These skills could be related to the task in hand, or they could be group skills such as leadership.

- **Develop group tasks that enable individuals to use their particular skills.** Your students may not all have learnt the same skills, or some may be more proficient in some areas than others. Carefully chosen group tasks can involve real teamwork in distributing tasks amongst the group so that people can use their skills effectively.

- **Use group tasks to help distribute skills.** Someone who is particularly proficient in a skill can help other members of a group to improve their skills. This has an additional benefit of making the skilled person think hard about what they can do in order to show another person how to do it.

- **Encourage computer communications between students as soon as possible.** In order to make effective use of computer communications, regular use is needed. If students can develop a culture of frequently checking e-mail and conferences, they will make very effective use of these media. If they only check occasionally, there will be a struggle to establish their effective use.

- **Set some simple tasks early on.** You could pair students up and give them a simple task that requires them to exchange ideas. They could then produce a joint word-processed report on what they have done. This would mean that they would need to communicate with each other and they could also need to exchange files attached to e-mail messages.

■ **Give everyone some practice at using computer conferencing.** If you plan to use computer conferencing to keep student group work going after a face-to-face course, or between elements of such a course, it is useful to use part of the course time to get everyone talking to each other electronically. Ideally you will need a room with networked terminals for each student. It can be useful to start everyone off with a common-interest topic, even one that has no relationship to your teaching programme, and allow your students to concentrate on the process of communicating with each other electronically, rather than thinking too hard about the content of their practice communications.

■ **Put out some important information only by e-mail or in conferences, to make people check for it.** Rather than sending out all the documents by mail, or as issued handouts, use computer communications for some of it. Warn your students that you are going to do this and keep doing it so that they continue to check their e-mail and conferences.

■ **Make sure some kind of backup is available.** If someone didn't receive a computer message because of technical problems, it could cause major problems for them. Some sort of safety net could be used: for example, you could send out a message to all students every week. Anybody who didn't receive the message would know to contact you so that you could try again or send a paper copy to them in the normal mail.

■ **Decide on your own access to group conferences.** The groups' conferences could be closed to you, so that you cannot read them and students can discuss any topic freely. This may help students to feel uninhibited about what they say in messages. Alternatively, you could have access to them so that you can monitor progress. Make sure that the students know what you have decided so that they can behave appropriately!

■ **Make use of any facilities the conference software has for tracking who has done what.** Most packages have features that show who has contributed, read or revised different items of a conference. These enable some checking over who has done what they were supposed to do.

■ **Make sure that somebody is in charge of the group.** It is easy for a group to encounter serious problems if there is no control over its activities. One person needs to take on the role of coordinating the whole group to make sure that all the tasks are progressing properly. When groups undertake several successive tasks, encourage the groups to decide who will coordinate their work on a rotating basis.

Chapter 4

Designing and using learning resources

Computer-based learning resources
18. *Choosing and using computer-based learning resources*
19. *Designing computer-marked assignments*
20. *Designing computer-generated feedback to students*

Making the most of the Internet
21. *Making effective use of e-mail*
22. *Helping students to get started with e-mail*
23. *Getting a computer-conference going*
24. *Putting the Internet to work for learning*
25. *Retrieving information from the Internet*
26. *Helping students to learn from the Internet*

This chapter is about resource-based learning in many of its forms. With growing emphasis on **flexible learning** pathways in college-based courses, wide-ranging suggestions are offered in this chapter about how to go about evaluating and **selecting existing materials** with the intention of adopting or adapting them to meet your students' needs. One of the problems with commercially available flexible learning materials is that some look good but just don't work, and others work well, but don't look attractive. Much published material falls between these two positions. What really matters is that the materials cause your students to learn successfully, but acceptable standards of appearance and style remain on the agenda. The checklist in this chapter may be a useful start when reviewing existing published materials, while exploring the possibility of adopting them or adapting them for your own students. and designing new flexible learning materials.

Next we move on to discussion of some of the main points to consider when **using videos and audiotape**.

Computer-based learning materials are widely used in teaching, and play a valuable part in flexible learning programmes. There may well exist computer-based packages which will be helpful to your own students, and it could be more cost-effective to purchase these and adopt them as they stand (or adapt them) than to design new materials of your own. The suggestions in this section may provide you with help in selecting computer-aided learning packages for your students.

The chapter ends with some suggestions on how to approach using perhaps the most significant and versatile learning resource yet invented, the **Internet**, to support student learning with technologies such as e-mail and computer-conferencing.

Students may be able to use the Internet at times of their own choice, in their own ways, at their own pace, and from anywhere that access to it is available to them. That said, it is not automatically a vehicle for productive and effective learning. Indeed, it is very easy to become sidetracked by all sorts of fascinating (or inappropriate!) things, and to stray well away from any intended learning outcome. The suggestions at the end of this chapter are not intended as starting points for setting out to *deliver* the curriculum through the Internet, but rather to help students to *use* the Internet to obtain material to use in connection with their studies, such as in assignments they are preparing. The suggestions may help you to help your students both to enjoy the Internet *and* to learn well from it.

1. What are the characteristics of resource-based learning?

■ **Resource-based learning can be considered to be open or flexible in nature.** Flexible learning packages are learning resources in their own right, whether they are print-based, computer-based, or multimedia in design. The learning that happens in resource-based learning usually opens up some freedom of time and pace, if not always that of place.

■ **Resource-based learning suggests that the subject content is provided to students through materials rather than via teaching.** The term 'resource-based' is often used as an opposite to 'taught'. Having said that, good practice in face-to-face teaching and learning often depends on students working with learning resources during sessions, as well at outside formal contact time.

■ **Learning resources can be quite traditional in nature.** With suitable study guides or briefing notes, resources such as textbooks, videos, audiotapes and journals can all be part of resource-based learning programmes, either when located in learning resources centres or libraries, or when issued to or borrowed by students.

■ **Resource-based learning usually accommodates a considerable amount of learning-by-doing.** Resources should provide students with opportunities to practise, and to learn by making mistakes in the relative comfort of privacy. Resource-based learning also depends on students being provided with feedback on how their learning is going. This feedback can be provided by tutors, or by interactive elements within the learning resources, where feedback to students may be provided in print or on-screen.

■ **Clearly expressed learning outcomes are important in all kinds of resource-based learning.** There may not be tutor support available at all times, and tone of voice, emphasis of tone, and facial expression may not be available to help students work out exactly what it is that they are expected to become able to do as they work with the resource materials. This means that the wording of the intended learning outcomes is crucial.

■ **Assessment criteria need to be clearly stated.** Students take important cues from the expected performance criteria, and indicators of the kinds (and extent) of the evidence they should accumulate to demonstrate that they have learned successfully from resource-based learning materials should be clearly set out.

■ **Resource-based learning often needs appropriate face-to-face debriefing.** It can be very worthwhile to reserve a whole-class session to review an element of resource-based learning, and to answer students' questions about the topics covered in this way. Such group sessions can also be used to gain useful feedback about the strengths and weaknesses of the materials themselves.

2. What sorts of flexibility are there?

Whether we think about flexible learning as used in distance-learning programmes, or for particular elements within traditional college-based programmes, there are several different aspects to flexibility. The following descriptions may alert you to which aspects of flexibility you particularly want to address in your own provision:

- **Flexibility can mean freedom of start-dates.** Many flexible learning programmes are described as 'roll-on, roll-off' systems. The key feature here is that students can more or less start at any time of the year, and finish when they are ready. There may be difficulties incorporating such an approach when flexible learning is being used for elements within college-based programmes, not least as most educational institutions don't operate on a 52-week year.

- **Flexibility can mean freedom of entry levels.** It is important to spell out clearly any prerequisite knowledge or skills, so that students can tell whether they are able to progress on to working with each package.

- **Flexibility can give students some choice about how much support they use.** Tutor support may well be available to all of the students on a programme, but some may make little use of this, and still succeed without difficulty. Some prefer to work on their own, and rise well to the challenge of sorting out their own problems. Those students who most need tutor support can then be accommodated.

- **Flexibility can mean freedom of pace.** This is one of the most attractive hallmarks of many flexible learning programmes. Especially when studied by mature, part-time students, freedom of pace may be an essential feature, allowing them to fit their learning into busy or unpredictable work patterns.

- **Flexibility can allow freedom of location and learning environment.** Flexible learning can allow students to continue their studies while away from the institution on work-placements, or on vacation, or even when confined to home by temporary illness. Students can have more choice about whether they work in a library or learning resources centre, or wherever they feel comfortable.

- **Flexibility can allow students freedom to determine how important a part information technology will play in their studies.** While sometimes it may be deemed necessary to involve students in using communications and information technology, for some students this can be a significant hurdle. With flexible learning, it can usually be arranged that there is more than one way of achieving most of the outcomes successfully.

- **Flexibility can mean freedom of end-points.** In some systems, students can go in for assessments (tutor-marked, computer-marked, and even formal exams) more or less when they feel that they are ready for assessment. This can allow high-fliers to try the assessments without spending much time studying the materials concerned, or students who find the material more demanding to wait until they are confident that they can succeed with the assessed components.

■ **Flexibility can allow students to work collaboratively or on their own.** Some students may not have much opportunity to work collaboratively, for example isolated students on distance learning programmes. For them, it may be possible to use electronic communication to allow them to make efficient (and cheap) contact with each other. For college-based students working through flexible learning elements alongside class-based ones, it is worthwhile to encourage them to collaborate, as they can often give each other useful feedback, and help each other to make sense of the more difficult ideas and concepts.

3. What lends itself to flexible learning?

It is worthwhile to think about which parts of the curriculum best lend themselves to an open or flexible approach. It is useful to start your flexible learning writing with such parts, and perhaps better still to experiment with adapting existing resources covering such curriculum areas towards a flexible learning format first. The following suggestions show that such starting points can be based on several different considerations, and are often linked to ways that flexible learning can augment face-to-face college-based programmes:

■ **Important background material.** In face-to-face programmes, a considerable amount of time is often spent near the start, getting everyone up to speed with essential knowledge or skills, to the annoyance of the students who already have these. Making such information the basis of a flexible learning package can allow those people who need to cover this material before the whole group starts, to do so in their own time and at their own pace, without holding up the rest of the group.

■ **'Need to know before …' material.** For example, when different students will be attempting different practical exercises at the same time, it could take far too long to cover all the prerequisite material with the whole group before introducing practical work. Designing separate, short flexible learning elements to pave the way to each practical exercise can allow these to be issued to students so that the practical work can be started much earlier.

■ **'Remedial material'.** In many courses, there are problem topics that can hold up a whole class while the difficulties are addressed by lecturers or tutors. This can lead to time being wasted, particularly by those students for whom there are no problems with the parts concerned. The availability of flexible learning packages addressing such areas can allow such packages to be used only by those students who need them, in their own time, so that the progress of the whole group is not impeded. Don't, of course, use a term as insulting as 'remedial' in the title of your package!

- **'Nice-to-know' material.** While 'need-to-know' material is more important, flexible learning elements can be particularly useful to address 'nice-to-know' material, and give such material to students without spending too much face-to-face time on it. This allows contact time to be saved for helping students with the really important material, and for addressing their problems.

- **Much-repeated material.** If you find yourself often covering the same ground, perhaps with different groups of students in different contexts or courses, it can be worth thinking about packaging such material in flexible learning formats. If you yourself get bored with things you often teach, you're not going to pass much enthusiasm for these topics on to your students, and it can be mutually beneficial to invest your energy into creating an alternative flexible learning pathway to cover such material.

- **Material which is best 'learnt-by-doing'.** Flexible learning is based on students answering questions, and doing tasks and exercises. Therefore it can be a useful starting point for a flexible learning package to base it on the sorts of activities that you may already be giving your face-to-face students. Standard assignments and activities already in use in traditionally delivered courses and programmes may be adapted quite easily for flexible learning usage, and have the strong benefit that they are already tried and tested elements of the curriculum.

- **Material where students need individual feedback on their progress.** A vital element of flexible learning is the feedback that students receive when they have attempted to answer questions, or had a try at exercises and activities. The kinds of feedback that you may already give your face-to-face students can be packaged into flexible learning materials.

- **Material that you don't like to teach!** It can be tempting to turn such elements of the curriculum into flexible learning materials, where students can work on them individually (or in untutored groups), and using face-to-face time more efficiently to address any problems that students find, rather than to teach them from scratch.

- **Material that students find hard to grasp first time.** In most subjects there are such areas. Developing flexible learning materials addressing these means that students can go through them on their own, as many times as they need. Effectively, the flexible learning material becomes their teacher. Students can then work through such materials at their own pace, and can practise with the learning materials until they master them.

- **Material that may be needed later, at short notice.** It is often the case that some topics are only really needed by students quite some time after they may have been covered in a course or programme. When such materials are turned into flexible learning formats, students can polish up their grip on the topics involved just when they need to.

4. Which students are particularly helped?

All sorts of people use flexible learning in distance-learning mode. The following categories of students are included as those who can be particularly helped in different ways. Many parallels may also be drawn with the use of flexible learning elements in college-based programmes, where similar benefits can be delivered to a variety of constituencies of the student population:

■ **High-fliers.** Very able students are often frustrated or bored by traditional class-based programmes, as the pace is normally made to suit the average student and may be much too slow for high-fliers. With flexible learning, they can speed through the parts they already know, or the topics they find easy and straightforward. They can work through a package concentrating only on the parts that are new to them, or which they find sufficiently challenging.

■ **Low-fliers.** The least able students in a group are often disadvantaged when the pace of delivery of traditional programmes is too fast for them. They can be embarrassed in class situations by being seen not to know things, or not being able to do tasks that their fellow students have no difficulty with. With flexible learning, they can take their time, and practise until they have mastered things. They have the opportunity to spend much longer than other students may take.

■ **Anxious students.** Some people are easily embarrassed if they get things wrong, especially when they are seen to make mistakes. With flexible learning, they have the opportunity to learn from making mistakes, in the comfort of privacy, as they try self-assessment questions and exercises, and learn from the feedback responses in an interactive learning package.

■ **Students with a particular block.** Students who have a particular problem with an important component of a course can benefit from flexible learning, in that they can work as often as they wish through materials designed to give them practice in the topic concerned. It can be useful to incorporate self-assessment exercises, with detailed feedback specially included for those students who have problems with the topic.

■ **Students needing to make up an identified shortfall.** For example, in science and engineering programmes, it is often found quite suddenly that some students in a group have not got particular maths skills. Rather than hold up the progress of a whole class, self-study components can be issued to those students who need to get up to speed in the areas involved. When the students have a sense of ownership of the need that these materials will address, they make best use of the materials.

■ **People learning in a second language.** In class situations, such students are disadvantaged in that they may be spending much of their energy simply making sense of the words, with little time left to make sense of the ideas and concepts. With flexible learning materials, they can work through them at their own pace, with the aid of a dictionary, or with the help of students already fluent in the language in which the materials are written.

- **Part-time students.** These are often people with many competing pressures on their time, or with irregular opportunities for studying, perhaps due to shift work, work away from home, or uneven demands being normal in their jobs. Flexible learning materials allow them to manage their studying effectively, and to make the most of those periods where they have more time to study.

- **People who don't like being taught!** Surprisingly, such people are found in college-based courses, but there are many more of these who would not consider going to an educational institution. Flexible learning allows such people to have a much greater degree of autonomy and ownership of their studies.

- **Students who only want to do part of the whole.** Some students may only want to – or need to – achieve a few carefully selected learning outcomes that are relevant to their work or even to their leisure activities. With a flexible learning package, they are in a position to select those parts they want to study, whereas in face-to-face courses they may have to wait quite some time before the parts they are really interested in are covered.

- **Students with special needs.** For example, people with limited mobility may find it hard to get to the venue of a traditional course, but may have few problems when studying at home. Students with other problems may be able to work through flexible learning materials with the aid of an appropriate helper or supporter. Open and flexible learning is increasingly being used to address the particular needs of diverse groups, including carers, prisoners, mentally ill people, religious groups, socially excluded people, and so on.

5. How will they work?

- **Look first at the intended learning outcomes.** If these are well expressed, and in language that your students will be able to understand easily, the materials are off to a good start in your interrogation.

- **Check how interactive the materials are.** There should be learning-by-doing opportunities throughout the materials. This is better than just having a collection of self-assessment questions or activities at the end of each section or module. Check whether the tasks and exercises are pitched at an appropriate level, so that they could give your students useful practice, and the chance to learn from anticipated mistakes.

- **Check how well the materials respond to students' efforts.** Look particularly at the responses to self-assessment questions. These should be considerably more than simply answers to the questions. Your students should be able to find out not only whether their own attempts at the questions were successful or not, but also what might have gone wrong with their own attempts when unsuccessful.

■ **Check the standards.** The standards to which the learning outcomes will be delivered should be most clearly evident from the levels of tasks in the materials. In particular, if tutor-marked assignment questions are included in the materials, see whether they are pitched at an appropriate level for your students, and decide whether you may indeed use them as they stand.

■ **Think about the tone and style of the materials.** Most flexible learning materials work better when the tone and style is relatively personal and informal. The materials should be involving, with students addressed as 'you', and when appropriate the authors talking to students as 'I'. Check, however, that the tone won't be found patronizing by your students. This is not necessarily the same as whether *you* may find the tone or style too informal – remember that you are not *learning* from the materials.

■ **Think about the ownership issues.** For example, if the materials are designed for students to write all over them, filling in answers to questions, entering calculations, sketching diagrams, and so on, students are likely to get a high degree of ownership of their learning from the materials. If the materials are more like textbooks, this ownership may be reduced, and students may not regard the materials as primary learning resources.

■ **Think ahead to what you may wish to add to the materials.** For example, when materials don't yet contain sufficient self-assessment questions, or when feedback responses are not yet self-sufficient enough for your students, you may well be able to bridge the gap by adding questions and responses of your own. This can be well worth doing if there are other aspects of the materials that make them particularly attractive as a starting point for your own fine-tuning.

■ **Look at the layout and structure of the materials.** For students to trust them, the materials should look professional and credible. They should be able to find their way easily backwards as well as forwards through the materials. There should be good sign-posting, showing how each section of the materials fits in to the whole, and linking the intended learning outcomes to the tasks and activities in the materials.

■ **See whether you can get feedback on how well the materials actually work.** Check whether there are other colleges or organizations already using the materials, and try to find out how well they are doing their job there. Reputable sources of published flexible learning materials will normally be only too pleased to provide details of major clients.

■ **Check the costs involved.** There are different ways of 'adopting' flexible learning materials. These range from purchasing copies in the numbers you require for your own students, to acquiring a site licence to reproduce your own copies. If you are dealing with a minority specialist option, the economics will probably favour buying copies directly. Bulk discounts may be available for significant purchases, and it can be worth buying in supplies to last for more than one 'run' of the materials, but this should only be considered when you are really certain that these are the materials that you want to use.

6. Is the content right?

It is important that time is devoted to checking-out the content of materials, and that such time is made available to those with this responsibility, or that someone appropriate is commissioned to evaluate the materials:

■ **Check carefully the match between the published learning outcomes, and those of your own programme.** It is normal to expect some differences. Some of your own learning outcomes may be absent from the published materials. The materials may at times go well beyond your own learning outcomes. It is important to establish what fraction of the published materials will be directly relevant to your own flexible learning programme. If it is less than half, this is normally a signal to continue searching elsewhere.

■ **Check that the published materials are compatible with other parts of your students' studies.** For example, check that they use subject-specific conventions or approaches that will be familiar to your own students.

■ **Seek out reviews of the learning materials.** Just as with textbooks, reviews can help you make decisions about which to adopt and which to reject. Reviews of flexible learning materials can be useful indicators of their quality. Reviews tend to concentrate more on the subject matter than the ways that the materials actually deliver successful learning, and are therefore useful in the context of establishing relevance.

■ **Decide whether the materials are sufficiently up to date.** A quick way to do this is to look for references to 'further reading', or tasks briefing students to make use of other reference books or articles on the topics covered. You will normally know of the most respected source materials, and any recent developments that should be encompassed within the flexible learning materials, or to which they should refer.

■ **Check that any resources that the materials depend upon are available.** For example, if the flexible learning materials are written with one or more set textbooks or articles to be used alongside them, make sure that these materials are still available. Even important set texts go out of print, often between editions, and the next edition may not lend itself to the particular tasks for which the flexible learning materials referred to it .

■ **Check the relevance of the learning-by-doing tasks in the materials.** Compare these with the sorts of tasks you would set students in conventional courses at the same level. Watch particularly for tasks which could be considered too basic, or 'missing the point' of important elements of learning. Also look out for tasks which may be too advanced, and which may stop your students in their tracks.

■ **Estimate the expected time that students may need to spend using the materials.** There are often indications of this built into flexible learning materials, but you may need to work out upper and lower limits that would reasonably relate to your own least able and most able students. Match these time-scales to the overall duration (or equivalent duration) of your flexible learning programme, and the relative importance of the topics addressed by the materials. For example, if a published workbook is expected to take the average student 12 hours to work through, but the topic concerned is only one-tenth of your 60-hour-equivalent module, you may need to look for a more concise package covering the same ground.

■ **Check that you can live with the ways the materials address important topics.** This includes equal opportunities approaches: for example, check how the materials portray male/female roles in the content of case studies and illustrations. Don't get into the 'not invented here syndrome'. If you really don't like the way the materials handle an important concept, you are probably well advised to look for other materials. Any distrust or reservations you have about learning materials may be quite infectious, and your students may quickly pick up doubts about the materials, and lose their confidence to learn from them.

■ **Work out how much you may need to add to the materials.** It is quite normal for published materials not to cover everything that you would include if you were designing them yourself. It is relatively easy to bridge small gaps, by designing handouts or small workbooks to address them.

■ **Work out how much you might wish to delete!** You don't want your students to waste their time or energy by doing things in published materials which are not connected to the learning outcomes of their own programmes, or which are not involved in their own assessment in some way. It is perfectly feasible to brief your students along such lines as 'Don't do anything with Section 9 unless you want to do so just for your own interest; it's not on your agenda.' To decide which published materials you may wish to adopt, make sure that there is not too much in this category.

7. Adopt, adapt, or start from scratch?

A vast amount of material has been written to support open and flexible learning. Some of this material looks good but does not work. Some looks bad but does work. The following questions and suggestions offer some help towards reaching a logical decision about some of the factors involved in deciding whether to embark on creating new flexible learning resource materials, or to prepare to adopt or adapt existing materials:

■ **Do you really want to start from scratch?** If your answer is a definite 'yes', this is probably a good enough reason for at least exploring in more depth the implications of creating new flexible learning materials. If the answer is a definite 'no!', it is probably worth your while to look carefully at some of the possibilities there may be of adopting existing materials, or adapting them to meet the needs of your particular open students.

- **Have you got time to start from scratch?** Designing open learning materials is a time-consuming activity, and usually takes quite a lot longer than is planned! In particular, materials need to be piloted and adjusted on the basis of feedback from students (and tutors, and mentors, and anyone else who sees how they work in practice). Such piloting should be done quite extensively, well before the materials are committed to their first 'published' form or made generally available. Starting from scratch can be really expensive if starting from a position of inexperience too.

- **Do you actually need to start from scratch?** Many institutions have developed their own policies, approaches and house styles relating to the production and support of open and flexible learning, and have staff development and training provision available. Such policies and training are often centrally resourced in the institution, and project management support may also be available. Before being tempted to start out on your own, it is important to make sure that you have checked out where your institution stands.

- **Have you got the skills to start from scratch?** If you have already developed highly successful open learning materials, you will not be in any doubt about your answer to this question. If, however, you have not yet gone up the learning curve involved in such development, you may not realize the diversity of skills that are involved.

- **Will you be a lone spirit, or a member of a cohesive team?** While it is indeed possible for one person to create and design an excellent open learning resource, the statistical probability of this happening is much less than when a committed team tackles the task. Members of such a team need to have broad agreement on the nature of most of the hallmarks of effective open learning materials, as well as time to work together on developing open learning alongside all the other things that they may be doing.

- **Will the right people be doing it for the right reasons?** When creating new open learning materials, everyone involved needs to believe in what they are doing, not just you! Team membership should not be dictated by who happens to have some slack in their timetable, or even by an identified need to establish a flexible learning pathway in topics taught by particular people.

- **Have you got the resources to start from scratch?** Creating new open learning materials involves more than skilled writers, who know both the subject involved and the problems that students have in learning it. Other things to consider include layout, production, reproduction, print-runs, design of media-based elements, administration, communication to students learning independently, monitoring student progress, and the design and implementation of related assessment elements.

- **Are you in a position to find out what exists already?** There is a wealth of published open learning material, increasingly accessible through catalogues and databases. There is an even greater wealth of material that is unpublished, but working effectively locally in colleges, universities, training organizations and elsewhere. There is no easy way of tracking down some of this material or of finding out how useful or relevant some of it may be to the needs of your own students. Most colleges have staff such as learning resources managers, and links to consortia, whereby progress can be made in tracking down and evaluating suitable resource materials.

- **Are you in a position to buy in identified suitable resources?** Almost anything that exists can be purchased for use in your own institution, but the cost–benefit analysis needs to be considered carefully. Detailed negotiations may need to be undertaken with the owners of the copyright of the work concerned, if you intend to mass-reproduce it. Site licences for local reproduction may need to be negotiated.

- **How important may the 'not invented here syndrome' be?** One of the biggest problems with adopting other people's materials is that the sense of ownership is lost. This may be reflected by a lack of trust in the materials. Reactions such as 'it's not the way I would have covered this topic' or 'this just isn't at the right level for my students' or 'this misses out some important points my students need to address' reflect genuine problems.

8. Planning how to adopt

Below are some practical suggestions about how to adopt materials that you have found to be suitable:

- **Work out whether students will be issued with their own personal copies.** Will students be able to keep their copies after they have finished working through them? If not, will there be a problem about students writing answers to self-assessment questions on the materials? It is obviously best if students can retain learning resource materials, as they can then relearn from them later when necessary. Is it feasible to offer a purchase-or-loan option to students themselves? If the materials are to be issued on a loan basis, how will you be able to get them back? What percentage can you expect to get back in a fit state for reissue? How many 'runs' may the materials survive?

- **Work out how many copies of the materials you will need.** This will normally be rather more than the flexible learners you expect in your first cohort. Even so, it can be quite difficult to estimate the number of copies to purchase, especially if your planning is for more than a single year.

- **Check out delivery dates firmly.** It is most unsatisfactory if at least the first parts of the materials you have chosen are not available at the start of your open learners' studies. Similarly, if the materials are bulky, you may not have space to store multiple copies for a long period of time.

■ **Take particular care with computer-based materials.** Something you've seen working well on someone else's network may not work on your hardware. There may be bugs to iron out. There may be incompatibility problems with other software, or with printers, modems and so on. Almost all such difficulties are solvable, but sometimes solutions take time. Get the computer-based elements up and running well before your flexible learners may need them.

■ **Protect at least one full copy of everything!** You never know when you will need that last available copy for an important purpose. The assignment booklet may be needed, for example, to show teaching quality reviewers or external examiners the level of the work expected from students. The installation instructions for computer software may be needed again when your system has to be cleared of a virus and programs need to be reinstalled. Keep all the essential papers and data in a safe place, and file them well so that everyone knows what is there.

■ **Work out exactly how you intend your students to make use of the adopted materials.** Work out how long they can expect to spend with each element of these materials. Clarify which intended learning outcomes are most relevant to them. Prioritize which tasks and exercises they should regard as central, and which as optional.

■ **Revisit the intended learning outcomes.** You will almost certainly need to restate these, fitting them in to the context of the overall outcomes your flexible learners are working towards. You may need to prioritize the published outcomes in the purchased materials, helping your students to see which ones are central, and which are more peripheral.

■ **Think ahead to how you will assess the learning outcomes.** Work out what proportion of the overall assessment will be linked to learning achieved through using the materials. Maybe start straightaway on designing tutor-marked assessment questions and related exam questions. Perhaps also design some indicative sample questions, which you can give out to students along with the materials, so they can see the standards they are expected to reach in their achievement of the outcomes.

■ **Compose briefing instructions for your open learners.** Introduce the adopted materials, explaining where they fit into the overall learning programme. If necessary, write short notes explaining any differences between the approaches used in the materials and in other resources they may be working with.

■ **Think about study skills advice.** It can be particularly helpful to flexible learners to have tailored suggestions for 'how to get the most out of …' both for print-based materials and computer-based ones. Such briefings can also suggest additional ways that students can make opportunities to practise the most important things you intend them to learn using the materials.

9. Planning how to adapt

Adapting existing flexible learning materials happens more frequently than adopting them as they stand. It is, not surprisingly, rare that someone else's package is exactly appropriate for your own students. If you are adapting published materials for use by your students, you will need to think about most of the suggestions in 'planning how to adopt'. Moreover, there will be the adaptations themselves to think about. Although this task may seem daunting, it becomes more manageable if broken down into the elements described below:

- **Regard adaptation positively.** It's a lot of work adapting a flexible learning package to make it directly meet the needs of your students, in the context of their overall study programme. However, there are benefits for you too. For a start, you will feel a stronger sense of ownership of the materials after you've done your work with them, than if you had used them in their original state.

- **Start with the intended learning outcomes.** If these are published within the package, rank them in terms of which are essential, which are desirable but not central, and which are optional for your own open learners. Then look carefully for anything important that is missed in the published outcomes. Look for outcomes that have not been stated, but that could be achieved using the materials as they stand. Then look for outcomes that are not covered by the materials, as these will become the focus of some of your adaptations.

- **Think early about other resource materials you may intend your students to use, alongside the adapted ones.** For example, there may be sections of textbooks, handouts you already use, or key articles that you would prefer them to work from than from parts of the materials you are adapting. Start clarifying in your own mind the parts of the materials that you are adapting that you *don't* want your flexible learners to work through.

- **Look carefully at the interactive elements.** Examine the learning that occurs through the self-assessment questions, exercises and activities. Decide which of these are really useful, as they stand, for your own students. Aim to keep these as they are. Then start looking for intended learning outcomes that are not yet matched by opportunities for learning-by-doing, and draft out further self-assessment questions and tasks as necessary. Adding such interaction is normally the most important stage in adapting materials for your own purposes.

- **Look at the quality of the responses to self-assessment questions and activities.** The feedback that students receive after engaging with the interactive elements is crucial for their learning. You may well decide to recompose the feedback components for a significant proportion of the self-assessment questions, particularly those you have already identified as central to the learning outcomes.

- **Think about adding some completely new self-assessment questions and feedback responses.** Consider how much practice your own students may need to make sense of the most important ideas, concepts and procedures covered by the learning materials. It is better to have too many good interactive elements, and then to whittle them down to realistic amounts, than to have too restricted a range at the outset.

■ **Review any tutor-marked assignments already in the materials.** You may well want to change these, fine-tuning them so that the tutor-marked agenda fits in with other such elements in different parts of your students' overall programme. You may be able to use tutor-marked assignments that you already use in face-to-face programmes instead.

■ **Consider writing a commentary to talk your students right through the materials as they use them.** This could be in a small booklet that they keep alongside them as they work through the materials. It is useful to use this as a guided tour through the materials. Specific comments such as 'I suggest you skip the exercise on p. 34 unless you had a problem with the question on p. 30', or 'only aim to remember the three most important factors listed on p. 51' can be very helpful to your students.

■ **Think about whether to do a 'cut-and-paste' job on the package being adapted.** Whether you can do this may depend upon the conditions on which you purchased or licensed your use of the package. However, it is worth if necessary negotiating with the authors, or owners of the copyright, of the material that you are adapting. A cut-and-paste job begins to become a preferred option when the changes, additions and deletions you decide to make reach more than a third of the original material. Be particularly careful, however, not to infringe copyright legislation regarding the material from the original package that remains intact.

■ **Plan a careful pilot of your adaptation.** It is quite likely that after the first 'run' you will wish to make substantial further adaptations, not least to the parts that you introduced yourself to the package. Beware of going into production of large numbers of copies of Adaptation Version 1. Even though it is more economical to do fairly large reprographic runs, it is false economy if you end up binning a lot of copies of a version that you have to change further.

10. Writing new flexible learning materials

The most difficult stage in starting out to design a flexible learning resource can be working out a logical and efficient order in which to approach the separate tasks involved. These suggestions should help you to avoid wasting too much time, and particularly aim to help ensure that the work you do is directly related to composing learning material rather than writing out yet another textbook:

■ **Think again!** Before really getting started on designing flexible learning resource material, it's worth looking back, and asking yourself a few basic questions once more. These include:

- Am I the best person to write this material?
- Is there a materials production unit in my institution that can help me?
- Are there any experienced materials editors there whose expertise I can depend upon?
- Is there graphics design help and support?
- Is there already an institutional house style?
- Can someone else produce the flexible learning materials, while I simply supply the raw material and notes on how I want it to work in flexible learning mode?

If, after asking these questions, you decide to press ahead with designing your own materials, the following steps should save you some time and energy:

- **Don't just start writing subject material.** A flexible learning package is much more than just the subject matter it contains, and is something for students to <u>do</u> rather than just something to read.

- **Get the feel of your target audience.** The better you know the sorts of people who will be using your flexible learning material, the easier it is to write for them.

- **Express your intended learning outcomes.** It is worth making a skeleton of the topics that your material will cover in the form of learning outcomes, at least in draft form, before writing anything else. Having established the learning outcomes, you are in a much better position to ensure that the content of your flexible learning material will be developed in a coherent and logical order.

- **Seek feedback on your draft learning outcomes.** Check that they are seen by colleagues to be at the right level for the material you are designing. In particular, check that they make sense to members of your target audience of students, and are clear and unambiguous to them.

- **Design questions, tasks and activities, firmly based on your intended learning outcomes.** Some of the outcomes may require several tasks and activities to cover them. It is also useful to plan in draft form activities that will span two or three learning outcomes simultaneously, to help pave the way towards integrating your package and linking the outcomes to each other.

- **Test your draft questions, tasks and activities.** These will in due course be the basis of the learning-by-doing in your package, and will set the scene for the feedback responses you will design. It is extremely useful to test these questions and tasks first, with anyone you can get to try them out, particularly students who may be close to your anticipated target audience. Finding out their most common mistakes and difficulties paves the way towards the design of useful feedback responses, and helps you adjust the wording of the tasks to avoid ambiguity or confusion.

- **Plan your feedback responses.** Decide how best you will let your students know how well, or how badly, they have done in their attempts at each of your tasks, activities and questions.

■ **Think ahead to assessment.** Work out which of the questions, tasks and activities you have designed will be self-sufficient as self-assessment exercises, where feedback responses can be provided to students in print in the learning package, or on-screen if you're designing a computer-based package. Work out which exercises need the skills of a tutor to respond to them, and will usefully become components of tutor-marked assignments.

■ **Map out your questions, tasks and activities into a logical sequence.** Along with the matching learning outcomes, this provides you with a strong skeleton on which to proceed to flesh out the content of your flexible learning material.

■ **Work out your main headings and subheadings.** It is wise to base these firmly on the things that your students are going to be doing, reflecting the learning outcomes you have devised. This is much better than devising headings purely on the basis of the subjects and topics covered, or on the original syllabus you may have started out with.

■ **Write 'bridges'.** Most of these will lead from the feedback response you have written for one question, task or activity, into the next activity that your students will meet. Sometimes these bridges will need to provide new information to set the scene for the next activity. It is important to ensure that these bridges are as short and relevant as you can make them, and that they don't run off on tangents to the main agenda provided by the skeleton you have already made. This also ensures that you make your writing really efficient, and save your valuable time.

■ **Write the introductions last.** The best time to write any introduction is when you know exactly what you're introducing. It is much easier to lead into the first question, task or activity when you know how it (and the feedback associated with it) fits into the material as a whole, and you know how and why you have arranged the sequence of activities in the way you have already devised. Although you may need to write draft introductions when first putting together your package for piloting, it is really useful to revisit these after testing out how students get on with the activities and feedback responses, and to include in the final version of each introduction suggestions to students about how to approach the material that follows, based on what was learned from piloting.

11. Writing self-assessment questions

Self-assessment questions, activities and exercises are one of the most important features of flexible learning materials, as they allow learning-by-doing, through practising, and also provide valuable opportunities for learning by trial and-error. It is normally safer to use structured question formats, rather than open-ended ones for self-assessment questions, as it is then much more possible to respond to exactly what your students *do* with each task. The following suggestions may help you to ensure that the self-assessment exercises you design are serving your students well:

- **Write lots of them!** Writing self-assessment questions gets quicker and easier with practice. Like most things, it is learned best by doing it. The more you write, the more you can select only the good ones to include in your material.

- **Make good use of existing materials.** If you are already teaching the topic concerned, you are likely to have accumulated quite a stock of class exercises, homework assignments, practice questions and so on. These have the great advantage that you already know they are relevant and important tasks. Many of these will lend themselves to being translated into self-assessment questions and feedback responses.

- **Look at as many samples of flexible learning material as you can.** This helps you see a variety of types and styles, and enriches your own writing of self-assessment components. Look at the examples you see from the student's point of view. In particular, look at the kinds of question where you feel that you are getting useful feedback if you make mistakes or don't actually choose the best or correct option in multiple-choice formats.

- **Keep your intended learning outcomes firmly in mind.** These should provide the agenda for all of the questions, tasks and activities that you set in your flexible learning material. If you find yourself tempted to use a question or exercise that is not directly related to the learning outcomes, check whether it would be a good idea to add new learning outcomes to your agenda to link such a question into your material properly.

- **Keep your tutor-marked assessment ideas firmly in mind.** Students who successfully work through all of your self-assessment questions, exercises and activities should be able to expect confidently that they will succeed in any other kinds of assessment they will encounter. The self-assessment components should provide them with all the practice they reasonably need, as well as allowing them to learn from mistakes in the comfort of privacy, before mistakes count against them.

- **Work out exactly what each question is intended to test.** There needs to be a good answer to: 'What's this question for?'. Sometimes the answer will be to allow students to confirm that they have mastered an idea, sometimes to introduce something new, and at other times it may be to alert them to something that they may have a problem with. It is important that students don't view the self-assessment questions as trivial – they may not even attempt them then.

- **Don't test too many things at once.** It is usually best to keep self-assessment tasks relatively straightforward and not too complex. This makes it much easier to design feedback responses, addressing anticipated problems that students may have found.

- **Have a feedback response in mind.** To work as a self-assessment activity, it has to be possible to respond to what your students actually do with it. This usually means that you will need to structure your questions carefully, so that you can *know* what your students are likely to do with them, and respond appropriately to students who succeed, and to students who don't.

- **Try multiple-choice formats, where they are suitable.** For example, with multiple-choice questions you can respond directly, and differently, to students choosing different distractors (wrong or less-good options), and to students who choose the correct or best option (the 'key').

- **Don't just use multiple-choice formats.** While these are very versatile, it can become tedious for students if this is the only kind of self-assessment question they meet. Ring the changes. Try some prioritizing or sequencing questions, where you ask your students to put given things in the best order of priority or the most logical sequence. Try some completion or filling-blanks questions, to help your students see whether or not they know what words should be added to complete the sense of sentences, definitions or statements.

- **Consider the use of at least some open-ended tasks as self-assessment questions.** While you can't guarantee to be able to respond to exactly what your students may have done with open-ended questions, there are ways of helping them to self-assess their own answers to these. The biggest danger is that students are quite likely not to go to the trouble of critically assessing their own answers, unless you make the self-assessment part of the exercise really valuable – and interesting – to them.

- **Try your questions out on students (and anyone else!).** The best way of finding out whether a question, task or activity will make a good self-assessment exercise is to see how people get on with it. You will find that this helps a great deal when you come to write the feedback responses, as you will be much more aware of the sorts of things that students may do incorrectly, or the most likely errors that they could make.

- **Discard lots of self-assessment questions!** Having gone to the trouble of designing self-assessment components, it is tempting to leave them in your materials even when you know from piloting and testing them that they are not too effective. It is better to start with a large number of possible questions, and select only those that work well. You can always recycle the discarded ones for usage in other contexts in which they will work better, such as in-class questions or tutorial exercises.

12. Writing feedback responses to structured questions

To capitalize on all the effort that goes into designing self-assessment questions, students need to be given really useful feedback every time they have a go at one. It is considerably easier to write feedback responses to structured questions than to open-ended tasks, as it is known to at least some extent the kinds of answers which students are likely to have given.

- **Check that you can actually *respond* to what students have done with each structured self-assessment question.** If you cannot actually be sure about the various possibilities, it probably will not work as a structured self-assessment question.

■ **Responses should be much more than just the answers to the questions.** In flexible learning materials, feedback responses are particularly important for those students who *need* some feedback on what they have done in their attempts at structured self-assessment questions – usually because the questions have helped to show them where their learning is not yet complete.

■ **Regard the responses to self-assessment tasks as the most important measure of the quality of your flexible learning materials.** Most people reviewing the quality of flexible learning materials turn straight to the responses to structured self-assessment questions. If these are really *responding* to students, rather than just giving the answers to the questions, the quality of the material as a whole is likely to be regarded as high.

■ **Ensure that each response addresses students' question: 'Was I right?'** Sometimes questions and tasks lend themselves to right and wrong answers. On other occasions there may be no right answer, but your feedback responses will still need to give students a frame of reference with which to judge the quality of their own attempts.

■ **Cater carefully for students who get things wrong.** When they get something wrong, there are two further questions they want answers to: 'What *is* the right (or best) answer?' and 'Why wasn't I right?' It is the latter of these two questions that is the most important for you to address through your feedback comments. It is not always enough to be pointed in the direction of the correct or preferred answer. Students want to know how their own answers (or choices of option) measure up, and what if anything they may have got confused about or wrong in their attempts at the question.

■ **Don't forget to praise good answers or choices.** Students who have attempted any self-assessment task successfully deserve a word or two of praise. But don't just say 'well done' every time; this gets very boring! Also, don't use superlatives such as 'splendid' except for the few tasks where students really deserve an accolade when successful. Milder forms of praise such as 'that's right …' or 'yes indeed …' have their place for responses to things that most students should be handling successfully.

■ **Give messages of sympathy for students who may be feeling daunted.** When it is expected that many students will make a particular mistake, it makes a great deal of difference to them if they read such phrases in your responses as 'Don't worry, most people have trouble with this idea at first' or 'This was actually quite a hard question.'

■ **Give the good (or bad) news straightaway.** As soon as students have attempted a self-assessment exercise, they want to know how they have done. It is very frustrating for them if they have to read through a rambling explanation before they begin to work out whether they did well or badly. Start the response crisply with the news. For example, when responding to a multiple-choice question it can be helpful to open with 'The best choice is Option C', then explain why, and what was wrong with the other options.

- **Start each part of your response with the verdict.** For example, if responding to a true–false question, remind your students along the following lines: 'It is *false* to say that ...' so that they know *that* it was false, and *what* exactly was false from the outset of your response. You can then elaborate and explain *why* it was false.

- **Make the responses worth reading.** If students just glance at your responses, or ignore them altogether, they are not getting the benefit of the feedback that you have planned for them. It can be a useful tactic to include at least some important ideas *only* in your feedback responses, and to refer in your main text to the fact that this is where the information is located.

- **Don't make mountains out of molehills!** Avoid the temptation to predict, and respond to, every possible thing that your students could do with your self-assessment questions. Students should be able to absorb your feedback to most questions within a few minutes.

13. Writing multiple-choice questions

As already hinted at above, one format of self-assessment question which can work particularly well in flexible learning materials is multiple-choice. The greatest advantage of these is that (when well designed) they can provide appropriate feedback to students whether or not they make correct (or best) selections from the options offered to them. A multiple-choice question has three main ingredients: the 'stem' setting the context, the 'key' which is the best option or the correct one, and 'distractors' – options containing faults or errors. The following suggestions should help you to get all three parts of multiple-choice questions working effectively:

- **Make sure that the key is definitely correct!** It should not be possible for students to find anything wrong or arguable in the key. It is often the most able students who spot something wrong with the key, and this can be frustrating to them when they see a response that does not acknowledge the level of thinking they exercised.

- **Make sure that the key does not stand out for the wrong reasons as being correct.** The key should not be given away by containing leading wording from the stem, nor should it be of significantly different length than the other options. Also make sure that any grammar links between the stem and the key don't give the key away. You may think such matters would rarely arise, but the last person to spot them is usually the author of the question!

- **Take care with 'definites' versus 'indefinites'.** It is alright to have sets of options including indefinite words such as 'sometimes, often, usually, rarely' or sets of definite words such as 'always, never, all, none', but it is not wise to combine the two kinds of words in a given question, as the indefinite options are more likely to be chosen as correct by anyone who is just guessing – and are probably correct too!

■ **Make sure that the stem provides a clear task.** For example, be clear about whether 'which …?' means 'which *one* …?' or 'which (one or more) …?'. There is no harm in asking 'which *two* of the following …?' when you really want students to pick two options, and are going to respond accordingly in your feedback.

■ **Avoid options that may let your students think too little.** It is best to avoid options such as 'all of these' or 'none of these'. These tend to be chosen as cop-out selections by students who are not thinking deeply enough to identify the best option. Having expressed this reservation, either of these options can be valuable if used *occasionally* where you really want to make a point about 'all of these' or 'none of these' being the best answer.

■ **Be careful with negative questions.** For example, if asking 'which one of the following is *not* true?' or 'which is an *exception* to the rule?', make it really stand out that it is a 'wrong' option that has to be selected in such questions; candidates become accustomed to looking for correct options.

■ **Make sure that there is something wrong with each distractor.** Remember that when you write a feedback response to a distractor you need to be able to explain convincingly what is wrong with it, or why the key is better.

■ **Choose distractors that represent likely errors.** There is no point in having distractors **that** are not chosen as 'correct' by at least someone! Distractors need to be as plausible as you can make them. That said, it is fine to inject a note of humour occasionally by using an 'unlikely' distractor!

■ **Let students help you to find better distractors.** It is worth posing the stem as an open-ended question to a face-to-face class if you have such an opportunity, and finding out what the most common wrong answers are. These can then form the basis of your distractors.

■ **Try questions out on a large group if you can.** For example, in a lecture, put the question up on the screen, and ask for a show of hands for each option in turn. When everyone chooses the correct (or best) option, your distractors may need to be made a bit more appealing! If you don't have the chance to work with large groups of students, it is still worth trying out your questions on as many people as you can, even if one at a time and at a distance (or electronically).

■ **Remember that multiple-choice questions are not restricted to simple formats.** For example, an extended set of options can be used, with the question asking students to decide which *combination* of options is correct or best ('a, d, e' or 'b, c, e' and so on). Browse through some flexible learning materials to explore the range of multiple-choice formats that is possible. The Science Foundation Course of the Open University in the UK has many excellent examples of sophisticated (and difficult!) multiple-choice questions.

14. Writing feedback responses to multiple-choice questions

Whatever form your multiple-choice questions take (print, computer-based, or test), students want (and need) to find out two things every time they make a choice: 'Was I right?' and 'If not, *why* not?'. The following suggestions may help your responses provide useful, quick feedback to students:

- **Think about when your response will be seen.** For example, students may see your response immediately on-screen after picking an option in a computer-based package, or at the back of a print-based package in the self-assessment question responses, or they may see it in print after completing a series of questions in a multiple-choice test.

- **Make it immediately clear whether the option was correct or not.** Instant feedback can be very useful, particularly when you can remind students of why they were right, or show them why they were wrong. Even if your students receive the response somewhat later, their first priority will still be to establish whether their choice was successful.

- **Give appropriate praise for the choice of correct options.** A few well-chosen words can be encouraging for students who made the correct choice. But make sure that 'well done' messages don't get boring or out of control! There are hundreds of ways of responding 'well done'. Save the 'splendid!' responses for right answers to really tricky questions. Milder forms of 'well done' include 'yes', 'right', 'of course', and so on.

- **Respond to students who choose distractors.** It's little use just saying to them 'Wrong, the correct option was A'. Students want (and need) to find out *why* the distractor was not the best option. If you can't respond to a distractor, take it as a sign that it was not a good distractor in the first place. Good distractors are wrong for a reason, not just wrong!

- **Acknowledge students who choose options that are partly correct.** When part of a distractor is correct, use words to remind students who have chosen it that they did indeed have some good reasons for their choices. For example: 'While it is true to say that …, it is not true to conclude that …..'

- **Let students choosing distractors off the hook gently.** They may well be working on their own, so don't leave them feeling that they must be the only people ever to have made such mistakes. Words like 'This was a tricky question', or 'Most people find this hard at first' can go a long way towards making it more acceptable to choose distractors. This can also help to build students' trust in the value of making mistakes in the comfort of privacy, then finding out why.

- **Give students the opportunity to give you feedback on your feedback.** Check particularly that when you explain what was wrong with distractors, students get your messages clearly. Ask your students to mark onto their materials any feedback responses that they cannot understand. Often the understanding will be about to dawn, and slowing down to identify exactly what it is that is not yet understood is all it takes to put things right. When this does not happen, it could be that the fault lies in the question or in the feedback, and some editing may be needed for the next edition.

- **Think of visual ways of responding.** Some students may wish to be responded to visually rather than with words – at least sometimes. Try to arrange coffee with a computer-graphics expert if you're designing responses for a computer-based package.

- **Keep the language of responses familiar and friendly.** Responses should address the student as 'you' and should use simple, accessible vocabulary. A sense of humour usually helps, but excessive humour (especially feeble puns!) can be counter-productive!

15. Writing study guides

Sometimes the quickest, and best, way to implement a flexible learning pathway is to collect and organize some relatively traditional materials, and to write a study guide to take students through them in a planned, structured way. Study guides are particularly useful for academic subjects where it may be necessary to get students to review a lot of case-study or research-based material. Writing study guide material involves many of the processes considered already in this section, but it is also important to think carefully about how students are briefed to use the traditional resources. The following suggestions should help you to ensure that your study guide helps students to make the most of such resources:

- **Make each study guide attractive and motivating.** The study guide may be the central document that students work with all of the time on your module, while they refer out from it to different books, articles, Web sites, videos and multimedia resources. Explain to students how the study guide is intended to help them balance the various activities that they will do in their studies.

- **Link the intended learning outcomes to the resources.** For example, when different textbooks or articles contain the reference material for your students' learning, it helps to indicate which learning outcome is addressed in each different resource material.

- **Link self-assessment questions to the respective resources.** One of the most important components of an effective study guide is the interaction, which plays the same part as self-assessment questions and feedback responses in self-standing flexible learning materials. With study guide materials, the subject matter is likely to be located in supporting texts or articles, and it helps to specify which source material(s) should best be used by students when working on the questions.

- **Link feedback responses to the respective resources.** Rather than write out detailed feedback responses, it is often possible to refer students to particular sections or paragraphs in their resource materials. However, it remains best to write the main response feedback, and to confine such references to 'further explanation' or 'see also the discussion in ...'.

■ **Don't refer students to large amounts of material at once.** For example, suggesting that students should read Chapter 4 of a textbook is not likely to cause them to learn much from their reading. It is better to brief them to focus their reading on particular pages or sections, and to legitimize the process of merely scanning less relevant or less important material.

■ **Use the study guide to suggest reasonable time-scales.** For example, when referring out to textbooks or computer-based learning packages, it can be useful to give your students a rough idea of the maximum and minimum times you expect them to spend with each source. This can help your students to avoid becoming sidetracked, and, for example, spending too much time working with one particular source.

■ **Give students an agenda *before* they read extracts from other resources.** For example, suggest that 'you should read Chapter 3, Sections 3.3–3.5 next, looking for answers to the following five questions ...'. When students have already got questions in their minds, their reading becomes considerably more active, and when they discover some information which answers one of their questions, they tend to learn it more successfully.

■ **Advise students on what *not* to read.** One of the problems with using external sources such as textbooks is that there is usually a significant amount that is not directly relevant to the intended learning outcomes of the flexible learning module. It can be helpful to advise students along the lines: 'There is no need for you to look at Chapters 4–5 of this source, unless you happen to be particularly interested in the content; this will not relate to any assessments in the present programme.' Most students are quick to take such hints!

■ **Consider setting tasks that cause students to compare and contrast different sources.** When the same topic is addressed in different ways in respective sources, rather than gloss over the difference, it can be valuable for students to make their own minds up about which approach they like best. Compare-and-contrast tasks may be better as part of tutor-marked assignments than as self-assessment exercises, as tutor feedback may add further value to students' own decisions about the different approaches they encounter.

■ **Include study-skills help.** Writing a study guide is about helping students with the *processes* they should aim to use to make the most of the resources with which they are working. It can be useful to have a separate commentary, including practicable suggestions about how to approach working with each different source or resource.

16. Using video recordings in your teaching

Video recordings play valuable roles in helping to show students things that they would not be in a position to explore on their own. You may already use video extracts in your teaching, or give students video materials from which to learn selected elements of their programme. With computer-based training, there are often video sequences embedded in multimedia programmes. However, the act of watching material on a television screen is not one of the most powerful ways through which students actually learn, unless the video extracts are carefully planned into their learning programme. The following suggestions may help you help your students to make the most of video:

■ **Decide what the intended learning outcomes directly associated with the video extracts will be.** It is important that any video extracts are not just seen as an optional extra by your students. The best way to prevent this from happening is to tell them exactly what they are intended to gain from each extract of video material.

■ **Decide why video is the best medium for your purposes.** Ask yourself 'What is this video extract doing that could not be done just as well in print?' Video extracts can be invaluable for showing all sorts of things that students could not experience directly, as well as for conveying the subtleties that go with body language, facial expression, tone of voice, and interpersonal interactions, skills and techniques.

■ **Decide *how* the video material is planned to help your students to learn.** Is it primarily intended to whet their appetites and stimulate their motivation? Is it designed to help them to make sense of some important ideas or concepts that are hard to learn without seeing things? Is it designed to give them useful briefings about things they themselves are intended to do after watching the material?

■ **Consider whether your students will need further access to the video.** If they are intended to watch the video a number of times, you may be able to arrange that the materials can be viewed on demand in a resources centre. If so, make sure that there are mechanisms enabling students to book a time-slot when they can see the video material.

■ **Decide what your students will take away after watching the video.** One of the dangers with video extracts is the 'now you see it, then it's gone' situation. If the video is serving important purposes for your students, they will need to have something more permanent to remind them of what they learned from it.

■ **Work out what (if anything) will be assessed.** If the video is just 'icing on the cake' and there is nothing arising from the video material that will be directly involved in any form of assessment, tell your students that this is the case. When things they derive from using the video elements *are* involved in their assessment, explain this to them, to help them give the video materials appropriate attention.

■ | **Use short extracts at a time.** People are conditioned to watch quite long episodes of television, but to do so in a relatively passive way. Make sure that your students approach video extracts in a different way than that which they normally use for watching television. It is better to split up a 30-minute video into half a dozen or so separate episodes if there are several different things you wish your students to get out of the material.

■ | **Set the agenda for your students before each episode of video.** Ensure that your students are set up with questions in their minds, to which the video extracts will provide answers.

■ | **Consider giving your students things to do while they view the video extracts.** You could brief them to note down particular observations, or to make particular decisions, or to extract and record specific facts or figures as they watch the video extracts.

■ | **Consider asking your students to do things after they've watched each extract.** This can help them to consolidate what they have gained from watching the extracts. It can also prompt them to have a further look at any extract where they may have slipped into passive viewing mode and missed important points.

■ | **Don't underestimate the importance of printed support materials.** To make the most of video elements, students need something in another medium to remind them about what they should be getting out of the video, and where it fits into the overall picture of their learning. Video recordings often work best when supported by a printed workbook, into which students write their observations and their interpretations of what they see. Their learning from such workbooks can be reviewed by looking again at them, even without looking again at the recording.

17. Using audiotapes in your teaching

Audiotape is so commonplace and cheap that its potential in teaching contexts is easily overlooked. In subject disciplines such as music, where sound is all-important, the use of audiotapes as a learning medium is already well developed. In multimedia packages, sound and images are often combined to good effect, yet audiotape can sometimes play a similar role at much less cost. The following suggestions may inspire you to put simple audiotape to good use to support your students:

■ | **Have good reasons for using audiotapes.** Always be in a position to explain to your students *why* an audiotape is being used alongside their other resource materials. Share with them information on what they should be getting out of using the audiotape.

■ | **Most students have access to audiotape.** Many students have portable cassette players, and may use these when travelling on public transport, or jogging, or driving, and in all sorts of circumstances. When elements of learning packages are available as audiotapes, there is the possibility that you will extend their learning to times when they would not otherwise be attempting to study.

■ **Label audiotapes informatively.** People who listen to tapes tend to accumulate lots of them, and it is easy for audiocassettes accompanying learning programmes to get lost amid those used for entertainment.

■ **Keep audiotape extracts short and sharp.** When there are specific intentions about what students should get out of listening to audiotapes, extracts should normally last for a few minutes rather than quarters of an hour! It is worth starting each extract with a recorded 'name' such as 'Extract 3, to go with Section 1, Part 2', and to have the same voice reminding students that when they have reached the 'End of extract 3, going with Section 1, Part 2', and so on.

■ **Use audiotape where tone of voice is important.** It can be particularly useful for students to hear messages where the emphasis that you place on key words or phrases helps them to make sense of material which would be harder to interpret from a printed page or from a computer screen.

■ **Sound can help students into subject-related jargon.** When there is new terminology, for example, it can be hard to tell how to pronounce a word just by seeing it in print, and it can be humiliating for students to find only when talking to a lecturer that they have got their pronunciation wrong! Audiotapes can introduce the vocabulary of a subject to students.

■ **Use audiotapes to bring learning to life.** Audiotapes can be invaluable for giving students the chance to hear people talking, discussing, debating, arguing, persuading, counselling and criticizing, and can capture and pass on to them many experiences and processes that would be difficult to capture in print.

■ **Clarify exactly when a recorded episode should be used.** If you are using audiotape alongside printed materials, it can be useful to have a visual 'flag' to indicate to your students when they should listen to a recorded extract.

■ **Turn students' listening into an active process.** Listening can all too easily be a passive process. Avoid this by setting your students things to think about before listening to a tape extract. Prime them with a few questions, so that they will be searching for the answers from what they hear.

■ **Consider using audiotape to give students feedback on their assignments.** It can be quicker to talk for a few minutes into a tape recorder, than to write all of your feedback down on your students' written assignments, or even to key in your feedback for e-mail transmission. The added intimacy of tone of voice can help you to deliver critical feedback in a more acceptable form. Students can also play the tape again and again, until they have understood each part of your recorded feedback. Always try to begin and end with something positive, just as you would do with written feedback.

■ **Combine audio and visual learning.** It can be useful to use audiotape to talk students through things that they are looking at in their resource materials. For example, complex diagrams or derivations in printed materials, or graphics, tables, spreadsheets shown on-screen in computer-based materials, can be brought to life by the sound of a human voice explaining what to look for in them.

18. Choosing and using computer-based learning resources

■ **Remember that it's harder to get a good idea of the effectiveness of computer-based materials than for paper-based ones.** This is not least because it is not possible to flick through the whole of a computer-based package in the same way as is possible with a printed package. It can be quite hard to get a feel for the overall shape of the learning that is intended to accompany a computer-based package.

■ **Choose your packages carefully.** The best computer-based learning packages are not always those that look most attractive, nor are they necessarily the most expensive ones. The best indicator of a good package is evidence that it causes learning to be successful. Where possible, try them out on students before committing yourself to purchasing them. Alternatively, ask the supplier or manufacturer for details of clients who have already used the packages, and check that the packages really deliver what you need.

■ **Prepare your own checklist to interrogate computer-based materials.** Decide the questions that you need to ask about each possible package, before committing yourself to purchase. Questions could include:

> Are the materials supplied with workbook elements?
> Do students themselves *need* these elements?
> Can support materials be freely photocopied?
> What is the standard of the equipment needed to run the packages effectively?
> What level of technical support and backup will be required?
> Does the software include individual student progress monitoring and tracking?
> Do the materials make good use of pre-test and post-test features?
> Can the materials run effectively on a network?
> Are there licensing implications if you wish to run the package on more than one machine?
> Can you afford multiple copies if the materials are multimedia, single-access packages?

■ **Try to establish the pedigree of the software.** Some computer-based packages have been thoroughly tested and developed, and have been updated and revised several times since their launch. Such packages normally give some details of the history of their development. Beware of packages, however well presented, that have been published or disseminated without real trialling.

■ **Find out about packages from colleagues in other institutions.** Use your contacts. Ask them what packages they know of, which work well and really help students to learn. Also ask them about packages that they don't rate highly, and about the factors that led them to this conclusion.

■ **Try before you buy.** Computer-aided learning packages can be quite expensive, especially if you need to purchase a site licence to use them on a series of networked computer terminals, or to issue students with their own copies on floppy disk. If you're considering buying a particular package, try to get a sample of your students to evaluate it for you. Their experience of using it is even more valuable than your own, as only they can tell whether they are learning effectively from it.

■ **Look at how the medium is used to enhance learning.** If the material does no more than to present on glass what could have been presented equally well on paper, it is probably not worth investigating further. The medium should do something that helps learning, such as causing students to engage in interaction that they might have skipped if the same tasks or questions were set in print.

■ **Get familiar with the package, before letting your students loose with it.** There is a learning curve to be ascended with most computer-based packages, and it is best if *you* go up this ahead of your students. They will need help on how to make best use of the package, as well as on what they are supposed to be learning from it. Find out what it feels like to use the package. By far the best way to do this is to work through the package yourself, even if you already know the subject that it covers. Find out what students will *do* as they use the package, and check whether the tasks and activities are really relevant to your students, and pitched at an appropriate level for them.

■ **Check the intended learning outcomes of the computer-based package.** The best packages state the intended learning outcomes clearly within the first few screens of information. The intended outcomes, and the level that the package is pitched at, should also be spelt out in supporting documentation that comes with the package. The main danger is that such packages address a wider range of intended outcomes than are needed by your students, and that they may become distracted and end up learning things that they don't need to, possibly interfering with their assessment performance.

■ **If necessary, rephrase the learning outcomes associated with the package.** It may be useful to tell your students exactly what the learning outcomes mean in the context of their particular studies. You may well need to redefine the standards associated with the outcomes.

■ **Think about access to equipment and software.** Some packages come with licence arrangements to use the package with a given number of students, either allowing multiple copies to be made, or the package to be used over a network. Ensure that the software is protected in order to prevent unauthorized copying, or unlicensed use on more than one machine.

■ | **Think how students will retain important ideas from the package, after they have used it.** Make sure that there is supporting documentation or workbook materials, as these will help students to summarize and remember the important things they gain while using computer-based packages. Where such resources don't already exist, you should consider the benefits of making a workbook or an interactive handout, so that students working through the package write down things (or record them) at important stages in their learning.

■ | **Ensure that learning-by-doing is appropriate and relevant.** Most computer-based packages contain a considerable amount of learning-by-doing, particularly decision making, choosing options, and entering responses to structured questions. Some of the tasks may not be entirely relevant to the intended learning outcomes of your programme, and you may need to devise briefing details to help students to see exactly what they should be taking seriously as they work through the package.

■ | **Check that students will get adequate feedback on their work with the package.** Much of this feedback may be already built into the package as it stands. However, you may need to think about further ways of keeping track of whether your students are getting what they should from their use of the package. It can be worth adding appropriate, short elements to tutor-marked assignments, so that there is a way of finding out whether particular students are missing vital things they should have picked up from the package.

■ | **Check how long the package should take.** The time spent by students should be reflected in the learning payoff they derive from their studies with the package, and this in turn should relate to the proportion of the overall assessment framework that is linked to the topics covered by the package.

■ | **Think ahead to assessment.** Work out what will be assessed, relating directly to the learning that is to be done using the computer-based materials. Express this as assessment criteria, and check how these link to the intended learning outcomes. Make sure that students, before working through the computer-based materials, know *what* will be assessed, *when* it will be assessed, and *how* it will be assessed.

■ | **Explore software that tracks students' progress.** This can involve pre-testing and post-testing, and storing the data on the computer system, as well as monitoring and recording the time taken by each student to work through each part of the package. Such data can be invaluable for discovering the main problems that students may be experiencing with the topic, and with the package itself.

■ | **Seek feedback from your students.** Ask them what aspects of the package they found most valuable, and most important. Ask them also what, if anything, went wrong in their own work with the package. Where possible, find alternative ways of addressing important learning outcomes for those students who have particular problems with the computer-delivered materials.

19. Designing computer-marked assignments

Computer-marked assignments can save human toil, and can be a means of giving much quicker feedback to students than is possible from human tutors. The following suggestions may help you to decide when and how to use computer-marked assignments:

- **Look at examples from a range of sources.** There are many examples of structured questions in published computer-marked assignments, and on the Internet. Seeing what other people have already done is the fastest way of working out what sorts of questions you could design for your own purposes.

- **Decide whether you are designing *computer-delivered* assignments, or just *computer-marked* ones.** Computer-marked assignments can be in print, with (for example) optical card-readers used to automate the marking, the printout of feedback to students, and the analysis of their scores and of the performance of the questions as testing devices. *Computer-delivered* assignments are where students enter their answers or choices directly into a computer or terminal, and may then get feedback and/or scores straightaway from the machine, or across the Internet or an intranet.

- **Don't become trapped into the belief that computer-marked assignments can only test lower cognitive knowledge.** Though such assignments are often used to test straightforward recall of information or simple decision making, well-designed assignments can test at a much deeper level. Look at the different things that can be tested, and the different question structures that are possible. Besides multiple-choice questions, computer-delivered assignments can be designed to use number-entry, text-entry, ranking, and a variety of other ways for students to enter their answers, judgements or decisions.

- **Decide which learning outcomes will be covered by the computer-aided assignment.** This is best done by working out which outcomes lend themselves best to testing using the range of formats available to you. Tell your students about this decision, so they are well informed about the content that they should prepare for the assignment.

- **Think about computer literacy implications.** If the assignment is print-based, and only the *marking* is to be done using computers, there is little to worry about, other than to make sure that the instructions regarding how to fill in the optically readable card or sheet are clear and straightforward. If, however, doing the assignment depends on sitting at a computer or terminal and interacting with it, students with highly developed keyboarding skills may be advantaged, as may those who have no fear of working with computers.

- **Decide whether your use of computer-marked assignments will be summative or formative.** Technology can be used for both purposes, and even if you decide that your primary purpose is to measure your students' achievements, you can still make use of the power of the technology to deliver feedback to your students.

■ **Explore the software options open to you.** There are several different software shells that support testing and feedback delivery. Which you choose will depend on how sophisticated your question design will be, and to some extent how easily you yourself can learn to handle the software. Alternatively, your responsibility may rest mainly in the area of designing questions and feedback, with someone else handling the task of entering your assignments into the software.

■ **Try out each question thoroughly before including it in an assignment.** You may be able to test out your questions with face-to-face groups of students, giving you a great deal of useful feedback about whether your questions are really testing them, and about which questions are too hard or too easy. Alternatively, you may be able to trial your questions in computer-based form as part of learning materials, and get the software to analyse how each question performs. This helps you to make a better-informed decision about which questions are good enough to include in a computer-marked assignment.

■ **Think about the security implications of assignments.** Where computer-delivered assignments count towards the overall assessment of students, ways may need to be found to prevent the correct answers from circulating around! Such ways include getting the cohort of students together at the same time, and maybe in the same room, and having them do the assignment in a way similar to a timed exam. Alternatively, ways may be found to keep students who have already done the exam demonstrably separated from those who have not yet done it. A further option is delaying any feedback or information on scores until all students have taken the test.

■ **Triangulate the results of computer-marked assignments.** At least until you know that a computer-marked assignment is performing reliably, and giving data that is consistent with *other* means of measuring your students' achievements, it is best to ensure that there are sufficient checks in the overall assessment system to find any snags with the computer-marked components. Be aware of the possibilities of some students being so apprehensive of computers that their performance is not representative of their achievement. Also beware of substitution, for example someone else doing the computer-marked component!

20. Designing computer-generated feedback to students

We've already looked at the principles of designing feedback for students, both as a key part of responding to self-assessment questions, and for responding to multiple-choice questions whether used primarily for testing or for feedback. The following suggestions aim to help you make computer-generated feedback as useful as possible to your students:

■ **Don't miss out on the opportunity to couple feedback with assessment.** Whether you are using computer-marked assignments or computer-delivered exams, the technology makes it possible to give each student feedback on each choice of option or each keyed-in answer.

- **Consider the pros and cons of instant feedback.** With computer-delivered exams, for example, it is possible for feedback to be given to students immediately after they have attempted each question. The positive feedback they gain when they answer questions successfully may boost their morale and lead to improved exam performance, but the opposite may happen if they get the first few questions wrong.

- **Consider 'slightly delayed' feedback.** It is useful if students can receive feedback while they still remember what they were thinking of when they answered the questions. In computer-delivered exams, feedback can be shown to students on-screen *after* they have completed all of the questions, and when it will not have any effect on their scores.

- **Think how best to give feedback if it is delayed more significantly.** For example, when sending computer-generated feedback printouts to students in response to their computer-marked assignments, there will normally be at least several days between students answering the questions and receiving feedback. It is then necessary to make sure that students are reminded of the context in which they answered each question.

- **Always remind students both of the question and of the options from which they have selected.** It is important, for example in multiple-choice formats, not only to remind students about the context surrounding the correct (or best) option, but also to remind them of the options that were wrong (or less good).

- **Use technology to write letters to students.** Particularly with computer-marked assignments, it is relatively straightforward to wrap up the feedback printed out for each question into a self-sufficient letter, commenting additionally on their overall performance.

- **Letters can be written for computer-delivered exams too.** It is possible for students doing a computer-delivered exam, in a formal examination room, to leave the room at the end of the exam and pick up a personal letter informing them not only of their overall performance, but also giving feedback where appropriate on each question they have attempted. Getting exam feedback so quickly, and in a form where it can be reread, is a powerful way of preventing this kind of formal examination from being a lost learning opportunity.

- **Start the feedback on a personal note.** Computers can be programmed to start a letter with 'Dear Alison …' rather than 'Dear Mrs Jones'. Most students prefer the personal touch, especially when the feedback is coming from a machine. It is, however, important to use familiar names only if you know what your students prefer to be called. The start of the letter can then give one of two or three 'openings', respectively designed for students who have respectively scored brilliantly, averagely, or not so well.

- **End the feedback letter with useful advice.** The computer can be programmed to search for topic areas where students' answers have shown particular strengths or weaknesses, and can offer topic-specific praise or suggestions. It is also useful to end a computer-delivered assignment feedback letter with something useful regarding preparation for the next assignment on the programme.

- **Don't make computer-generated feedback anonymous!** When the name of the tutor who designed the assignment is printed at the end of computer-generated feedback letters, this person is likely to receive quite a few communications from students (even if the name was made a fictitious one!). Especially if the tone of each feedback response is warm and helpful, students don't feel that the feedback was dreamt up by a machine.

21. Making effective use of e-mail

E-mail is the simplest form of communicating by computer. Electronic communication is addictive! To most people who have already climbed the learning curve of finding out how to use e-mail, the apprehension they may have experienced on their first encounters fades into insignificance. Computers can be linked up to a network and the users are issued with e-mail addresses. A user can use e-mail software to type a message and send it to any other user. The message is stored on a central computer until the recipient collects it. This can be on a computer network within the institution or it can be via the Internet, which enables users anywhere in the world to exchange messages. Once you are connected to the Internet, sending e-mail is cheaper than sending a letter or making a telephone call and is much quicker. The following suggestions may help you to get started with e-mail yourself, and to maximize some of the benefits that e-mail can offer to you and to your students:

- **Find out what e-mail facilities your institution has available.** Most lecturers already have access to e-mail facilities in their institutions. Check whether you can log in anywhere on the network. Can you log in from home? What are the security arrangements?

- **Arrange to have your own e-mail address.** It is much better to be able to collect your e-mail separately from the rest of your organization. This will help avoid e-mail being lost within the organization and will help others feel that they are communicating with you directly.

- **Choose your e-mail address carefully.** You may be able to choose the first part of your own address. Make sure that it uses the name you usually use for your communications. It is common for IT managers to issue e-mail addresses to people based on their names from a personnel file. As an example, if your name is *Keith Robert Simpson*, the first part of the e-mail address you are issued might be *KR Simpson*. If you are generally known as *Bob*, people will not recognize you from the e-mail address. If it is possible, insist that the name part of your e-mail address is what you want it to be.

- **Include your e-mail address on written communications and tell people what it is when you are on the telephone.** Make the address part of your letterhead to make it widely known. Encourage people to e-mail you, rather than writing to you or telephoning you.

- **Take care to let people know if your e-mail address changes.** If you move from one service provider to another, for example, or if your institution changes its address details, your e-mail address will change. It can be worth the time spent to e-mail everyone in your address book with details of any forthcoming change, and then to e-mail them from your new address again as soon as the change is implemented.

- **Ask other people if they have e-mail and what their addresses are.** Most e-mail software includes an electronic address book. You can enter the e-mail addresses into it when you are told them. When you want to send an e-mail message, you can just select whom you want to send it to and the computer will fill the address in for you.

- **Make sure that students get started with e-mail.** Write careful, step-by-step briefing instructions for your students. The computer-literate people may hardly do more than glance at these before getting into the swing of using e-mail. However, for those people who lack confidence or experience with computers, these instructions can be vital and comforting until they become familiar with the medium.

- **Decide what you really want to do with e-mail.** There are numerous purposes that e-mail can serve, and you need to ensure that the purpose is always clear to your students. If they know *what* it is being used for, and *why* e-mail has been chosen for this, they are much more likely to get more out of it.

- **Make the most of e-mail.** Although you may just want to use e-mail for routine communication with (and between) students and colleagues, there are many more uses that the medium can lend itself to. Think about the possible uses of sending attached files, such as documents, assignments, digitally stored images, sounds and video recordings. All of these can be edited or marked, and returned to students, in the same ways as simple messages.

- **Collect your e-mail frequently and reply quickly.** If you don't collect your e-mail frequently and respond promptly, you will lose out on the benefits of fast communications and other people will be less inclined to send you e-mail in future.

- **Make the most of the lack of time constraints.** One of the most significant advantages of e-mail as a vehicle for feedback is that students can view the feedback when they have time to make sense of it. They can store it until such time becomes available. They can also look at it as often as they wish to, and you can keep copies of exactly what you said to each individual student.

- **Be available!** When students are accustomed to e-mail, they expect quick replies to their queries. If you're going to be away from your access to the system for more than a day or two at a time, it is worth letting all your students know when you will be back online.

- **Make the most of the speed.** Giving feedback by e-mail to students at a distance obviously reduces delays. The sooner students get feedback on their work, the more likely it is that their own thinking is still fresh in their minds, and the feedback is therefore better understood.

■ **Keep e-mail messages simple.** Some e-mail systems have very limited editing facilities and can only handle straightforward text. They don't allow different fonts or typestyles and diagrams are not possible, so messages tend not to look attractive. The reason for this is to let a very wide variety of systems communicate in a very simple way.

■ **Keep most messages brief and to the point.** People are actively discouraged by long e-mail messages. If something takes more than one screen, most readers either dump them or file them. Encourage your students also to make economical use of the medium, and to send several short messages rather than try to cram lots of points into a single missive.

■ **When you send a long e-mail, explain why, and what to do with it.** For example, from time to time you may want to send students something that you don't expect them to treat as a normal e-mail message, but perhaps to print out and study in depth. It makes all the difference if they know what they are expected to do with longer messages.

■ **Send more detailed messages as attached files.** If you want to send more detailed communications, you can produce them in another, more flexible computer package. If you save the file you produce, you can then send this with a short e-mail message explaining what you are sending.

■ **Make sure the recipient has software to read attached files.** If you send a complex file such as a word-processed document or a spreadsheet, make sure the recipients can read them. Ideally they would have the same version of the program that you used to create it, but it may be possible to send a file which is saved in a format compatible with the recipient's software even if it isn't the same.

■ **Make use of mailing lists to send copies to more than one recipient at the same time.** Most e-mail software makes it very simple to send extra copies of a message to other people. It is also often possible to create lists, or groups, of people and to send messages to all the members of the groups at the same time. These groups can also be saved for future mailings.

■ **Encourage students to reply about your feedback.** When you are using e-mail to give specific feedback to students, it is important that you know that you have got through to them all. Asking them to reply to you gives them the chance to let you know how they *feel* about the feedback you have given them, or the mark or grade that you have awarded them.

■ **Use e-mail to keep a dispersed or distant group of students together.** Sending out circular notes not only helps individuals to feel part of a community of students, but also reminds them about important matters such as assessment deadlines, or problems that have arisen with course materials, or updates to interesting materials that have been discovered on the Internet.

■ **Remember those students whose access to e-mail is difficult or impossible.** One of the disadvantages of using e-mail as a means of communication is that if some students have problems with access, they can become significantly disadvantaged. You may need to find ways of compensating through other means for those things they miss out on.

■ | **Take particular care with your e-mail message titles.** It can take ages to search for a particular e-mail if it is not clear what each message is about. The computer software can sort messages by date, and by sender, but it is more difficult to track down topics. Two or three well-chosen keywords make the most useful titles.

■ | **Keep track of your e-mails.** Good filing is as important with electronic communication as it is with written forms. You may need to refer back to a previous e-mail you have sent, or use it as evidence. Print backup copies of the most important e-mails you send or receive, as well as electronic copies.

■ | **Don't let the privacy of the medium lead you into trouble!** Don't put anything in an e-mail that you would not be able to defend in front of a jury! Be careful with what you say; most institutions have standards of behaviour, such as for appropriateness of language, and potentially libellous discussion. Your e-mails may be monitored, and will probably remain accessible from the server.

22. Helping students to get started with e-mail

Having explored how *you* can get started with e-mail, next we look at ways you can help your students to take the plunge. People who would not have been thought to be computer literate often take their first steps into the area because they are attracted by the benefits of e-mail. Some, perhaps many, of your students are likely to be up to speed with computers and e-mail, but the following suggestions may help you to whet the appetites of those who have not yet become 'mouse-trained':

■ | **Tell students not to worry about hitting the wrong keys.** Mention how unlikely it is that they will break the computer! For those students who are reluctant to get into computer usage, there is often a concern that they may do something drastic and irreversible to expensive equipment. Remind students that the only thing they are likely to risk when using computers is losing some of the work they have done with the machine, and even this risk is quite small, with 'undo' commands in most computer software, and with good habits about saving work to disk every few minutes.

■ | **Point out that e-mail is a way of practising useful written communication skills.** Getting students to communicate with each other, and with you, using e-mail helps them to develop their written command of the language. Seeing their own words on-screen rather than on paper can make them more aware of their strengths and weaknesses with the language.

■ | **Promote the benefits of computer confidence.** The information technology revolution has meant that a much greater proportion of people need to use computers in their everyday work and lives. Being computer literate also means that people don't have to rely on other people to perform various tasks for them. For example, students who have mastered word-processing don't have to pay someone to process their reports or memos, and can keep editorial control over them, making it much easier to change them whenever they receive some useful feedback about draft versions.

■ **Remind students that an e-mail message need not be sent until they are completely happy with it.** This allows them to edit and polish their writing. If they were to attempt so much editing on a hand-written message, it could either look very messy, or have to be written out several times before the same number of adjustments had been achieved.

■ **Remind students that e-mail can be viewed as environment-friendly.** The saving of paper can be significant. If the computing facilities are already available, it can be argued that using e-mail incurs negligible costs.

■ **Point out to students that they can save and keep their own e-mail communications in an organized way.** By copying each e-mailed message to their own files or disks, they can keep track of all the messages they have composed and sent. Keeping similar track of handwritten messages is less likely, or would involve the trouble and expense of photocopying. Students looking back at a range of e-mails they have composed can see for themselves how their skills with the language are developing.

■ **Remind students that e-mail can be a way of them keeping in touch with their friends elsewhere.** Most libraries or colleges have Internet facilities available to students, making it possible for them to send messages to anywhere in the world. Such facilities are sometimes free of charge to library users, and in any case the actual costs are insignificant once the equipment has been installed.

■ **Help students to get started.** Probably the best way to do this is for you to *require* all of your students to e-mail something short to you, with a time deadline. It can be worth thinking about using a short written exercise for this purpose, in which case you can attach at least some marks to the task. This can make all the difference to students who might otherwise not get round to finding out how to log into the system and send an e-mail.

■ **Make students' efforts worthwhile.** If you've asked all members of a group to e-mail something to you, try to respond *immediately* (within a day or two) to each message as it arrives. The fact that students get a little individual feedback via e-mail from you, and quickly, helps them to see for themselves the potential of e-mail as a communication medium.

■ **Encourage students to write very short e-mails!** One of the problems with e-mail communication is that people tend to read only the beginning of a message. If an incoming message is too long for immediate reading, people tend either to file them away for later reading (and forget them!) or simply delete them.

23. Getting a computer-conference going

The success of a computer-conference depends upon its value to students, and how well they can make good use of it. This in turn depends significantly on the design and structure of the conference, and on the degree of ownership students develop about it. In Chapter 3, some of the advantages of computer-conferences were explored in the context of virtual groups. The following suggestions may help you to tread sensitively regarding moderating a conference, while setting it up so as to maximize its value to students:

- **Explain to students the benefits of participating in computer-conferences.** Students can exchange a lot of information, both study-related and social, through such conferences. They can get peer-feedback on their own ideas, and even on selected parts of their work. Participating in computer-conferences helps students to develop computer-related skills, and can quickly help them to speed up their keyboarding skills.

- **Provide good 'start-up' messages.** These are the initial messages within a conference, to which students can append their own messages as replies. Each 'start-up' message should have a definite purpose, so that replies and ensuing discussion is focused rather than rambling. The messages should state the main topics of the conference, and are listed sequentially in the main directory of the conference. Conferencing takes place when participants add 'replies' to these messages. Modern conferencing software looks and feels more like Internet pages than the heavily linear, text-based systems that were formerly used.

- **Make each screen speak for itself.** Especially with 'start-up' messages, which introduce each topic in the conference, it is best that the essence of the main message takes up less than a single screen. If students have to scroll down more than one page before finding out what is being addressed, they are less likely to read the 'start-up' message, and therefore unlikely to reply. Further detail can be added in the next few pages (or 'replies'). Encourage students contributing their own replies to keep them to a single screen whenever possible, and to send several replies with different titles rather than one long reply addressing a number of different aspects.

- **Choose the titles of 'start-up' messages carefully.** When students are looking at the directory of a computer-conference, they will see the titles of these pages arranged as an index, in the order in which the pages were originally entered. Aim to make these titles self-explanatory, so that students can tell what each section of the conference is about straight from the directory, rather than having to read the whole of a 'start-up' page before finding out whether they wish to explore the topic further.

- **Don't cover too much in a 'start-up' message.** It is better if each section of the conference is relatively self-contained, and prescribed, rather than having topic pages which cover several different aspects. As new matters arise from students' replies to 'start-up' messages, decide whether to introduce new 'start-up' messages to carry these matters forward separately. Add your own responses directing students who may be following the conference themes regarding where in the conference each theme is being developed further.

■ **Choose the topics within your conference carefully.** Think about the structure you want the conference to take and set up a topic for each main area. Topics that are too general may end up with messages that are not clearly focused and discussions may not develop well. Start with a small number of topics and only add more when they are needed. It is confusing to have too many topics at first, so only have a few at the beginning.

■ **Make sure messages are put into the correct topic.** If messages are put into the wrong topic, the structure of the discussions will suffer. Encourage conference members to think about where to put messages at a very early stage and try to establish a culture of well organized discussion. If some members consistently place messages in the wrong place, send them an e-mail explaining what they have done and what would be better. If they persist in doing this, you may need to use your moderating powers to move messages to the correct place.

■ **Encourage students to reply with messages that are short and only contain one point.** Long messages are difficult to read on computer screens, so discourage any that are more than one screen long. If messages contain discussion of more than one point, the structure of the conference can break down, so encourage members to send several short messages, addressing one point each.

■ **Leave a message every time you log on.** One of the concerns that computer-conference users have is that nobody is reading their messages. Use the conference as frequently as you can and always leave some kind of message to show that you have been logging in. Ideally your messages should answer questions or raise some important issue, but a trivial message in the 'chat' topic is better than nothing.

■ **Use the conference as a notice board.** Get into the habit of making the conference *the* best way to keep up with topical developments in the field of study, as well as administrative matters such as assessment deadlines, guidance for students preparing assessments, and so on. Try to make it necessary for students to log on to the conference regularly; this will result in a greater extent of active contribution by them. A conference can provide you with a quick and efficient way to communicate detailed information to the whole of a class. Students themselves can print off and keep anything that is particularly important to them.

■ **Use the conference as a support mechanism.** This can save a lot of tutor time. Elements of explanation, advice or counselling that otherwise might have had to be sent individually to several different students can be put into the conference once only, and remain available to all. Whenever your reply to an enquiry or problem raised by a student warrants a wider audience, the conference is there to do this.

■ **Make the conference a resource in its own right.** Add some screens of useful resource material, maybe with 'hot-links' to other Internet sources that are relevant. It is useful if some such material is *only* available through the computer-conference; this ensures that all your students will make efforts to use it.

■ **Try to get students discussing and arguing with each other via the conference.** The best computer-conferences are not just tutor–student debates, but are taken over by the students themselves. They can add new topics, and bring a social dimension to the conference.

■ **Set up a 'chat' topic for general conversation.** Conference members might want to discuss matters that are less serious than the topic-related aspects of the conference. Set up an area for them to do this and encourage them to 'chat' in that area. Other names for 'chat' conferences might be 'café' or 'pub': choose a name to suit the tone you are trying to establish for your conference.

■ **Encourage members to use e-mail where it is more appropriate.** E-mail is more private and so it should be used for messages that are for individuals rather than for general distribution to all conference members. There is also no point in making others read messages that are not relevant to them. Most systems will allow private 1:1 communication, as well as 1:many and 1:selected others.

■ **Try to moderate with a light hand.** If people are putting messages in the wrong topic or are not using e-mail appropriately, provide gentle guidance about what to do in future. As far as you can, keep the ownership of the content and structure of the conference with the participants themselves, rather than being tempted into editing the conference too much.

■ **Be prepared to moderate rigorously if necessary!** For example, remove anything offensive or inappropriate before it is likely to be seen by many students. If particular students misuse the conference, treat the issue seriously, and seek them out and warn them of the consequences of such actions, for example loss of computer privileges. It is useful to recruit student moderators from those students who are particularly computer literate, and who may be only too willing to become conference moderators, editing and rearranging contributions to keep the structure of the conference fluent and easy to follow.

■ **Consider having some assessed work entered onto the conference.** If students *have to* make some contributions, they are more likely to ascend the learning curve regarding sending in replies, and to do so more readily in non-assessed elements too. One advantage in having an assessed task 'up on the conference' is that each student can see everyone else's attempts, and the standards of work improve very rapidly.

■ **Consider allocating some of the coursework marks for participation in a computer-conference.** This is one way of ensuring that all the students in a class engage with a class conference. Once they have mastered the technique of contributing to a conference, most students find that they enjoy it enough to maintain a healthy level of participation.

24. Putting the Internet to work for learning

- **Play with the Internet yourself.** You need to pick up your own experience of how it feels to tap into such a vast and varied database, before you can design ways of using it to deliver some meaningful learning experiences to your students.

- **Decide whether you want your students to use the Internet, or an intranet.** An intranet is where a networked set of computers talk to each other, using Internet conventions, but where the content is not open to the rest of the universe. If you are working in an organization which already has such a network, and if your students can make use of this network effectively, there will be some purposes that will be better served by an intranet. You can also have *controlled* access to the Internet via an intranet, such as by using hot-links to predetermined external sites.

- **Use the Internet to research something yourself.** You may well of course have done this often already, but if not, give it a try before you think of setting your students 'search and retrieve' tasks with the Internet. Set yourself a fixed time, perhaps half-an-hour or even less. Choose a topic that you're going to search for, preferably something a little offbeat. See for yourself how best to use the search engines, and compare the relevance and efficiency of different engines. Find out for yourself how to deal with 4,593 references to your chosen topic, and how to improve your searching strategy to whittle them down to the 10 that you really want to use!

- **Don't just use the Internet as a filing cabinet for your own teaching materials!** While it is useful in its own way if your students can have access to your own notes and resources, this is not really *using* the Internet. Too many materials designed for use in other forms are already cluttering up the Internet. If all you intend your students to do is to download your notes and print their own copies, sending them e-mailed attachments would do the same job much more efficiently.

- **Think carefully about your intended learning outcomes.** You may indeed wish to use the Internet as a means whereby your students address the existing intended outcomes associated with their subject material. However, it is also worth considering whether you may wish to add further outcomes, to do with the processes of searching, selecting, retrieving and analyzing subject material. If so, you may also need to think about whether, and how, these additional outcomes may be assessed.

- **Give your students specific things to do using the Internet.** Make these tasks where it is relevant to have up-to-the-minute data or news, rather than where the 'answers' are already encapsulated in easily accessible books or resources.

- **Consider giving your students a menu of tasks and activities.** They will feel more ownership if they have a significant degree of choice in their Internet tasks. Where you have a group of students working on the same syllabus, it can be worth letting them choose different tasks, and then communicating their main findings to each other (and to you) using a computer-conference or by e-mail.

- **Let your students know that the process is at least as important as the outcome.** The key skills that they can develop using the Internet include designing an effective search, and making decisions about the quality and authenticity of the evidence they find. It is worth designing tasks where you already know of at least some of the evidence you expect them to locate, and remaining open to the fact that they will each uncover at least as much again as you already know about!

- **Consider designing your own interactive pages.** You may want to restrict these to an intranet, at least at first. You can then use dialogue boxes to cause your students to answer questions, enter data, and so on. Putting such pages up for all to see on the Internet may mean that you get a lot of unsolicited replies!

- **Consider getting your students to design and enter some pages.** This may be best done restricted to an intranet, at least until your students have picked up sufficient skills to develop pages that are worth putting up for all to see. The act of designing their own Internet material is one of the most productive ways to help your students develop their critical skills at evaluating materials already on the Internet.

25. Retrieving information from the Internet

The Internet has enormous potential as a source of information for a vast range of tasks. It can also, however, lead to problems and it needs to be used with care. Passing some of this guidance on to students will help them avoid pitfalls:

- **Choose your times carefully.** If you plan to give students information retrieval tasks using the Internet during course time, make sure that you plan so that the system will not be too congested at the time. When the system is busy, it becomes very slow and communications can even break down. If possible, use it when the USA is asleep (in the mornings for UK users).

- **Think about the time it might take and what the costs might be for your students to find information.** The Internet is generally cheap to use, but costs can mount up. If students are using a modem to make their connection, encourage them to do it at weekends or in the evenings to reduce costs. Make sure they have the opportunity to search at these times. You might need to give students some hints about where they should search so that they don't waste too much time.

- **Use 'local' sources when possible.** A number of organizations have sites in different parts of the world. If you can find one in the same country (or even continent) that you are working from, communications can be faster at busy times.

■ **Use a good search engine to help you find information.** There are quite a few search engines available on the Internet. Choose one that seems to perform quickly and that produces a good range of results. Once again, some search engines have sites in different parts of the world, so using a 'local' one may be faster.

■ **Learn to use the advanced facilities of a search engine to refine searches.** Simple searches on almost any single word produce too many matches to be useful. Search engines usually allow you to carry out more refined searches in order to home in more accurately on the information you are looking for. Many of these engines include tutorials that will help you to use them effectively.

■ **Be prepared to use the rest of the Internet, as well as the World Wide Web.** Most Internet users are most familiar with the graphical user interface of the World Wide Web (WWW). This is the easiest part of the Internet to use, but some of the other parts make a wider range of information available and (because they don't use graphics widely) are much faster in operation. If the WWW doesn't have the information you need, try to find out about using FTP (File Transfer Protocol), Gopher servers and Veronicas. They may seem difficult to use, but they give access to a wide range of information.

■ **Be cautious about the quality of the information available on the Internet.** It is very cheap and easy to set up pages, particularly on the WWW. As a result, the quality of the information is very variable. Before relying on it, check out the reliability of the source of the information. The information could have been put there by students as a prank, by a fundamentalist group or by a company for sales purposes. Ideally, you should only use information that provides some means (such as references) for verifying it.

■ **Insist that students acknowledge their sources of information.** If a source is used, students should give the address of the page where it was found. This enables the source to be verified and discourages plagiarism.

■ **Be aware that information on the Internet can change or be moved.** It is quite common for links from one page to another page, or another site, to change. A page can also be moved to a different server. Before directing students to a source of information, make sure it is still there.

■ **Make sure students don't drift around on the surf.** It is very easy to follow interesting links around the Internet and to spend a lot of time unproductively. Warn your students against this danger and give them some idea how much time should be spent on Internet tasks.

■ **Alert students to their responsibilities.** Point out that they should not store anything on the hard drive that they would not want to defend in court! Most institutions have rules about 'inappropriate material', and ways of checking who put it there.

26. Helping students to learn from the Internet

The Internet is the electronic highway to the largest collection of information, data and communication ever constructed by the human species. Playing with the Internet is easy, but *learning* from it is not always straightforward. The following suggestions may help you to point your students in directions where they will not only enjoy playing with the Internet, but also develop their techniques so that they learn effectively from it too. Some of these suggestions may also help *you* to learn more from it:

- **Consider starting small.** For example, you might be able to download selected information from the Internet onto individual computers, or a locally networked series of terminals. You can then give your students specific 'search' tasks, where it will be relatively easy for them to locate specific information.

- **Get your students to induct each other.** Learning from the Internet need not be a solo activity. Indeed, it can be very useful to have two or three students working at each terminal, so that they talk to each other about what they are finding, and follow up leads together. Encourage them to take turns at working the keyboard, so that they all develop their confidence at handling the medium, and are then equipped to carry on working on their own.

- **Give your students exercises that help them to improve their selection of search words.** Show them how choosing a single broad search word leads to far too many sources being listed, and makes it very slow and boring to go through all of the sources looking for the information they really want. Get them to experiment with different combinations of search words, so that the sources that are located become much more relevant to their search purposes.

- **Allow your students to find out about the different speeds at which information can be found on the Internet.** For example, let them experiment at different times of the day, so they can see when the Internet is heavily used and slower. Also, let them find out for themselves how much slower it can be waiting for graphics to be downloaded than for mainly text materials. Help them to become better at deciding whether to persist with a source that is highly relevant but slow to download, or whether to continue searching for sources that may download more quickly.

- **Remind your students that finding information is only the first step in learning from it.** It is easy to discover a wealth of information during an Internet search, only to forget most of it within a very short time. Encourage your students to download and edit the materials that they think will be most relevant, or even to make conventional handwritten or word-processed notes of their own while they use the Internet.

- **Help your students to learn to keep tabs on what they have found.** Entering 'bookmarks' or 'favourites' is one of the most efficient ways of being able to go back easily to what may have turned out to be the most relevant or valuable source of information during a search. Get your students to practise logging the sites that could turn out to be worth returning to. Also help them to practise clearing out bookmarks that turn out to be irrelevant, or that are superseded by later finds.

■ **Give your students practice at recording things that they have found during searches.** It can be useful to design worksheets to train them to note down key items of information as they find it, and to train them to be better at making their own notes as a matter of routine when exploring a topic using the Internet.

■ **Consider getting your students to experiment with a learning log.** This can be done for a few hours of work with the Internet, and then looked back upon for clues about which tactics proved most successful. It can be even better to get students to compare notes about what worked well for them, and where the glitches were.

■ **Help your students to develop their critical skills.** For example, set them a task involving them reviewing several sources they find on the Internet, and making decisions about the authenticity and validity of the information that they locate. Remind them that it is not possible to tell whether information is good or bad just by looking at the apparent quality of it on the screen. Remind your students that information on the Internet may not have been subjected to refereeing or other quality-assurance processes normally associated with published information in books or journal articles.

■ **Remind students to balance playing with the Internet and learning from it.** It is perfectly natural, and healthy, to explore, and to follow up interesting leads, even when they take students far away from the purpose of their searches. However, it is useful to develop the skills to ration the amount of random exploration, and to devote 'spurts' of conscious activity to following through the specific purposes of searches.

Chapter 5

Assessment

Putting assessment into context
1. What should assessment be?
2. Why should we assess?
3. When should we assess?
4. Plagiarism, cheating and assessment
5. Monitoring the quality of your assessment processes

Setting and marking exams
6. Designing questions for traditional exams
7. Setting open-book exam questions
8. Designing exam marking schemes
9. Marking examination scripts
10. Using exam questions as class exercises
11. Conducting vivas
12. Designing multiple-choice exams
13. Helping students to cope with exam failure

Making the most of your external examiners
14. External examiners: before they start
15. External examiners: when they arrive
16. Becoming an external examiner yourself

Diversifying assessment
17. Assessing essays
18. Assessing reports
19. Assessing practical skills
20. Assessing presentations

This is the longest chapter in this book, and in many ways the most important, not least from the point of view of students themselves. Although this chapter is essentially about 'how to assess', the suggestions offered range much further than simply giving advice on how to go about measuring students' achievements. In each of the assessment varieties addressed, consideration is given to ways of setting it up so that it helps students to learn deeply, satisfyingly and relevantly.

The chapter begins by **putting assessment into context**, with suggestions on formal assessment processes such as exams and vivas, including advice on making your own tasks associated with such scenarios less burdensome.

It often surprises lecturers that they can be set loose **setting and marking exams** even without having had any real training or practice in the processes involved. The suggestions in the next part of this chapter aim to give some guidance to how these critically important duties can be approached.

External examining is often cited as a crucial plank in the quality assurance structure. It can indeed work very well, but care needs to be taken to optimize the benefits that the processes involved can deliver. The suggestions in the next section may alert you to ways in which you can ensure that external examining works well in the contexts of the courses you teach and assess.

Next, suggestions are offered on a wide range of assessment scenarios, with the main aim being to encourage you to **diversify assessment** of your students, avoiding the situation where their assessment is dominated by just a few processes and instruments. What can we assess? And how? The range of assessment methods to choose from is much wider than is often realized. Yet more than 80 per cent of assessment in universities comprises essays, reports, and traditional time-constrained exams. Assessment that is 'fit for purpose' uses the best method of assessment appropriate to the context, the students, the level, the subject and the institution. The suggestions below illustrate how a wide range of products of students' work can be assessed. While each of the subsections below provides suggestions on how to go about assessing, they also include numerous suggestions about how to help students prepare successfully for each of the kinds of assessment discussed. Assessment is one of the most important aspects of the work of most lecturers, and therefore a significant portion of this book of 2,000 tips is related to ways of helping to make assessment fair, efficient and valid.

The chapter continues with suggestions on how best to help students to benefit from various forms of assessment by giving them detailed and helpful **feedback** on their work. Communications technologies such as e-mail and computer-conferencing can help to make some feedback processes more efficient, and at the same time more informal.

The next section contains tips on how to **reduce your load**.

The chapter concludes with some specific suggestions on ways of **involving students in their own assessment**, particularly to deepen their learning.

Nothing affects students more than assessment, yet they often claim that they are in the dark as to what goes on in the minds of their assessors and examiners. Involving students in peer- and self-assessment can let them into the assessment culture they must survive. Increasingly peer-assessment is being used to involve students more closely in their learning and its evaluation, and to help to enable students to really understand what is required of them. It is not a 'quick fix' solution to reduce staff marking time, as it is intensive in its use of lecturer time at the briefing and development stages. It can have enormous benefits in terms of learning gain. The suggestions in the last section of this chapter may help you get started with student peer-assessment.

1. What should assessment be?

When snowed under by the amounts of assessment we have to do, it is only too easy to dive into the task without taking the time to think out our moral or ethical stance for the task. This section begins by identifying some values as a starting point on this mission. Several later parts of this section give further detail on how these values can be met.

- **Assessment should be valid.** It should assess what it is that you really want to measure. For example, when attempting to assess problem-solving skills, the assessment should not be dependent on the quality and style of the production of written reports on problem solving, but on the quality of the solutions devised.

- **Assessment should be reliable.** If we can get the task briefings, assessment criteria and marking schemes right, there should be good inter-tutor reliability when more than one lecturer marks the work, as well as good intra-lecturer reliability (lecturers should come up with the same results when marking the same work on different occasions). All assignments should be marked to the same standard.

- **Assessment should be fair.** Students should have equivalence of opportunities to succeed even if their experiences are not identical. This is particularly important when assessing work based in individual learning contracts. It is also important that all assessment instruments and processes should be *seen to be fair* by all students.

- **Assessment should be equitable.** Assessment practices should not discriminate between students, and should disadvantage no individual or group. Obviously, students may prefer and do better at different kinds of assessment (some love exams and do well in them, while others are better at giving presentations, for example), so a balanced diet of different means of assessment within a course will ensure that no particular group is favoured over any other group.

- **Assessment should be formative – even when it is also intended to be summative.** Assessment is a time-consuming process for all concerned, so it seems like a wasted opportunity if it is not used as a means of letting students know how they are doing, and how they can improve. Assessment that is primarily summative in its function (for example, when only a number or grade is given) gives students very little information, other than frequently confirming their own prejudices about themselves.

- **Assessment should be timely.** Assessment that occurs only at the end of a learning programme is not much use in providing feedback, and also leads to the 'sudden death' syndrome, where students have no chance to practise before they pass or fail. Even where there is only end-point formal assessment, earlier opportunities should be provided for rehearsal and feedback.

- **Assessment should be incremental.** Ideally, feedback to students should be continuous. There is sense therefore in enabling small units of assessment to build up into a final mark or grade. This avoids surprises, and can be much less stressful than systems when the whole programme rests on performance during a single time-limited occasion.

- **Assessment should be redeemable.** Most universities insist that all assessment systems contain within them opportunities for the redemption of failure when things go wrong. This not only is just, but also avoids high attrition rates.

- **Assessment should be demanding.** Assessment systems should not be a pushover, and the assurance of quality is impossible when students are not stretched by assessment methods. That is not to say that systems should only permit a fixed proportion of students to achieve each grade: a good assessment system should permit all students considered capable of undertaking a course of study to have a chance of succeeding in the assessment, provided they learn effectively and work hard.

- **Assessment should be efficient.** Brilliant systems of assessment can be designed, but they are often completely unmanageable because of ineffective use of staff time and resources. The burden on staff should not be excessive, nor should be the demands on students undertaking the assessment tasks.

2. Why should we assess?

If we think clearly about our reasons for assessment, it helps to clarify which particular methods are best suited for our purposes, as well as helping to identify who is best placed to carry out the assessment, and when and where to do it. Some of the most common reasons for assessing students are referred to below:

- **To classify or grade students.** There are frequently good reasons for us to classify the level of achievements of students individually and comparatively within a cohort. Assessment methods to achieve this will normally be summative and involve working out numerical marks or letter grades for students' work of one kind or another.

- **To enable student progression.** Students often cannot undertake a course of study unless they have a sound foundation of prior knowledge or skills. Assessment methods to enable student progression therefore need to give a clear idea of students' current levels of achievement, so they – and we – can know if they are ready to progress.

- **To guide improvement.** The feedback students receive helps them to improve. Assessment that is primarily formative need not necessarily count towards any final award and can therefore be ungraded in some instances. The more detailed the feedback we provide, the greater is the likelihood that students will have opportunities for further development.

- **To facilitate students' choice of options.** If students have to select electives within a programme, an understanding of how well (or otherwise) they are doing in foundation studies will enable them to have a firmer understanding of their current abilities in different subject areas. This can provide them with guidance on which options to select next.

■ **To diagnose faults and enable students to rectify mistakes.** Nothing is more demotivating than struggling on, getting bad marks and not knowing what is going wrong. Effective assessment lets students know where their problems lie, and provides them with an essential dimension of the toolbox to put things right.

■ **To give us feedback on how our teaching is going.** If there are generally significant gaps in student knowledge, this often indicates faults in the teaching of the areas concerned. Excellent achievement by a high proportion of students is often due to high-quality facilitation of student learning.

■ **To motivate students.** As students find themselves under increasing pressure, they tend to become more and more strategic in their approaches to learning, only putting their energies into work that counts. Assessment methods can be designed to maximize student motivation, and prompt their efforts towards important achievements.

■ **To provide statistics for the course, or for the institution.** Universities need to provide funding agencies with data about student performance, and assessment systems need to take account of the need for appropriate statistical information.

■ **To enable grading and final degree classification.** Unlike some overseas universities, UK universities still maintain the degree classification system. However, some universities are already debating the introduction of a no-classifications system coupled with the production of student portfolios.

■ **To add variety to students' learning experience, and add direction to our teaching.** Utilizing a range of different assessment methods spurs students to develop different skills and processes. This can provide more effective and enjoyable teaching and learning.

3. When should we assess?

We have all encountered those stressful periods in an academic year when students feel overburdened with assessment, and when we feel overstretched with marking. The following suggestions provide some alternatives to this:

■ **Spread the assessment out throughout the semester or year.** Bunching all assessments towards the end makes it very difficult for any formative feedback to be given to students. Without this, for example, students giving poor conclusions to essays could end up being marked down for the same fault on five or six occasions.

■ **Assess a little rather than a lot.** Save yourself time. Choose carefully what you really want to measure, and design tasks that measure this primarily. Don't measure the same knowledge or skills again and again. You can often get just as good a comparative picture of how a class is doing from short assignments as you can from long comprehensive ones.

■ **Ask students to decide on agreed hand-in dates.** Then adhere to deadlines firmly. For example, say that a given assignment can only be marked if handed in on time. Offer to provide feedback, but no marks, when work is handed in late. In practice, however, make exceptions for documented illness, genuine crises, and so on.

■ **Remember that students have a social life too!** Giving a test on the last day before a vacation is not the most effective time to plan assessment, and is certainly not popular with students. Choose hand-in deadlines at 1600 on Tuesdays! This allows late-running students a weekend to catch up in, and allows students who are weekending away a Monday to travel back on.

■ **Sometimes design assignments on things that students have not yet covered.** This can be a very effective way of alerting students to what they need to learn in due course. It helps students become more receptive when the topics concerned are addressed later in the taught programme.

■ **Try to time your assignments to avoid the 'week 7 nightmare'.** Students often report the phenomenon of everyone giving them coursework at the same time, and this often falls around midway through a semester in modularized systems. In some universities, assessment dates are preplanned and timed to avoid such clashes, and are published at the beginning of each module.

4. Plagiarism, cheating and assessment

We must not forget that things can go wrong when students don't approach their tasks in the ways in which we intend them to do so. For assessment to work fairly, all parties must play the game. Plagiarism is usually interpreted as 'unfair or inappropriate usage of other people's work', while cheating is somewhat more sinister – though the borderlines between the two are impossible to define precisely. The following suggestions may help you to ensure that your students know their responsibilities regarding fair play:

■ **Distinguish between malicious and inadvertent plagiarism.** Punitive action may be quite inappropriate when plagiarism is the consequence of students' lack of understanding of acceptable practice regarding citing the work of others.

■ **Debate issues and solutions with the whole class.** Establish ground rules for fair play, and agreed procedures for dealing with any infringements of these ground rules. It is important that such discussions should take place before the first assessment.

- **Act decisively when you discover copying.** One option is to treat copying as collaborative work, and mark the work as normal but divide the total score by the number of students involved. Their reactions to this often help you find out who did the work first, or who played the biggest part in doing the work.

- **Be alert when encouraging students to work together.** Make sure that they know where the intended collaboration should stop, and that you will be vigilant in checking that later assessed work does not show signs of the collaboration having extended too far.

- **Help students to understand the fine line between collaborative working and practices that the university will regard as cheating**. Sometimes it can come as a shock and horror to students to find that what they thought of as acceptable collaboration is being regarded as cheating.

- **Don't underestimate your students!** Clever students will always find a way to hack into computer-marked assessments. Bear this in mind when considering whether to use such processes for assessment or just for feedback.

- **Anticipate problems, and steer round them.** When collaboration is likely to occur, consider whether you can in fact turn it into a virtue by redesigning the assessments concerned to comprise collaborative tasks for students in groups.

- **Be aware of cultural differences concerning acceptable behaviour regarding tests.** Bring the possibility of such differences to the surface by starting discussions with groups of students. Acknowledge and discuss the extreme pressures to avoid failure to which some students may feel themselves subject.

- **Get students to devise a code of practice.** Students actually *want* fair play, and can be very rigorous if asked to devise systems to guarantee this. Draw links between the systems they devise and the Assessment Regulations extant in your university. Make sure that students understand what the regulations mean!

- **Remember how difficult it can be to prove that unfair practices have occurred.** Study the 'Appeals Procedures' of your university. Remember that when things go wrong, not all the blame will lodge firmly with any students who were guilty; when the blame hits the fan, it can land on you too!

5. Monitoring the quality of your assessment processes

However good we are at assessing students, we do well to monitor our effectiveness, and keep a watching brief on what works well and what does not, so that we too can learn from our triumphs and mistakes, and can address problems. Quality reviewers, both internal and external, also look for evidence of how assessment quality is monitored. The following suggestions may be useful:

- **Keep an overview of the marks you are giving.** In a small sample it won't be possible to get a set of results which plot into a normal distribution curve on a graph. However, if you notice that all of your marks are bunching too tightly at the median point, or that everyone is getting top marks, this may indicate that something is awry. It may help you to use a spreadsheet or other visual means to keep an eye on what's going on.

- **Get students to give you feedback on how well they feel you are assessing them.** You may not always want to hear their answers, but you could ask questions including 'Am I giving you enough feedback?', 'Do you find it helps you to improve?', 'Is the turnaround fast enough for you?', 'Is there any way in which I can improve my assessment?', 'How useful are the questions I am setting?', and so on.

- **Get help from colleagues.** Especially when work is not double-marked, sampled or moderated, it is useful to get colleagues to take a look at some of your grades, particularly when you are inexperienced regarding assessment. Pick scripts including a strong one, a weak one and an average one, and ask an experienced colleague or two to confirm that they agree with your evaluation.

- **Keep notes from year to year.** As you assess sets of work, note any difficulties you experience which may have arisen from the timing of the assessment or how you briefed the students. Note also difficulties of interpretation. Use these notes to help you design better assessments in future years.

- **Remember how valuable data on student performance is in its own right.** Use such data to identify areas where students generally showed strengths and weaknesses. Such data represents important evidence for subject review. Think ahead regarding how future assessments may be adjusted to help students to address areas of weakness next time round.

- **Beware of upward-creeping standards.** The more experienced you become in teaching and assessing a subject, the greater the risk is that you gradually expect or demand higher levels of performance from successive groups of students.

- **Tune in to other universities.** Build up your list of friends and colleagues in other colleges, and exchange with them past exam papers, assignment briefings and marking schemes. This can help you to design new tasks more easily for your own students, and also gives you the chance to seek feedback from such people on your own assessment practices.

- **Stand back and ask 'What did that really measure?'** When reflecting on data from assignment performances or exam results, check that you did in fact succeed in measuring those aspects of student performance that you intended to assess. Also, however, ask 'What *else* did I measure?'. Decide whether to make such additional agendas more explicit next time, if they are valuable (or if not valuable, how to steer assessment tasks away from such agendas).

■ **Use comments from external assessors.** Quality auditors or reviewers, external examiners and others may well provide you with comments on how effective they perceive your assessment methods to be. Use such feedback to help you to improve continuously, rather than seeing it as a personal attack. Make sure that you continue to include those elements that they praise or commend, and develop such elements further when appropriate.

■ **Become an external assessor yourself.** Once you have developed expertise in your own university, an excellent way to learn from the experiences of other institutions is to become involved in external examining or quality reviewing yourself. What you learn about the excellence (or otherwise) of others' means of assessment can then be transferred to your own context.

6. Designing questions for traditional exams

Setting exams always seems to be required at the last moment! Yet this is one of the most important tasks lecturers ever do. The words you choose when setting questions will have far-reaching effects on the lives and careers of your students. The following suggestions may help you to choose your words carefully, and check your questions thoroughly before they appear on exam papers:

■ **Don't do it on your own!** Make sure you get feedback on each of your questions from colleagues. They can often spot whether your question is at the right level more easily than you can. Having someone else look at one's draft exam questions is extremely useful. It is better still when all questions are discussed and moderated by teams of staff. Where possible, set questions with your colleagues. This allows the team to pick the best questions from a range of possibilities, rather than use every idea each member has.

■ **Ask colleagues: 'What would you say this question really means?'** If they tell you anything you hadn't thought of, you may need to adjust your wording a little. Ask one or two colleagues to paraphrase or summarize your exam questions. Perhaps choose one colleague who knows the subject well, and one from a different area. Look at how their wording is different to yours, and decide which versions or combinations may be the most appropriate to use.

■ **Keep your sentences short.** You're less likely to write something that can be interpreted in more than one way if you write plain English in short sentences. This also helps reduce any discrimination against students whose first language is not English.

■ **Work out what you're really testing.** Is it decision making, strategic planning, problem solving, data processing (and so on), or is it just too much dependent on memory? Most exam questions measure a number of things at the same time. Be up-front about all the things each question is likely to measure.

■ **Set questions that seek to discover what has been learned, rather than what has been taught.** Avoid testing basic information recall, and try to set questions that require students to make use of their knowledge, and to reinterpret it intelligently.

■ **Keep the language simple.** Students have enough to cope with in the terror and stress of exam conditions, without having to cope with linguistic and syntactical complexity!

■ **Make the rubric unambiguous.** More students fail exams because they do not follow the instructions appropriately on number of questions and length of answers, than through lack of knowledge. Try your paper out on a 'naive reader' (rather than on a colleague who knows the form), and see if it is easy to understand exactly what the rubric is instructing candidates to do.

■ **Avoid trick questions.** Such questions tend to demonstrate the cleverness of the examiner rather than the true worth of the students. Exams should always aim to test ability fairly, rather than to play games with students.

■ **Don't measure the same things again and again.** For example, it is all too easy in essay-type exam questions to measure repeatedly students' skills at writing good introductions, firm conclusions and well-structured arguments. Valuable as such skills are, we need to be measuring other important things too.

■ **Liaise with your external examiner.** You are likely to get really useful feedback and advice on marking protocols, model answers and marking schemes, as well as on issues of level and content.

■ **Include data or information in questions to reduce the emphasis on memory.** In some subjects, case-study information is a good way of doing this.

■ **Make the question layout easy to follow.** A question with bullet points or separate parts can be much easier for (tense) candidates to interpret correctly than one that is just several lines of continuous prose.

■ **Don't overdo the standards.** When you're close to a subject, it's easily possible that your questions get gradually harder year by year.

■ **Write out an answer to your own question.** This will be handy when you come to mark answers, but also you'll sometimes find that it takes *you* an hour to answer a question for which candidates have only half an-hour.

■ **Use the question to show how marks are to be allocated.** For example, put numbers in brackets to show how many marks are attached to various parts of the question (or alternatively, give suggested timings such as 'Spend about 10 minutes on Part 2').

■ **Try your questions out.** Use coursework and student assignments to give components of your future exam questions pilot runs, and use or adapt the ones that work best for exams.

- **When setting questions, think about what students would need to do to answer them effectively.** Prepare your marking brief at the same time. Even open-ended questions should be written with a clear view of what would constitute evidence of successful achievement.

- **Consider making the mark scheme explicit.** When students can see details of the marking scheme on the question paper, they can spend more time on the parts of the exam that carry most marks, and avoid wasting a lot of time on less important areas.

- **Don't expect students to write too much.** While word limits can provide useful guidance in continuous assessment, in exams unrealistic word-length guidance can cause extra and unnecessary stress.

- **Take into account that many students don't write well or quickly by hand any more.** Many students nowadays work mostly on word processors, and find the process of writing by hand slow and unwieldy, with no opportunities for online editing. This may be the main cause of work that looks scrappy or full of amendments on scripts.

- **Be creative.** Think about the possibility of allowing students to write one question of their own in an exam, and even a marking scheme for it, then answer it. It is obviously harder to mark the range of totally different products such a process gives, but it allows students to demonstrate their strengths.

7. Setting open-book exam questions

Many of the suggestions above regarding setting traditional exam questions continue to apply. In addition:

- **Tell students what you expect them to do.** Many may not understand the difference between this kind of exam, the first time that they encounter one, and traditional ones. This may result in students just trying to write out material, rather than do things with it as a resource.

- **Decide whether to prescribe the books students may employ.** This is one way round the problem of availability of books. It may even be possible to arrange supplies of the required books to be available in the exam room.

- **Provide photocopies of extracts from relevant set texts.** However, seek advice to ensure that you don't violate photocopying copyright regulations.

- **Set questions that require students to do things with the information available to them,** rather than merely summarizing it and giving it back.

■ **Make the actual questions particularly clear and straightforward to understand.** The fact that students will be reading a lot during the exam means that care has to be taken that they don't read the actual instructions too rapidly.

■ **Focus the assessment criteria on what students have done with the information**, and not just on them having located 'the correct information'.

■ **Expect shorter answers.** Students doing open-book exams will be spending quite a lot of their time searching for, and making sense of, information and data. They will therefore write less per hour than students who are answering traditional exam questions 'out of their heads'.

8. Designing exam marking schemes

Making a good marking scheme can save you hours when it comes to marking a pile of answers. It can also help you to know that you are doing everything possible to be uniformly fair to all students. In addition, as your marking schemes will normally be shown to people including external examiners and quality reviewers, it's important to make schemes that will stand up to such scrutiny. The following suggestions should help:

■ **Write a model answer for each question.** This can be a useful first step towards identifying the mark-bearing ingredients of a good answer. It also helps you see when what you thought was going to be a 30-minute question turns out to take an hour! If you have difficulties answering the questions, the chances are that your students will too! Making model answers and marking schemes for coursework assignments can give you good practice for writing exam schemes.

■ **Make each decision as straightforward as possible.** Try to allocate each mark so that it is associated with something that is either there or absent, or right or wrong, in students' answers.

■ **Aim to make the scheme usable by a non-expert in the subject.** This can help your marking schemes be useful resources for students themselves, perhaps in next year's course.

■ **Aim to make it so that anyone can mark answers, and agree on the scores within a mark or two.** It is best to involve colleagues in your piloting of first-draft marking schemes. They will soon help you to identify areas where the marking criteria may need clarifying or tightening up.

■ **Allow for 'consequential' marks.** For example, when a candidate makes an early mistake, but then proceeds correctly thereafter (especially in problems and calculations), allow for marks to be given for the correct steps even when the final answer is quite wrong.

■ **Pilot a marking scheme by showing it to others.** It's worth even showing marking schemes to people who are not closely associated with your subject area. If they can't see exactly what you're looking for, it may be that the scheme is not yet sufficiently self-explanatory. Extra detail you then add at this stage may help you to clarify your own thinking, and will certainly assist fellow markers.

■ **Make yourself think about honourable exceptions.** Ask yourself whether your marking scheme is sufficiently flexible to accommodate a brilliant student who hasn't strictly conformed to your original idea of what should be achieved. There are sometimes candidates who write exceptionally good answers which are off-beam and idiosyncratic, and they deserve credit for these.

■ **Consider having more than 20 marks for a 20-mark question.** Especially in essay-type answers, you can't expect students to include all the things you may think of yourself. It may be worth having up to 30 or more 'available' marks, so that students approaching the question in different ways still have the opportunity to score well.

■ **Look at what others have done in the past.** If it's your first time writing a marking scheme, looking at other people's ways of doing them will help you to focus your efforts. Choose to look at marking schemes from other subjects that your students may be studying, to help you tune in to the assessment culture of the overall course.

■ **Learn from your own mistakes.** No marking scheme is perfect; when you start applying it to a pile of scripts, you will soon start adjusting it. Keep a note of any difficulties you experience in marking according to your scheme, and take account of these next time you have to make one.

9. Marking examination scripts

The following suggestions may help you approach the task of marking exam scripts efficiently, while still being fair and helpful to students:

■ **Be realistic about what you can do.** Marking scripts can be boring, exhausting and stressful. As far as constraints allow, don't attempt to mark large numbers of scripts in short periods of time. Put scripts for marking into manageable bundles. It is less awesome to have 10 scripts on your desk and the rest out of sight than to have the whole pile threatening you as you work.

■ **Avoid halo effects.** If you've just marked a brilliant answer on a script, it can be easy to go into the same student's next answer seeing only the good points and passing over the weaknesses. Try to ensure that you mark each answer dispassionately.

■ **Watch out for prejudices.** There will be all sorts of things you like and dislike about the style and layout of scripts, not to mention handwriting quality. Make sure that each time there is a 'benefit of the doubt' decision to be made, it is not influenced by such factors.

■ **Recognize that your mood will change.** Every now and then, check back to scripts you marked earlier, and see whether your generosity has increased or decreased. Be aware of the middle-mark bunching syndrome. As you get tired, it feels safe and easy to give a middle-range mark. Try as far as possible to look at each script afresh.

■ **Remind yourself of the importance of what you're doing.** You may be marking a whole pile of scripts, but each individual script may be a crucial landmark in the life of the student concerned. Your verdict may affect students for the rest of their careers.

■ **Take account of the needs of second markers.** Many universities use a blind double marking system, in which case you should not make any written comments or numbers on the scripts themselves, to avoid prejudicing the judgement of a second marker. You may find it useful to use post-its or assessment pro-formas for each script, so you are able to justify the marks you give at any later stage. Such *aides-mémoire* can save you having to read all the scripts again, rethinking how you arrived at your numbers or grades.

■ **Write feedback for students.** In most exams, the system may not allow you to write on the scripts the sort of feedback you would have given if the questions had been set as assessed coursework. However, students still need feedback, and making notes of the things you would have explained about common mistakes can help you prepare some discussion notes to issue to students after the exam, or can remind you of things to mention next time you teach the same subjects.

■ **Devise your own system.** You may prefer to mark a whole script or just Question 1 of every script first. Do what you feel comfortable with, and see what works best for you.

■ **Provide feedback for yourself and for the course team.** As you work through the scripts, note how many students answered each question, and how well they performed. You may begin to re-alize that some questions turned out to have been very well written, while others could have been framed better. You will find out which questions proved to be the hardest for students to answer well, even when all questions were intended to be of an equal standard. Such feedback and re-flection should prove very useful when designing questions for next time round.

■ **Set aside time for a review.** Having marked all the scripts, you may wish to capture your thoughts, such as suggestions about changes for part of the course or module, or the processes used to teach it.

10. Using exam questions as class exercises

Answering exam questions well is still the principal skill that students need to develop to succeed in their education. In our attempts to increase the learning payoff of taught sessions, we can help students to develop their exam skills by making use of exam questions. The following suggestions may help you to build related activities into lectures and tutorials:

■ **Let a class have a try at an exam question under exam conditions.** Then ask students to exchange their answers, and lead them through marking their work using a typical marking scheme. This helps students to learn quickly how examiners' minds work.

■ **Issue two or three old exam questions for students to try in preparation for a tutorial.** Then lead them through assessing their work using a marking scheme during the tutorial. Ask them to prepare lists of questions on matters arising from the exercise, both on subject content and requirements for exams, and use their questions to focus tutorial discussion.

■ **Display an exam question on-screen in a large-group lecture.** Ask students in groups to brainstorm the principal steps they would take in the way they would approach answering the question. Then give out a model answer to the question as a handout, and talk the class through the points in the model answer where marks were earned.

■ **In a lecture or a tutorial, get students in groups to think up exam questions themselves.** You can base this on work they have already covered, or on work currently in progress. Ask the groups to transcribe their questions onto overhead transparencies. Display each of these in turn, giving feedback on how appropriate or otherwise each question is in terms of standard, wording, length and structure. (You will get many questions this way that you can later use or adapt!).

■ **Use exam questions to help students to create an agenda.** In a lecture or tutorial, give out two or three related exam questions as a handout. Ask students in groups to make lists of short questions to which they don't yet know the answers. Then allow the groups to use you as a resource, quizzing you with these questions. You don't have to answer them all at once – for some your reply will be along the lines 'We'll come to this in a week or two', and for others 'You won't actually be required to know this.'

■ **Get students to make marking schemes.** Give them a typical exam question, and ask groups of students to prepare a breakdown of how they think the marks should be allocated. Ask them to transcribe the marking schemes to overhead transparencies. Discuss each of these in turn with the whole group, and give guidance on how closely the marking schemes resemble those used in practice.

■ **Get students to surf the Net.** Ask them to access the Internet to see if they can find appropriate exam questions on the subjects they are studying. Suggest that they work in twos or threes, and bring the questions they find to the next class session. You can encourage them to download the questions they find, and make an electronic question bank.

■ **Ask students in groups to think up a 'dream' question.** Ask the groups to make bullet-point lists of the 10 most important things that they would include in answers to these questions. These questions will give you useful information about their favourite topics.

■ **Ask students in groups to think up 'nightmare' questions.** With these, you can open up a discussion of the causes of their anxieties and traumas, and can probably do a lot to allay their fears, and point them in the right direction regarding how they might tackle such questions.

■ **Ask students to think of way-out, alternative questions.** Suggest that they think of questions which are not just testing of their knowledge and skills, but which get them to think laterally and creatively. This encourages deeper reflection about the material they are learning, and will probably give you some interesting ideas to use in future exams.

11. Conducting vivas

Vivas are used for a variety of purposes, and with varying degrees of importance. The following suggestions may help you prepare yourself for conducting vivas, as well as helping your students have a better experience of them:

■ **Remind yourself what the viva is for.** Purposes vary, but it is important to be clear about it at the outset. For example, the agenda could include one or more of the following: confirming that the candidates did indeed do the work represented in their dissertations, or probing whether a poor examination result was an uncharacteristic slip, or proving whether students' understanding of the subject reached acceptable levels.

■ **Prepare your students for vivas.** Explain to them what a viva is, and what they will normally be expected to do. It helps to give them opportunities to practise. Much of this they can do on their own, but they will need you to start them off on the right lines, and to check now and then that their practice sessions are realistic.

■ **Think about the room layout.** Sitting the candidate on a hard seat while you and your fellow-assessors sit face-on behind a large table is guaranteed to make the candidate tremble! If possible, sit beside or close to the candidate. Where appropriate, provide students with a table on which to put any papers they may have with them.

■ **Think about the waiting room.** If candidates are queuing together for long, they can make each other even more nervous. If you're asking the same questions of a series of students (in some situations you may be *required* to do this for fairness), the word can get around about what you're asking.

■ **Prepare yourself for vivas!** Normally, if you're a principal player at a viva, you will have read the student's work in some detail. It helps if you come to the viva armed with a list of questions you may ask. You don't have to ask all of them, but it helps to have some ready! Normally, you may need to have a pre-viva discussion with other members of the examining panel, and you need to be seen to have done your homework.

■ **Prepare the agenda in advance, and with colleagues.** It is dangerously easy (and unfair to students) for the agenda to develop during a series of interviews with different students. Prepare and use a checklist or pro-forma to keep records. Memory is not sufficient, and can be unreliable, especially when different examiners conducting a viva have different agendas.

- **Do your best to put the candidate at ease.** Students find vivas very stressful, and it improves their confidence and fluency if they are greeted cheerily and made welcome at the start of a viva.

- **When vivas are a formality, indicate this.** When students have done well on the written side of their work, and it's fairly certain that they should pass, it helps to give a strong hint about this straightaway. It puts students at ease, and makes for a more interesting and relaxed viva.

- **Ensure there are no surprises.** Share the agenda with each candidate, and clarify the processes to be used. You are likely to get more out of candidates this way.

- **Ask open questions which enable students to give full and articulate answers**. Try to avoid questions which lead to minimal or 'yes/no' replies.

- **Let students do most of the talking.** The role of an examiner in a viva is to provoke thought and prompt candidates into speaking fluently about the work or topics under discussion, and to spark off an intellectual dialogue. It is not to harangue, carp or demonstrate the examiner's intelligence, or to trick candidates!

- **Prepare to be able to debrief well.** Write your own notes during each viva. If you are dealing with a series of such events, it can become difficult to remember each feedback point that you want to give to each student. Vivas can be very useful learning experiences, but much of the experience can be lost if time is not set aside for a debrief. Such debriefing is particularly useful when students will encounter vivas again.

- **When debriefing, ask students for their opinions first.** This can spare them the embarrassment of having you telling them about failings they already know they have. You may also find useful food for thought when students tell you about aspects of the vivas that you were unaware of yourself.

- **Be sensitive.** Vivas can be traumatic for students, and they may have put much time and effort into preparing for them. Choose words carefully, particularly when giving feedback on aspects that were unsuccessful.

- **Be specific.** Students will naturally want to have feedback on details of things they did particularly well. As far as you can, make sure you can find something positive to say even when overall performance was not good.

- **Consider recording practice vivas on video.** This is particularly worthwhile when one of your main aims is to prepare students for more important vivas to follow. Simply allowing students to borrow the recordings and look at them in the comfort of privacy can provide students with useful deep reflection on their performance. It is sometimes more comfortable to view the recordings in the atmosphere of a supportive student group.

- **Run a role-play afterwards.** Ask students to play both examiners and candidates, and bring to life some of the issues they encountered in their vivas. This can allow other students observing the role-play to think about aspects they did not experience themselves.

- **Plan for the next step.** Get students to discuss strategies for preparing for their next viva, and ask groups of students to make lists of 'do's and don'ts' to bear in mind next time.

- **Get students to produce a guidance booklet about preparing for vivas and taking part in them.** This may be useful for future students, but is equally valuable to the students making it as a way of getting them to consolidate their reflections on their own experience.

12. Designing multiple-choice exams

When multiple-choice questions are used for exams rather than just for self-assessment, feedback or diagnostic testing, much more care needs to be taken regarding the design and validation of the questions. The following suggestions may help you to devise effective multiple-choice exams:

- **Check the performance of each question with large numbers of students before including it in an exam.** The most suitable questions are those that discriminate between the able and less able candidates. There are statistical packages that can help you work out the 'facility-value' of questions (how easy or difficult they are) and the 'discrimination index' of questions (how well they separate the best candidates from the rest). Ideally, all questions should have been through trialling with hundreds of students before using the most suitable questions in a formal exam.

- **Make the most of the opportunity to give students quick feedback.** An advantage of multiple-choice exams is that it is perfectly possible to arrange that students get not only their scores very quickly, but also detailed feedback reminding them of their correct decisions, and explaining why other decisions were incorrect.

- **Make sure that candidates aren't going to be getting questions right for the wrong reasons.** Look for any give-aways in the keys or context of the questions. During trialling, if too many students get a question right, it could be that the question is too easy to serve a useful purpose in testing, or it is sometimes the case that something is giving away the correct option to choose.

- **Watch out for cases where the best candidates choose a distractor.** This usually happens when they can see something wrong with the option that is supposed to be undeniably correct, or 'best'. This can be done manually, by scanning the responses from a large group of students, and with prior knowledge of who the most able students are. Computer software can normally help by identifying all students who have got a particular question wrong, and can be programmed to search for candidates with a high overall score who get these particular questions wrong.

- **Start the exam with some relatively straightforward questions.** This helps anxious candidates to get into their stride, and is better than having such candidates thrown into a panic by an early tricky question.

■ **Help candidates to develop their skills at tackling multiple choice exams.** Give candidates past papers to practise on, and provide advice on the most effective techniques for tackling this form of exam.

■ **Get the timing right.** Decide whether you really want an against-the-clock exam. Find out how long candidates take on average. With a timed exam, there is some tendency for candidates to rush their decision making, and even if they have plenty of time left over, they are still left with a hangover legacy of questions where they made wrong decisions.

■ **Make sure that distractors are plausible.** If no one is selecting a given distractor, it is serving no useful purpose. Distractors need to represent anticipated errors in students' knowledge or understanding.

■ **Try to avoid overlap between questions.** If one question helps students successfully to answer further questions, the possibility increases of students picking the right options for the wrong reasons.

■ **Remember that students can still guess.** The marking scheme needs to take into account the fact that students will score some marks by pure luck! Computer-based assessment software can help to ensure that different marks are awarded for different distractors, to ensure at least that not every guess is equally weighted! Otherwise, if most of the questions are, for example, four-option ones, the average mark that would be scored by a monkey would be 25 per cent, so the real range lies between this and 100 per cent. It is important that people are indeed allowed to get 100 per cent in such structured exams, and that this does not cause any problems when the marks are blended with more traditional exam formats where written answers in some subjects still attract marks only in the 70s even when they're reckoned to be first-class answers.

■ **Ensure that students are well practised at handling multiple-choice questions.** Answering such questions well is a skill in its own right, just as is writing open answers well. We need to ensure that students are sufficiently practised, so that multiple-choice exams measure their understanding and not just their technique.

■ **Look at a range of published multiple-choice questions.** For example, several Open University courses have multiple-choice assignment questions, as well as multiple-choice exams. You may be surprised how sophisticated such questions can be, and may gain many ideas that you can build into your own question-design.

■ **Gradually build up a large bank of questions.** This is best done by collaborating with colleagues, and pooling questions that are found to be working well. It then becomes possible to compose a multiple-choice exam by selecting from the bank of questions. If the bank becomes large enough, it can even be good practice to publish the whole collection, and allow students to practise with it.

■ **When you've got a large bank of questions, there is the possibility of on-demand exams.** Students can then take a multiple-choice test with a random selection of questions from the bank, at any time during their studies, and 'pass' the component involved as soon as they are able to demonstrate their competence with the questions.

■ **Look for ways of making marking quick and easy.** When large numbers of candidates are involved, it is worth looking at optical mark-reading techniques or computer-aided testing formats.

■ **Get some colleagues to take your exam.** They may be surprised at things they find that they did not know, and they may give you some surprises too about what you *thought* were cut-and-dried questions.

13. Helping students to cope with exam failure

Of course, we'd all prefer that such help was not needed. However, in most exam systems, casualties seem inevitable. The fact that some students did not pass does not mean that they could not pass. The following suggestions may help you to guide students who failed towards future successes:

■ **Help students to come to a position where they can see failure as an opportunity for learning.** This is better than the natural instinct, which leads people to regard failure as a major disaster. Failing an exam can be a strong demotivator, but can also be an opportunity to seek feedback, providing a stimulus for deeper learning.

■ **Take account of the feelings of students.** Students who fail exams often take it as a blow to their self-esteem. Be prepared for a whole range of resultant emotions, including anger, inertia, disbelief, and inconsolable grief. For students who have done well at school, failing exams at university may be their first experiences of failure, and may give them a profound shock. For those who struggled to get to university, exam failure may confirm their underlying thoughts that they were never quite up to it in the first place.

■ **Concentrate on what students can do in future to improve, rather than railing over their failings.** Let students see a range of examples of satisfactory and good work (rather than just model answers, which imply the need for perfection).

■ **Let students have further opportunities for practising under simulated exam conditions.** Ideally, this can give students the chance to experience success before they next experience real exams.

■ **Let students play examiner.** Give students the chance to apply assessment schemes to examples of good, bad and indifferent exam scripts (and if possible to their own scripts which failed). Such a process rapidly increases students' awareness of the rules of the exam game.

■ **Help students to identify what went well.** Even in a failed exam, most students display strengths in some parts of some questions. Help them not to dismiss these strengths in the context of their overall failure, and encourage them to extend the areas of success on future occasions.

■ **Help students develop revision and exam techniques.** There are plenty of books, learning packages and computer packages available to help students to build up confidence.

■ **Encourage students in pairs to set each other questions and mark them.** Informally talking through their answers to each other can motivate them, and help them improve their self-confidence.

14. External examiners: before they start

■ **Help external examiners to get to know your team.** A 'photo gallery' with brief details of areas of responsibility for each member of your team can help external examiners to tune in to your course even before their first visit. The same information may well be useful for the course handbook.

■ **Make sure they are informed of key dates such as those of exam boards well in advance.** Let them know when they may expect work to moderate, questions to review, and the dates by which you will need to have things back from them. External examiners tend to be busy people, so make sure that they have leeway to negotiate alternative dates with you. Send them not only the general regulations regarding assessment, but also any particular information showing how assessment works in your course.

■ **Help them to see the background and context of your course.** Tell them about the history of the course, and changes that have already been made to its structure and the way that it is assessed. Show them how the course relates to other programmes that may feed into it, and to follow-on programmes. Give them details of future ambitions regarding the development of the course.

■ **Involve your external examiners in developments.** Send them minutes of Course Board meetings, particularly when assessment issues are featured. Don't present them with a *fait accompli* when changes are made; they may well have views which could usefully be addressed.

■ **Be truthful!** External examiners are experienced people, and trying to pull the wool over their eyes is not the best way to cement good working relationships with them!

■ **Invite external examiners to a training day.** Pay them appropriately for their time and participation. Some universities run half-day or full-day training programmes for external examiners to brief them collectively, and to give them the chance to see round the campus and facilities. Such programmes can be combined with visits to your course team and department.

15. External examiners: when they arrive

■ **Arrange for examiners to be met.** If train travel is involved, it can be much appreciated if you meet them at the station and take them the rest of the way. If not, make sure that as soon as they arrive at the university there is someone to meet them. They may have been travelling for some time, and a friendly face to meet them, and a tea or coffee, makes a lot of difference.

■ **Plan the day carefully.** Try to build in some spare time. Things may not always go according to your plans. Examiners can be delayed by late trains or traffic problems, and it's worth making sure that any preliminary meetings can still take place. Involve examiners in the planning of the day. They may have things they want to discuss, especially after seeing a selection of student work.

■ **Think carefully about breaks and refreshments.** We all function better with a few regular breaks, and the availability of light refreshments during the day is usually welcomed, especially on arrival if a long distance has been travelled.

■ **Arrange for examiners to meet some students.** It is useful to draw up a brief agenda for such meetings, so both examiners and students have a shared idea of the purposes of such meetings. You may need to put students' minds at rest, as they often become anxious, especially if it is the first time they have met an examiner.

■ **Arrange for examiners to meet members of the course team.** Consult with examiners and find out whether any areas of the work they have seen already are areas for praise or concern, and whether they want to discuss particular aspects of the course with the people involved in teaching it.

■ **Try to avoid surprises.** Examiners don't like being put on the spot during meetings, for example if they are asked for their views on proposed developments to the course, or on how problems should be addressed. It is helpful to them if such issues are shared with them before their visit.

■ **Regard the day as an opportunity for expert consultancy.** External examiners are chosen for their breadth of experience and expertise. Don't let the situation intimidate you. Listen to their advice. Solicit their suggestions and respond creatively rather than negatively to any criticisms they offer. After all, the whole aim of the external examiner system is to maintain and improve quality.

16. Becoming an external examiner yourself

- **Regard it as a compliment.** It is flattering to be approached to undertake external examining. It is a recognition of your standing in your field, and of the experience you bring to your work. However, it is not all glory (and not usually well paid!).

- **Think about your commitment.** Have you enough time? What will your duties involve in practice? How many days will you need to be away from your own job? Can you afford the time? Talk to other external examiners. Compare approaches to the role. Build up a picture of which actions are reasonable and appropriate.

- **Put dates in your diary as soon as you get them!** At the beginning of a new academic year, enter all of the dates you will be required to attend meetings into your diary, If you don't yet know what these dates are likely to be, it's worth asking for them, or choosing some dates yourself which you will keep available for meetings.

- **Check the university regulations.** Many institutions are in the process of changing their regulations, so don't assume that regulations will be the same as in your own university or even that they will be the same as they were last year if you are continuing as an examiner. If you have not been sent a copy of the regulations, ask for one.

- **Take the job seriously.** Both sides benefit when external examiners approach their work with appropriate professionalism. If you've been sent scripts to look at for comments on standards, return them promptly with your conclusions. Set aside time at an appropriate point to write your report.

- **Keep in touch with the course.** Developing your relationship with the course team can give you a good feel for the course. Ask to be sent, for information, minutes of course team meetings. Find out whom is your most appropriate point of contact, for example whether it should be the course leader you communicate with, or the head of the department responsible for the course.

- **Find good things to say about the course.** Work out which features of the course should be commended and encouraged. Avoid the feeling that your main job is to spot things that are wrong.

- **Back up any critical comments with practical, positive suggestions.** When a course team faces problems, external examiners can be a really valuable source of advice, so make sure that you're sufficiently tuned in to the course to be able to offer suggestions when asked, or when help is needed.

- **Your report is serious stuff!** External examiners' reports are a very public side of assessment. The words you may write when composing such reports may be analysed and probed into very deeply by course teams – and quality assessors! The following suggestions may help you make best use of the responsibility you bear when writing such reports, especially if you are taking on external examining for the first time.

■ **Get hold of your predecessor's reports.** External examiners normally serve for between three and five years, so it should be possible to see how your predecessor handled the role. It is particularly valuable to look for recommendations made in previous reports. You can check whether they are now being implemented by the course team, and you can include appropriate acknowledgement of this in your own report.

■ **Look for the main headings to address.** They may or may or may not have appeared as headings as such in previous reports, but (for example) the first paragraph often addresses whether the standard of the course is comparable with similar courses in other institutions.

■ **Comment on trends.** It is best not to go into too much specific detail in your reports: you can always save elaborations for your verbal contributions to the exam board.

■ **Keep your report simple.** External examiners' reports are often scrutinized by people who know little about the specific subject (for example, a 'Quality and Standards Committee'), and such people need to be able to identify the main messages in your report.

■ **Keep your report short.** If it's too long, your main points may get lost amid other details. Don't feel that you have to prove you've done a good job of being an external examiner by writing a very detailed report. The most valuable reports are ones that are concise and strong, and that make any recommendations very clearly.

■ **Make gentle recommendations.** It is far more acceptable to say 'It may be worthwhile for the course team to consider …' rather than 'It is essential that the following changes be implemented at once'.

■ **Consider getting informal feedback on your draft report.** For example, it is useful to send a copy of your draft to the course leader, and invite comments about anything you've missed, and suggestions for rewording. Sometimes course leaders can help you to include in your report appropriately phrased comments which will in due course help the course team to make improvements to the operation of the course.

■ **Build continuity into your reports.** When you are following up previous reports you have written for the course, look carefully for evidence showing that your earlier recommendations have been acknowledged and followed through.

17. Assessing essays

- **Don't assess essays too often.** Any assessment form advantages those students who happen to be skilled at delivering what is being measured. This applies to essays too, and there is a significant danger that those students who happen to become good at planning and writing essays continue to be advantaged time and time again.

- **Help students to see exactly how essays are marked.** Alert students to the credit they gain from good structure and style. One of the best ways of doing this is to involve classes of students in looking at examples of past (good, bad and indifferent) essays, and applying assessment criteria. This can be followed by involving students in peer-assessment of each other's essays.

- **Subdivide essay questions into several parts, each with marks publicly allocated.** This helps to prevent students from straying so far off the point that they lose too many of the marks that they could have scored.

- **Give word limits.** Even in exams, it can be useful to suggest to students that an essay answer should lie between (for example) 1,500 and 2,000 words. This helps to avoid the quantity-versus-quality issue, which leads some students into simply trying to write a lot, rather than thinking deeply about what they are writing – and it also helps reduce the time it takes to mark the essays.

- **Have a clear, well-structured marking scheme for each essay question.** This can save a lot of time when marking, and can help guarantee that students' answers are assessed fairly and consistently.

- **Don't assume that longer equals better.** It is often harder for students to write succinctly than to just ramble on. However, students need to be briefed on how best we want them to develop their art in writing briefly.

- **Help students develop the skills required to assemble the 'content' for essays.** One of the best ways of doing this is to set class or coursework tasks that require students to prepare essay plans rather than fully finished masterpieces. A concept map or diagram can show a great deal about the eventual 'worth' of students' essays, and can avoid distraction from the elements of style and structure. Students can put together maybe half-a-dozen essay plans in the time it would take them to complete one essay, and do far more thinking and learning.

- **Consider involving students in peer-assessing some essays or essay plans.** This helps them to put their own efforts into perspective, and to learn things to emulate (and things to avoid!) by seeing how other students go about devising essays.

- **Help students to improve their technique through feedback.** Consider the range of approaches you can use to give students useful feedback on their essays, including statement banks, assignment return sheets and e-mail messages, and try to minimize the time you spend writing similar feedback comments onto different students' essays.

■ **Use some class time to get students to brainstorm titles for essays.** This helps them to think about the standard they could anticipate for essay questions in forthcoming exams, and gives them topic areas to base their practice on.

18. Assessing reports

Reports are among the most frequent of the various assignments given to students as continuous assessment work. In many subjects, some of the most important learning occurs in laboratories, and in associated work done before and after practical sessions. It is important to try to assess this learning carefully. The following suggestions may help your students get the most out of such work:

■ **Give clear guidance regarding the format of reports.** For example, issue a sheet listing principal generic section headings, with a short description of the purpose and nature of each main section in a typical report.

■ **Get students to assess subjectively some past reports.** Issue students with copies of some good, bad and indifferent reports, and ask them to mark them independently, simply giving each example an impression mark. Then facilitate a discussion where students explain why they allocated the marks in the ways they did.

■ **Get students to assess objectively some past reports.** Issue groups of students with good, bad and indifferent reports, along with a sheet listing assessment criteria and a mark scheme. Ask each group to assess the reports. Then initiate discussions and comparisons between groups.

■ **Make explicit the assessment criteria for reports.** Help students to see the balance between the marks associated with the structure of their reports, and those given to the content and the level of critical thinking and analysis.

■ **Ask students for full reports less often.** For example, if during a course students tackle eight pieces of work involving report writing, ask students to write full reports for only two of these, and ask for summary or 'short-form' or 'memorandum' reports for the remaining assignments. These shorter reports can be structured in note form or bullet points, and can still show much of the evidence of the thinking and analysis that students have done.

■ **Accommodate collaboration.** One way round the problems of collaboration is to develop approaches where students are required to prepare reports in groups – often closer to real life than preparing them individually.

■ **Involve students in assessing each other's reports.** When marks for reports 'count' significantly, it may be desirable to moderate student peer-assessment in one way or another, but probably the greatest benefit to derive is that students get a good deal more feedback about their work than hard-pressed staff are able to provide. It is far quicker to moderate student peer-assessment than to mark all the reports from scratch.

■ **Consider asking students to write (or word-process) reports onto pre-prepared pro-formas.** This can help where there are significant 'given' elements such as equipment and methodology. You can then concentrate on assessing the important parts of their writing, for example interpretation of data.

■ **Publish clear deadlines for the submission of successive reports.** In the case of practical work, allow only one or two weeks after the laboratory session. It is kinder to students to get them to write up their reports early, rather than to allow them to accumulate a backlog of report writing, which can interfere (for example) with their revision for exams.

■ **Prepare a standard assessment/feedback grid, to return to students with marked reports.** Include criteria and marks associated with (for example) the quality of data, observations, calculations, conclusions, references and verdicts.

■ **Allocate practical work in advance of the sessions, and include some assessed pre-laboratory preparation.** For example, pose half-a-dozen short-answer questions for students to complete before starting a piece of laboratory work. This helps students know what they are doing, rather than follow instructions blindly. It also avoids wasting time at the start of a laboratory session working out only then which students are to undertake each experiment.

■ **Include some questions linked closely to practical or fieldwork in examinations.** For example, tell students that two exam questions will be based on work they will have done outside the lecture room. This helps to ensure that practical work isn't forgotten when students start revising for exams.

■ **Get students to design exam questions based on practical work.** Set groups of students this task. Allocate some marks for the creativity of their questions. When done over several years, the products could be turned into a bank of questions, which could be placed on computer for students to consult as they prepared for exams.

■ **Consider the use of computers in the laboratories and other practical work situations.** Where facilities are available, arrange that students can input their experimental data directly onto a computer or network. Many universities now enable students to write up their reports straight into a word processor alongside the laboratory bench, using a report template on disk. Such reports can be handed in immediately at the end of the laboratory session, and marked and returned promptly.

19. Assessing practical skills

Reports may only be indirect evidence of the development of practical skills The skills themselves are important in many subject areas. This importance is often reflected by the time students spend in laboratories, workshops, and other situations where they practice and develop such skills. Some questions and suggestions are listed below:

- **What exactly are the practical skills we wish to assess?** These may include a vast range of important skills, from deftness in assembling complex glassware in a chemistry laboratory to precision and speed in using a scalpel on the operating table. It is important that students know the relative importance of each skill.

- **Why do we need to measure practical skills?** The credibility of our courses often depends on what students can do when they enter employment. It is often said by employers that students are very knowledgeable, but not necessarily competent in practical tasks.

- **Where is the best place to try to measure these skills?** Sometimes practical skills can be measured in places such as laboratories or workshops. For other skills, students may need to be working in real-life situations.

- **When is the best time to measure practical skills?** When practical skills are vitally important, it is probably best to start measuring them very early on in a course, so that any students showing alarming problems with them can be appropriately advised or redirected.

- **Who is in the best position to measure practical skills?** For many practical skills, the only valid way of measuring them involves someone doing detailed observations while students demonstrate the skills involved. This can be very time-consuming if it has to be done by staff, and also can feel very threatening to students.

- **Is it necessary to establish minimum acceptable standards?** In many jobs, it is quite essential that everyone practising does so with a high level of skill (for example, surgery). In other situations, it is possible to agree on a reasonable level of skills, and for this to be safe enough (for example, teaching!).

- **How much should practical skills count for?** Students often spend a considerable proportion of their time developing and practising practical skills. It is important to think clearly about what contribution to their overall assessment such skills should make, and to let students know this.

- **May student self-assessment of practical skills be worth using?** Getting students to assess their own practical skills can be one way round the impossible workloads that could be involved if staff were to do all the requisite observations. It is much quicker for staff to moderate student self-assessment of such skills than to undertake the whole task of assessing them.

- **May student peer-assessment of practical skills be worth using?** Involving students in peer-assessment of practical skills can be much less threatening than using tutor assessment. The act of assessing a peer's practical skills is often very good for peer-assessors, in terms of improving similar skills of their own.

- **Is it necessary to have a practical examination?** In some subjects, some sort of end-point practical test may be deemed essential. Driving tests, for example, could not be wholly replaced by a written examination on the Highway Code.

- **Reserve some marks for the processes.** Help students to see that practical work is not just reaching a defined end point, but is about the processes and skills involved in doing so successfully.

- **Ask students to include in their reports 'ways I would do the experiment better next time'.** This encourages students to become more self-aware of how well (or otherwise) they are approaching practical tasks.

- **Include some 'supplementary questions'.** Make these questions that students can only answer when they have thought through their own practical work. For example, students can be briefed to compare their findings with a given published source, and comment on any differences in the procedures used in the published work from those used by the students.

- **Design the right end products.** Sometimes it is possible to design final outcomes which can only be reached when the practical work itself is of high quality. For example, in chemistry, the skills demonstrated in the preparation and refinement of a compound can often be reflected in the purity and amount of the final product.

20. Assessing presentations

Being able to speak convincingly and authoritatively are useful career skills for students. One of the best ways of helping them develop such skills is to involve them in giving assessed presentations. The following suggestions may help your students get the most from such activities:

- **Be clear about the purposes of student presentations.** For example, the main purpose could be to develop students' skills at giving presentations, or it could be to cause them to do research and reading and improve their subject knowledge. Usually, several such factors may be involved together.

- **Make the criteria for assessment of presentations clear from the outset.** Students will not then be working in a vacuum and will know what is expected of them.

■ **Get students involved in the assessment criteria.** This can be done either by allowing them to negotiate the criteria themselves or by giving them plenty of opportunities to interrogate criteria you share with them.

■ **Ensure that students understand the weighting of the criteria.** Help them to know whether the most important aspects of their presentations are to do with they *way* they deliver their contributions (voice, clarity of expression, articulation, body language, use of audio-visual aids, and so on) or the *content* of their presentations (evidence of research, originality of ideas, effectiveness of argument, ability to answer questions, and so on).

■ **Give students some prior practice at assessing presentations.** It is useful, for example, to give students a dry run at applying the assessment criteria they have devised to one or two presentations on video. The discussion that this produces usually helps to clarify or improve the assessment criteria.

■ **Let the students have a mark-free rehearsal.** This gives students the chance to become more confident and to make some of the more basic mistakes at a point where it doesn't count against them. Constructive feedback is crucial at this point so that students can learn from the experience.

■ **Involve students in the assessment of their presentations.** When given the chance to assess each other's presentations they take them more seriously and will learn from the experience. Students merely watching each other's presentations tend to get bored and can switch off mentally. If they are evaluating each presentation using an agreed set of criteria, they tend to engage themselves more fully with the process, and in doing so learn more from the content of each presentation.

■ **Ensure that the assessment criteria span presentation processes and the content of the presentations sensibly.** It can be worth reserving some marks for students' abilities to handle questions after their presentations.

■ **Make up grids using the criteria that have been agreed.** Allocate each criterion a weighting, and get all of the group to fill in the grids for each presentation. The average peer-assessment mark is likely to be at least as good an estimate of the relative worth of each presentation as would be the view of a single tutor doing the assessment.

■ **Be realistic about what can be achieved.** It is not possible to get 12 five-minute presentations into an hour, and presentations always tend to over-run. It is also difficult to get students to concentrate for more than an hour or two of others' presentations. Where classes are large, consider breaking the audience into groups, for example dividing a class of 100 into four groups, with students presenting concurrently in different rooms, or at different timetabled slots.

■ **Think about the venue.** Students do not always give of their best in large, echoing, tiered lecture theatres (nor do we!). A more intimate flat classroom is less threatening particularly for inexperienced presenters.

- **Consider assessing using videotapes.** This can allow the presenters themselves the opportunity to review their performances, and can allow you to assess presentations at a time most suitable to you. Viewing a selection of recorded presentations from earlier rounds can be useful for establishing assessment criteria with students. This sort of evidence of teaching and learning is also useful to show external examiners and quality reviewers.

- **Start small.** Mini-presentations of a few minutes can be almost as valuable as 20-minute presentations for learning the ropes, especially as introductions to the task of standing up and addressing the peer-group.

- **Check what other presentations students may be doing.** Sometimes it can seem that everyone is including presentations in their courses. If students find themselves giving three or four within a month or two, it can be very demanding on their time, and repetitious regarding the processes.

21. Assessing student projects

In many courses, one of the most important kinds of work undertaken by students takes the form of individual projects, often relating theory to practice beyond the college environment. Such projects are usually an important element in the overall work of each student, and are individual in nature. Setting, supporting and assessing such work can be a significant part of the work of a lecturer, and the following suggestions should help to make these tasks more manageable:

- **Choose the learning-by-doing to be relevant and worthwhile.** Student projects are often the most significant and extended parts of their courses, and it is important that the considerable amount of time they may spend on them is useful to them and relevant to the overall learning outcomes of the courses or modules with which the projects are associated.

- **Work out specific learning outcomes for the projects.** These will be of an individual nature for each project, as well as including general ones relating to the course area in which the project is located.

- **Formulate projects so that they address appropriately higher-level skills.** The aims of project work are often to bring together threads from different course areas or disciplines, and to allow students to demonstrate the integration of their learning.

- **Give students as much opportunity as possible to select their own projects.** When students have a strong sense of ownership of the topics of their projects, they put much more effort into their work, and are more likely to be successful.

- **Include scope for negotiation and adjustment of learning outcomes.** Project work is necessarily more like research than other parts of students' learning. Students need to be able to adjust the range of a project to follow through interesting or important aspects that they discover along the way. Remember that it is still important to set standards, and the scope for negotiation may sometimes be restricted to ways that students will go about accumulating evidence to match set criteria.

■ **Make the project briefings clear, and ensure that they will provide a solid foundation for later assessment**. Criteria should be clear and well understood by students at the start of their work on projects.

■ **Keep the scope of project work realistic.** Remember that students will usually have other kinds of work competing for their time and attention, and it is tragic when students succeed with project work, only to fail other parts of their courses to which they should have devoted more time alongside their projects.

■ **Liaise with library and information services colleagues.** When a number of projects make demands on the availability of particular learning resources or information technology facilities, it is important to arrange this in advance with such colleagues, so that they can be ready to ensure that students are able to gain access to the resources they will need.

■ **Ensure that a sensible range of factors will be assessed.** Assessment needs to relate to work that encompasses the whole of the project, and not be unduly skewed towards such skills as writing-up or oral presentation. These are likely to be assessed in any case in other parts of students' work.

■ **Collect a library of past projects.** This can be of great help to students starting out on their own projects, and can give them a realistic idea of the scope of the work likely to be involved, as well as ideas on ways to present their work well.

■ **Arrange staged deadlines for projects.** It is very useful for students to be able to receive feedback on plans for their project work, so that they can be steered away from going off on tangents, or from spending too much time on particular aspects of a project.

■ **Allow sufficient time for project work.** The outcomes of project work may well include that students develop time-management and task-management skills along the way, but they need time and support to do this. Arrange contact windows so that students with problems are not left too long without help.

■ **Consider making projects portfolio-based.** Portfolios often represent the most flexible and realistic way of assessing project work, and allow appendices containing a variety of evidence to be presented along with the more important parts showing students' analysis, thinking, argument and conclusions.

■ **Encourage students to give each other feedback on their project work.** This can be extended to elements of peer-assessment, but it is more important simply to get students talking to each other about their work in progress. Such feedback can help students sort out many of the problems they encounter during project work, and can improve the overall standard of their work.

■ **Think about the spaces and places which students will use to do their project work.** Some of the work may well occur off-campus, but it remains important that students have access to suitable places to write up and prepare their project work for assessment, as well as facilities and support to help them analyze the data and materials they accumulate.

■ **Include a self-evaluation component in each project.** This allows students to reflect on their project work, and think deeper about what went well and where there may have been problems. It can be particularly useful to students to get feedback about the quality of their self-evaluation.

22. Assessing dissertations and theses

Students invest a great deal of time and energy in producing dissertations and theses, usually in their final year. We therefore owe it to them to mark them fairly and appropriately:

■ **Make sure that the assessment criteria are explicit, clear, and understood by the students.** This may seem obvious! However, theses and dissertations are normally very different in the topics and themes they address, and the assessment criteria need to accommodate such differences. Students will naturally compare marks and feedback comments. The availability of clear criteria helps them see that their work has been assessed fairly.

■ **Get students to assess a few past dissertations.** You can't expect them to do this at the same level as may be appropriate for 'real' assessment, but you can (for example) issue students with a one-sided pro-forma questionnaire to complete as they study examples of dissertations. Include questions about the power of the introduction, the quality and consistency of referencing, and the coherence of the conclusions.

■ **Offer guidance and support to students throughout the process.** Dissertations usually take students quite some time to complete. Students appreciate and need some help along the route. It is worth holding tutorials both individually and with groups. This takes good planning, and dates need to be set well in advance, and published on a notice board or handout to students.

■ **Ensure that student support mechanisms are available.** With large class sizes, we cannot afford to spend many hours of staff time with individual students. However, much valuable support can be drawn from the students themselves, if we facilitate ways of them helping each other. Consider introducing supplemental instruction processes, or setting up friendly yet critical student syndicates. Running a half-day workshop with students counselling each other can be valuable.

■ **Beware of the possibility of bias.** Sometimes dissertations involve students writing on topics with a sensitive cultural or political nature. We need to be aware of any prejudices of our own, and to compensate for any bias these could cause in our assessment. Whenever possible, dissertations should be second-marked (at least!).

■ **Can you provide students with equal opportunity regarding selecting their dissertation themes?** Research for some dissertations will involve students in visiting outside agencies, finding materials for experiments, building models and so on. With resource limitations becoming more severe, students may be forced to avoid certain topics altogether. Try to suggest topics where financial implications are manageable to students.

■ **Check whether dissertations always have to be bound.** This may depend on which year of the course they are set in. It may be worth reserving binding for final year dissertations, to help save students money.

■ **Help students to monitor their own progress.** It helps to map the assessment criteria in a way that helps students to keep track of their own progress and achievements. Computer programs are now available which help students work out how they are getting on, and prompt them to the next steps they should be considering at each stage.

■ **When assessing dissertations, collect a list of questions to select from at a forthcoming viva.** Even of there is not going to be a viva, such lists of questions can be a useful addition to the feedback you return to students.

■ **Use post-its while assessing dissertations and theses.** These can be placed towards the edges of pages, so that notes and questions written on the post-its can be found easily again. They help you avoid having to write directly on the pages of the dissertation or thesis (especially when your questions are found to be addressed two pages later!).

23. Assessing reviews and annotated bibliographies

In seeking to extend the range of methods by which we develop students' information retrieval skills, critical reviews of books and articles are frequently set as assignment tasks. Getting students to compile annotated bibliographies helps increase the breadth of their reading, and alerts them to sources they may not otherwise have seen. In assessing these forms of task, the following points are worth addressing:

■ **Promote variety.** Ask students to select their own subject for research, and give them a wide range of topics to choose from.

■ **Prompt awareness of audience.** Ask students to write reviews of different kinds of publication, so that they become aware of the differences in tone and style of writing which are appropriate for different audiences.

■ **Get students to assess existing reviews.** For example, issue students with a selection of existing reviews, and ask them to identify features of the best reviews, and faults of the worst ones.

■ **Help students to see that reviewing is not just a matter of summarizing what everyone has said.** You only have to look at book reviews in journals to see how some reviewers make up their contributions by summarizing the 'contents' pages of the material that they are reviewing. This is not a high-level intellectual activity.

■ **Decide about credit to be awarded to 'search' tasks.** It is useful to get students both to locate all relevant major resources addressing a field, and to prioritize (for example) the most important or most relevant half-dozen sources.

■ **Consider limiting the parameters.** Getting students to do a short comparative review of two or three important sources can be easier (and fairer) to assess than when the reviews are done without any restrictions. When such focused review tasks are coupled with a general search, it is possible to measure information retrieval skills as well as the higher-level 'compare and contrast' skills, without the agenda for the latter remaining too wide for objective assessment.

■ **Set a tight word-limit for the review.** The art of writing a good, short review is more demanding than writing long reviews. When students' reviews are of equal length, it becomes easier to distinguish the relative quality of their work. However, brief students on how to draft and redraft their work, to ensure the quality of short reviews.

■ **Think about combining collaborative and individual work.** For example, suggest that groups of students do a search collaboratively, and identify the most relevant sources together. Then suggest they write individual reviews of different sources. Finally, consider asking them to share their reviews, then write individual comments comparing and contrasting the sources.

■ **Ask students to look at the same texts, but give them different focuses.** For example, students could look at a series of articles on pollution, and write different reviews of them aimed to be separately useful to conservationists, parents, individualists and general consumers.

■ **Emphasize the importance of brevity.** It is much more difficult to write a concise pithy review than to ramble on with opinion and narrative at unspecified length. Short reviews are also quicker to mark (but make sure that students don't adopt the 'stop when you've written a thousand words' approach).

■ **Encourage qualitative judgement.** Prompt students to write on not only what a book or article is about, but also about how effective it is in providing convincing arguments, and how well it is expressed.

■ **Involve your library or information services staff.** It's a mean trick to send off groups of students to rampage through the library, without giving notice to the staff there of what you are doing. Discussing your plans with your faculty librarians, for example, gives them a chance to be prepared, and gives opportunities for them to make suggestions and give advice to you on the nature of the task, before you give it to students.

■ **Think hard about resource availability.** Make sure that there won't be severe log-jams with lots of students chasing particular library resources. Widen the range of suggested resources. Consider arranging with library staff that any books that will be in heavy demand are classified as 'reference only' stock for a specified period, so that they can remain in the library rather than disappearing on loan.

■ **Consider setting annotated bibliographies as group tasks.** This can encourage students to collaborate productively in future information-seeking tasks, and can reduce the drudgery sometimes experienced in tasks such as literature searching.

■ **Make the final product 'publishable'.** Aim to compile collections of the best reviews and annotated bibliographies, for example to use in next year's Course Handbook, or as the basis of an assessed task for next year's students.

■ **Consider delegating assessment to library staff (with their agreement!).** Library staff may be willing and able to assess annotated bibliographies and reviews in parallel with yourself, or may be willing to provide additional feedback comments to students.

24. Assessing performances

In many universities there are courses in subjects such as creative writing, dance, music, drama and so on where an element of performance is an integral part of the process. These elements are often regarded as more challenging to assess than, for example, written exams. The following suggestions may be helpful:

■ **Clear criteria for assessed performances are absolutely vital.** In the aesthetic domain, it is sometimes difficult to articulate these criteria without reducing them to absurdities. The key is to produce criteria that assess the essence of the performance rather than the easy-to-measure elements.

■ **Learn from the experience of others.** To develop expertise in assessing performances, it is invaluable to work alongside more experienced colleagues and learn from the ways in which they make evaluations or judgements.

■ **Ensure that the evidence of the elements of the performances is recorded.** Use video, audio-tape, notation or other methods, so there is evidence available for moderation subsequently.

■ **Stage assessment over a period of time.** It is often helpful to have an incremental element to the assessment so that 'work in progress' assessed at intermediate points contributes to the final grade.

■ **Require students to keep careful records of their preparations for the performances.** This makes it possible for their reflections on the processes, by which their performances were developed, to contribute to their assessment.

■ **Include peer-assessment.** Other students on a course can contribute to the assessment of each other's performances, so long as the assessment criteria are explicit, and evidence of successful outcomes is required. Intra-group peer-assessment can also be helpful, for example with students who are performing together in a play or dance performance.

■ **Minimize competition.** Students in the performing arts move in a competitive world, and assessment schemes which prioritize 'the best' and 'winning' can be counter-productive in contexts where peer support and peer-assessment are interdependent.

■ **Use audiences to contribute to the assessment.** Performances often provide excellent opportunities for gaining a range of views of achievement. Beware, however, of candidates packing audiences with their fans and friends, and devise criteria that are quantifiable as well as qualitative.

■ **Accommodate issues relating to style and personal taste.** Where there are such issues in play, assessors should make these explicit at the outset. This will at least provide information to enable students to make choices about how they prefer to perform.

■ **Be aware of the stresses that performances can put on candidates.** In addition to the performance anxiety that is common in most kinds of assessment, there are further stresses that can occur. Examples include when scenery falls, instruments get damaged, audio-visual equipment fails, and injuries befall performers. Aim to develop styles of assessment that can accommodate glitches, and ensure that such happenings don't necessarily indicate failure.

25. Assessing poster-displays and exhibitions

When students are asked (individually or in groups) to synthesize the outcomes of their learning and/or research into a self-explanatory poster, which can be assessed on the spot, it can be an extremely valuable process. More and more conferences are providing poster-display opportunities as an effective way of disseminating findings and ideas. This kind of assessment can provide practice in developing the skills relevant to communicating by such visual means:

■ **Use the assessment process as a showcase.** Students are often rather proud of their achievements and it can be invaluable to invite others in to see what has been achieved. Think about inviting moderators, senior staff, students on parallel courses, and employers. Gather their impressions, either using a short questionnaire, or verbally asking them a couple of relevant questions about their experiences of seeing the display.

■ **Use posters as a way to help other students to learn.** For example, final year students can produce posters showing the learning they gained during placements. This can be a useful opportunity for students preparing to find their own placements to adjust their approaches and base them on others' experiences.

■ **Get students to peer-assess each other's posters.** Having undertaken the task of making posters themselves, they will be well prepared to review critically the work of others. This also provides chances for them to learn from the research undertaken by the whole cohort rather than just from their own work.

■ **Consider asking students to produce a one-page handout to supplement their poster.** This will test a further set of skills, and will provide all reviewers with an *aide-mémoire* for subsequent use.

■ **Give sufficient time for the debrief.** Lots of learning takes place in the discussion during and after the display. The tendency is to put poster-display and exhibition sessions on during the last week of the term or semester, and this can give little time to unpack the ideas at the end.

■ **Make careful practical arrangements.** Large numbers of posters take up a lot of display space, and to get the best effect they should be displayed on boards. Organizing this is possible in most universities, for example by borrowing publicity display boards, but it needs to be planned in advance. Allow sufficient time for students to mount their displays, and make available drawing pins, Blu-Tack, tape, Velcro sticky pads, demountable display equipment, and so on.

■ **Stagger the assessment.** Where peers are assessing each others' posters, to avoid collusion, 'fixing', and outbursts of spite, it is valuable to arrange that half the display is in one room and the rest in another, or to run successive displays at different times. Number the posters and get one half of the group to assess the odd-numbered posters and the other half to assess the even-numbered ones, and average the data that is produced.

■ **Consider getting groups to produce a poster between them.** This encourages collaborative working and can reduce the overall numbers of posters – useful when student numbers are large. You could then consider getting students within the group to peer-assess (intra) their respective contributions to the group as well as to assess collaboratively the posters of the other groups (inter-peer-group assessment).

■ **Link assessment of poster-displays to open days.** Students coming to visit the institution when they are considering applying for courses may well get a good idea about what students actually do on the courses, from looking at posters on display.

- **Prepare a suitable assessment sheet.** Base this firmly on the assessment criteria for the exercise. Provide space for peers' comments. This paves the way towards plenty of opportunity for peer feedback.

- **Use assistance.** When working with large numbers of peer-assessed posters, you may need help in working out the averaged scores. Either get the students to do the number work for themselves or for each other (and advise them that the numbers will be randomly checked to ensure fair play), or alternatively, press-gang colleagues, partners, administrators or progeny to help with the task.

- **Provide a rehearsal opportunity.** Let the students have a practice run at a relatively early stage, using a mock-up or a draft on flipchart paper. Give them feedback on these drafts, and let them compare their ideas. This can help them to avoid the most obvious disasters later.

- **Let everyone know why they are using poster-displays.** This method of assessment may be unfamiliar to students, and to your colleagues. It is therefore valuable if you can provide a clear justification of the educational merits of the method to all concerned.

- **Brief students really carefully about what is needed.** Ideally, let them see a whole range of posters from previous years (or some mock-ups, or photographs of previous displays) so that they have a good idea about the requirements, without having their originality and creativity suppressed.

- **Use the briefing to discuss criteria and weighting.** Students will need to know what level of effort they should put into different elements such as presentation, information content, structure, visual features, and so on. If students are not clear about this, you may well end up with brilliantly presented posters with little relevance to the topic, or really dull, dense posters that try to compress the text of a long report onto a single A1 sheet.

- **Give students some practical guidelines.** Let them know how many A1 sheets they can have, where their work will be displayed, what size of font the text should be to be readable on a poster, what resources will be available to them in college, and how much help they can get from outsiders such as friends on other courses who take good photographs or who have the knack of writing in attractive script.

- **Attach a budget to the task.** In poster-displays, money shows! If you were to give a totally free hand to students, the ones with best access to photocopiers, photographic resources, expensive papers, word processors and so on might well produce better looking products than students who have little money to spend on their posters or displays (although it does not always turn out this way). Giving a notional budget can help to even out the playing field, as can requiring students to use only items from a given list, with materials perhaps limited to those provided in workshops in the college.

- **Keep records of poster-displays and exhibitions.** Take photographs, or make a short video. It is not possible to retain complete displays and exhibitions, but a handy reminder can be very useful for use when planning the next similar event. Evidence of the displays can also be interesting to external examiners and quality reviewers.

■ **Get someone (or a group) to provide a 'guide booklet' to the exhibition.** This helps the students undertaking this task to make relative appraisals of the different items or collections making up the exhibition as a whole.

■ **Consider turning it into a celebration as well.** After the assessment has taken place, it can be pleasurable to provide some refreshments, and make the display or exhibition part of an end-of-term or end-of-course celebration.

26. Assessing seminars

Assessing student seminars can add to the diversity of assessment methods, and allow for instant feedback, providing a valuable learning experience. As seminar groups are smaller than lecture groups, it is possible to employ some different assessment methods. Assessing seminars often includes an element of assessing presentations, but can be extended much further than this in scope. The following suggestions may help your students derive more benefit from seminars:

■ **Brainstorm assessment possibilities with students.** Get groups of students to draw up lists of the possible ways their seminars could be assessed. Collect and collate the contents of the lists, and ask the whole group to vote on the three best ways.

■ **Get students to identify criteria by which to assess seminars.** For example, show a video of a previous seminar and ask the students first to give it an impression rating. Then help them identify some objective criteria that could be used to assess it, and which also could be extended to assess their own forthcoming seminars.

■ **Prepare a seminar of your own, and get students to assess it.** Try to include in your seminar the good practice features that you wish students to emulate. Be prepared, however, to learn some home truths about your own performance, and don't get cross when you receive critical comments!

■ **Get students themselves to peer-assess seminars.** Ask small groups of students to organize and prepare a seminar. Keep the presentations short and snappy (not a whole hour each!). Get the whole group to write assessment criteria, and decide on the relative weightings for these, and draw up assessment sheets using these. Allow the groups to assess each other's presentation (inter-peer-group assessment). You could try as a first stage getting students to give marks on two aspects of each seminar: content and presentation, and use number cards as in ice skating or ballroom dancing competitions.

■ **Use the time carefully.** Getting students to plan the organization of both the seminars and the assessment can enable the timetabled sessions to be used effectively.

■ **Consider assessing small tasks within the seminar.** For example, ask all students observing each seminar to write an article on the topic under discussion for a newspaper. Collect the articles and distribute them. The individual marks for the articles can contribute towards the seminar assessment mark.

■ **Get students to write their own reflective logs about their contributions to the seminar programme.** Get the students to self-assess these logs. Students are remarkably honest about how well they feel they have contributed, although they will probably need some briefing and support regarding how to assess themselves.

■ **Keep records of students' interactions, and give them grades for them.** At its simplest, this means that a student who failed to attend a sufficient proportion of the seminars would be deemed to have failed the seminar element of the overall assessment programme. More sophisticated systems would allow you to differentiate students in terms of pass, merit or distinction, based on criteria you made public to the students at the outset. If you do this, it is important to make it clear that 'hogging the air' does not constitute good performance, whereas 'enabling the contribution of others' does.

■ **Use parallel seminar groups to assess each other's presentations.** This can take time to set up, but can enable students to learn from each other, particularly when differentiated seminar topics are given.

27. Assessing work-based learning

Many courses include a placement period, and the increasing use of accreditation of prior experiential learning in credit accumulation systems means that we need to look at ways of assessing material produced by students in work contexts, rather than just things students write up when back at college after their placements. The following suggestions may help:

■ **Involve employers, professional supervisors and colleagues.** They will need careful briefing, and negotiation may also be required to achieve their full cooperation, as they are often very busy people. Ways of involving them include asking them to produce testimonials, statements of competence, checklists, grids and pro-formas, or simply to sign off students' own statements of competence or achievement.

■ **Be clear about the purpose of the assessment.** Is the assessment being done to satisfy a funding body, the university or employers? Or is the assessment primarily to aid students' learning? Or is the assessment primarily designed to help students develop skills and experience that will aid their future careers? Clarifying the purposes can help you decide the most appropriate forms of assessment.

- **Get the balance right.** Work out carefully what proportion of students' overall assessment will be derived from their placements. Decide whether the related assessment should be on a pass–fail basis, or whether it should be attempted to classify it for degrees.

- **Expect placements to be very different.** If a group of students are spread through a number of companies or organizations, some will have a very good experience of placement, and others through no fault of their own can have an unsatisfactory experience. It is important that factors outside students' control are not allowed to prejudice assessment.

- **Consider carefully whether a mentor is well placed to assess.** There can sometimes be complex confusions of role if the person who is the professional supporter or friend of the assessee is also the person who has to make critical evaluations for assessment purposes.

- **Decide carefully whether to tutor-assess during workplace visits.** Visiting students on placement certainly gives tutors opportunities to gather data that may be relevant to assessment, but if assessment is on the agenda the whole nature of such visits changes.

- **Include assessment of a work log.** Some professions prescribe the exact form that such a log or work diary should take; in other work contexts it is possible for the course team or the students themselves to devise their own formats. It is often helpful if such logs include lists of learning outcomes, skills or competences that students are expected to achieve and demonstrate, with opportunities to check-off these and add comments as appropriate.

- **Ask students to produce a reflective journal.** This can be a much more personal kind of document, and might include hopes, fears and feelings as well as more mundane accounts of actions and achievements. Assessing reflective journals can raise tricky issues of confidentiality and disclosure, but ways round such issues can be found, particularly if students are asked to submit for assessment edited extracts from their reflective journals.

- **Consider using a portfolio.** A portfolio to demonstrate achievement at work can include suitably anonymized real products from the workplace (with the permission of the employer) as well as testimonials from clients, patients, support staff and others.

- **Help to ensure that assessment does not blind students to their learning on placement.** Consider asking students who have completed work placements to write their experiences up in the form of a journal article, perhaps for an in-house magazine or journal. A collection of these can help to disseminate their experiences. Joint articles written with employers are even more valuable, and help make links with employers better.

28. Assessing action research

Since action research is about improving students' professional experience through reflection *and* action, its assessment is both interesting and challenging. Importantly, action research has value in itself to the researcher, and therefore needs to be assessed with reference to the students' own workplace. The following questions point to the essence of action research, and provide the main criteria for its assessment:

- **Does the research proposal identify a problem or issue clearly?** Does this directly link with the students' own professional practice?

- **Have the students reflected on their own beliefs and values?** Has this been shown to help them to understand the problems and issues under investigation in the research?

- **Has the evidence collected by students been derived from investigations carried out within their workplace?** Is the evidence sufficiently specific, so that it is clear that it has not been collected from available sources elsewhere?

- **Is there evidence of students' involvement at a personal level in the research process?** It is worth checking that the individuality of students shows through in the processes they chose for their research, and the ways that they interpret and communicate their findings.

- **Is the research directed towards improving the quality of the students' practice?** It is important to ensure that the research does not stray towards what has been readily researchable rather than what is directly relevant to the fields in which the students will practise.

- **Has the search for new knowledge been determined by the nature of the improvements to practice sought by the students?** It is useful to examine how students have defined their aims and objectives for their research, and how relevant these are in terms of seeking pointers towards improved practice.

- **Is there evidence of relating theory to improvements in students' practice?** Has appropriate theoretical underpinning been identified, and have concepts been integrated developmentally?

- **Has the collection of evidence been largely the result of observation, discussion and reflection?** Is it subjective and qualitative rather than objective and quantitative?

- **Has the research shed light on the possibilities for students' ongoing professional development?** Does this extend well beyond the immediate outcomes of the programme of action research undertaken?

29. Assessing portfolios

Portfolios provide a valuable method of assessing students' achievements, particularly in contexts outside the learning institution. They enable students to provide evidence of achievement of specified competences, sometimes as a result of a learning contract, from a variety of contexts including work, leisure and home, and from independent study as well as the university itself. Portfolios can become unwieldy if students are not given guidance on the range, volume and form of presentation of materials, and can be difficult and time-consuming to assess. The following suggestions should help you minimize these risks, and help your students get the most from portfolios:

- **Specify or negotiate intended learning outcomes clearly.** Ensure that students have a shared understanding of the level expected of their work.

- **Propose a general format for the portfolio.** This helps students demonstrate their achievement of the learning outcomes in ways that are more easily assembled.

- **Specify or negotiate the nature of the evidence that students should collect.** This makes it easier to assess portfolios fairly, as well as more straightforward for students.

- **Specify or negotiate the range and extent of the evidence expected from students.** This helps students plan the balance of their work effectively, and helps them avoid spending too much time on one part of their portfolio while missing out important details on other parts.

- **Don't underestimate the time it takes to assess portfolios.** Also, don't underestimate their weight and volume if you have a set of them to carry around with you!

- **Prepare a pro-forma to help you assess portfolios.** It is helpful to be able to tick off the achievement of each learning outcome, and make decisions about the quality of the evidence as you work through a portfolio.

- **Use post-its to identify parts of the portfolio to which you may want to return.** This can save a lot of looking backwards and forwards through a portfolio in search of something you know you've seen in it somewhere!

- **Consider using post-its to draft your feedback comments.** You can then compose elements of your feedback as you work through the portfolio, instead of having to try to carry it all forward in your mind till you've completed looking at the portfolio.

- **Put a limit on the physical size of the portfolio.** A single box file is ample for most purposes, or a specified size of ring-binder can provide guidance for the overall size.

- **Give guidance on audio or video elements.** Where students are to include video or audio-tapes, it is worth limiting the duration of the elements they can include. Insist that they wind the tapes to the point at which they want you to start viewing or listening, otherwise you can spend ages trying to find the bit that they intend you to assess.

■ **Provide interim assessment opportunities.** Give candidates the opportunity to receive advice on whether the evidence they are assembling is appropriate.

■ **Quality not quantity counts.** Students should be advised not so submit every piece of paper they have collected over the learning period, otherwise the volume of material can be immense.

■ **Get students to provide route-maps.** Portfolios are easier to assess if the material is carefully structured, and accompanied by a reflective account, which not only outlines the contents but also asserts which of the criteria each piece of evidence contributes towards.

■ **Get students to provide a structure.** Portfolio elements should be clearly labelled and numbered for easy reference. If loose-leaf folders are used, dividers should be labelled to enable easy access to material. All supplementary material such as audiotapes, videos, drawings, computer programs, tables, graphs and so on should be appropriately marked and cross-referenced.

■ **Be clear about what you are assessing.** While detailed mark schemes are not really appropriate for portfolios, it is still necessary to have clear and explicit criteria, both for the students' use and to guide assessment.

■ **Structure your feedback.** Students may well have spent many hours assembling portfolios and may have a great deal of personal investment in them. To give their work number marks only (or pass/fail) may seem small reward. Consider using an assessment pro-forma so that your notes and comments can be directly relayed to the students, particularly in cases where required elements are incomplete or missing.

■ **Encourage creativity.** For some students, this may be the first time they have been given an opportunity to present their strengths in a different way. Hold a brainstorming session about the possible contents of portfolios, for example which may include videos, recorded interviews, newspaper articles, and so on.

■ **Provide opportunities for self-assessment.** Having completed their portfolios, a valuable learning experience in itself is to let the students assess them. A short exercise is to ask them: 'In the light of your experience of producing a portfolio, what do you consider you did especially well, and what would you now do differently?'

■ **Assess in a team.** If possible set aside a day as a team. Write your comments about each portfolio, and then pass them round for others to add to them. In this way, students get feedback that is more comprehensive, and assessors get to see a more diverse range of portfolios.

■ **Set up an exhibition.** Portfolios take a long time to complete and assess. By displaying them (with students' permission) their valuable experience can be shared.

■ | **Think about where and when you will mark portfolios.** They are not nearly as portable as scripts, and you may need equipment such as video or audio playback facilities to review evidence. It may be helpful therefore to set aside time when you can book a quiet, well-equipped room where you are able to spread out materials and look at a number of portfolios together. This will help you get an overview, and makes it easier to get a feel for standards.

30. Assessing reflective logs

Reflective logs, by their very nature, are made in different ways by different students. Where it is intended to assess such work, it is useful to specify the format and structures within which candidates can demonstrate their reflections. Reflective logs may be a significant element in assessed portfolios:

■ | **Set the brief clearly in advance.** It is easier to mark reflective logs if students have a clear idea of what they are trying to achieve. This will avoid you having to plough through endless ramblings that are irrelevant to the assessment task.

■ | **Identify clearly what evidence will demonstrate achievement of the assessment criteria.** Ensure that the criteria used are measurable. It is difficult, for example, to assess whether a piece of writing represents 'an honest personal account' when all that is available is the candidate's work, without a framework against which to judge it.

■ | **Quantify the amount of evidence required.** For example, specify 'three examples of ...' or 'illustrations of applying four methods to ...'. This makes it much simpler to give fair assessments to a range of different candidates, each approaching the task of producing reflective logs in their own ways.

■ | **Consider whether it is necessary to grade or give marks.** Conscientious engagement with the task may be all that you need to see evidence of. This may be sufficient for a pass/fail assessment outcome. If some kind of grade is required, it may be best to go for a system of banding (for example, fail, pass, merit, distinction). However, where this is the case, it will be essential to provide students (and fellow-assessors) with an assessment protocol to give guidance on what exactly would constitute the kind of performance necessary for each level of achievement.

■ | **Consider permitting the submission of extracts for assessment, rather than the whole reflective log.** Some areas of work may lead students to write personal or confidential matters into what becomes a really meaningful reflective journal. They may not wish to reveal these areas to their assessors, moderators and external examiners.

■ | **Give students reflective logs to assess, and ask them to formulate assessment criteria.** This helps them to identify good practice to apply to their own future reflective logs.

■ **Give students the chance to develop their skills.** It is best to introduce reflective logs early in a course, so that students have time to acquire the appropriate skills.

■ **Start small.** Build up confidence gradually. Even a very short reflective exercise can be extremely valuable, especially when students get plenty of feedback on it. It is easier to give a lot of feedback on a short exercise!

■ **If time allows, skim-read the whole reflective log first.** Then read more closely, looking for evidence of the criteria being achieved.

■ **Consider letting students in groups make reflective logs.** Students can generate greater levels of reflection when bouncing ideas off each other, and discussing matters arising.

31. Assessing groups

The ability to work as an effective member of a team is a key skill required in most careers. The development of this skill can be encouraged by including student group-work in courses. When facilitated effectively and assessed sensitively, student group-work can be most productive and can also be fun:

■ **Set the scene appropriately.** Help students to understand how beneficial group-work can be to them. Share your thinking with colleagues as well as students. It is important that everyone is aware how the student group-work is to be assessed. Assessing such work without any explanation can be a devastating experience for the students assessed.

■ **Introduce assessed group-work early.** Don't wait until the final year of a course. This is partly because students may have become fixed in their expectations regarding assessment, and also because in many courses much depends on students' final year performance, and it would be unfair to change the assessment practices at this late stage. When group-work assessment is introduced early in a course, students are more likely to see it as natural and non-threatening.

■ **Don't allocate marks early on.** Too much detail about marks can detract from the main purpose of using group-work assessment – that of developing students' skills at working together. Before setting assessed group-work tasks, introduce a few exercises to help students develop and reflect on group skills.

■ **Use exercises such as 'building a paper tower' to develop a team spirit.** Give each group six sheets of paper, scissors and sticky tape, and ask them to build the tallest free-standing tower. Don't allow cheating! Then get the students to discuss how their groups worked together. Allocating a non-participating observer to each group can be useful.

■ **Introduce assessment criteria slowly.** Set an activity for the students and give them some of the criteria. Ask them to add two further criteria of their own, and to decide how many marks should be associated with each criterion.

■ **Allow time for debriefing.** The most important part of the learning payoff is when students analyse their successes, and some of the 'could have done better by …' aspects of their activities in the group.

■ **Be clear about what you are trying to assess.** Work out whether you are assessing the product or outcome of the group-work, or whether it is the processes that are being measured. Processes and product can be quite different, and require different approaches to assessment. In some group activities only products may lend themselves to assessment, while in other activities it may be only processes which can be assessed.

■ **Let students choose their own criteria.** This is best done after students have already had some experience of group-work. Each group could be briefed to do the same activity, but asked to devise its own set of criteria, using which other groups will mark them. This is usually a very positive learning experience, leading to greater awareness among students of the importance of the clarity of assessment criteria.

■ **Be aware of dangers associated with assessing individuals in a group.** This can lead to great traumas and heated debates. If individual contributions are to be assessed it is very important that the criteria are known, discussed and agreed at the outset. It is usually better to assess such contributions after the team has developed confidence and trust.

■ **Consider the assessment implications of the various ways of forming groups.** Do you wish students to choose their own groups? (They tend to self-select by ability, with able students strategically choosing each other, leaving the less able to make up their own teams later.) Do you want to allocate students randomly, to provide an element of fairness? (This works well on small-scale projects where the teams can be rotated.) Or do you want to put students into *learning* teams, where you select groups to ensure a balance of the mixture of experience, ability and skills? This is particularly useful in providing a productive cooperative learning experience, but takes a higher level of organizational skill for you to arrange it.

32. Assessing flexible learning

In many ways, good assessment practice for flexible learning overlaps with many of the suggestions throughout this chapter, particularly regarding the provision of feedback. However, such feedback needs to be articulated even more carefully for flexible learners than for conventional students, as it may well be delivered without face-to-face contact:

■ | **Get to know your students.** Sometimes, in distance education, tutors and students may never actually meet. Even then, exchanges of correspondence can open up good communication, and this is best done well before the more formal role of assessing comes in.

■ | **Make the first assignment a dry run.** It can take much of the pressure off students, if they know that the first tutor-marked assignment is essentially a setting-the-parameters exercise.

■ | **Remember how distance students may feel about sending in their first assignments for assessment.** For many, it may be the first time for years they've submitted written work to a lecturer for assessment. They can be anxious, excited, vulnerable and fearful about the prospect of having someone assess their work.

■ | **Remember how important feedback is.** Feedback from lecturers is all the more crucial for open and distance students. Your comments on written assignments may be the main way (or the only way) that such students receive feedback from an expert. Ticks and crosses are not nearly enough.

■ | **Mind your language.** Remember that even such simple words such as 'but', 'however' and 'although' are usually followed by bad news of one kind or another, and can cause students' feelings to sink. Students can't see the reassuring smile on your face or the twinkle in your eye when they've only got your words to look at.

■ | **Be careful not to demotivate completely!** Try to avoid altogether using words such as 'failed', 'have not grasped', 'misunderstood', or even 'adequate' or 'satisfactory'. Such words can come across very negatively to students who are taking every word you write seriously.

■ | **Use assignment return sheets or letters for your main comments.** It's important that students don't get their work back covered with your comments between the lines. Give yourself space to explain things clearly and legibly.

■ | **Keep a copy of your substantive comments.** It's all to easy to forget exactly what you've said to each student when you're returning their marked work to them. A copy of your assignment return sheet or letter can be really helpful to you when you may need to follow up further some issues, for example in telephone discussions with students or in subsequent assignments.

■ | **Try to return marked work as quickly as possible.** Students get much more value from your feedback when they get your comments while they can still remember the detail of the thinking they put into their assignments.

■ | **Invite students to tell you more about what they want from your feedback.** Some may specifically ask you for comments on their style or grammar. Some may want particular comments about whether they were successful in tackling areas they found difficult.

■ | **Consider preparing model answers or discussion notes to return to students with their marked work.** This can save you having to repeat the same comments over and over again to different students, and can be very useful to students in helping them see the standards you're expecting of them.

- **Be particularly clear about the wording of assignment questions.** When working with distance students, it is often sensible to redraft assignments on the basis of your experience of marking the first batch from students.

- **Save examples of good assignments.** With their owners' permission, it can be helpful to be able to send good examples to students who had particular problems with an assignment.

- **If you're marking alongside other lecturers, take particular care with inter-tutor reliability.** It's useful to check that your feedback and standards are similar to those of other lecturers marking the same assignments.

- **Ask your students regularly how they're finding your marking.** It's useful to know whether they are getting what they need from your comments and explanations, and they will often surprise you about areas where you thought you had made yourself quite clear!

- **Consider being an open learner yourself.** It can be very valuable to subject yourself to the experience of having *your* work marked by someone else! Most lecturers who experience this find that it affects the way they communicate with students.

- **Keep good records.** Especially if you're dealing with students who may telephone you, or who may meet you face to face from time to time, it's important for you to be able to tune in rapidly to where each individual is in their work.

- **Ask students to set you questions.** Some students will do this anyway, but it is worth encouraging the rest to write down in the form of questions anything that they are having difficulty with in their studies. This will of course increase your workload, but it can pay off in terms of your students' success in their studies.

- **Don't be over-defensive regarding the learning materials.** Often, students' questions and problems will reveal deficiencies in the learning materials, and it can often pay you to write a 'replacement page 25' to overcome a particular problem to which several students have alerted you.

- **Give study-skills advice.** Students working through flexible learning pathways often miss out on the informal tips and wrinkles lecturers pass on in face-to-face sessions. Students may welcome particularly advice about revision strategies and exam technique.

33. Learning contracts and assessment

Learning contracts are a particularly valuable way to ensure that students receive relevant feedback on their work. They also enable students to negotiate how they will satisfy the assessment requirements of a course, either by devising their own learning outcomes, or by discussing what kinds of evidence they will need to assemble in order to satisfy specified learning outcomes in a more structured course. Learning contracts are useful in that they enable students to demonstrate individuality, gain credit for prior experience, and concentrate on what they *can* do rather than what they cannot do:

■ **Consider calling them 'learning agreements' rather than 'contracts'.** This can make them somewhat less threatening for students to negotiate, and emphasizes the ethos that everything in such an agreement is subscribed to by both sides.

■ **Start by looking at the students' entry profiles.** This can be done by using a self-rating pro-forma to be completed by students, by discussion with lecturers, or by other means of recognizing prior achievement.

■ **Consider where the learning programme needs to lead.** Think about what final level of achievement is being targeted, and what kinds of evidence will be needed to demonstrate this.

■ **Plan for action.** Students and lecturers will need to consider how students can progress towards the required learning outcomes, ideally expressing these processes in the form of action plans which include particular activities, deadlines, check points, and agreed means of collecting evidence.

■ **Evaluate achievement.** Students and lecturers will need to monitor performance to see how the targets have been met from time to time. This will almost certainly be a cyclical process, with students going back to their original agreements for rethinking and replanning.

■ **Renegotiate.** Few learning contracts ever go completely to plan. They should be sufficiently flexible for students who have achieved more than they originally thought they would to incorporate this in the assignments, and to cope with the inevitable delays, pitfalls and disappointments that befall us all.

■ **Make your availability clear.** If effective monitoring of the learning agreements is to take place, there will need to be contact between lecturers and students, and this should be fixed in advance. An open-door policy is not ideal, as under-confident students may well be perpetually knocking on your door, and the fiercely independent students may reject support because they don't realize when they need it.

■ **Stand back a bit.** Students learning independently need a different kind of support from those in traditional learning contexts. It is often difficult to balance the need to let students develop independently against our tendency as lecturers to be directive and offer all the answers. Learning contracts are designed to let students take a more autonomous role in learning.

- **Be supportive.** Students working on learning contracts will still need advice, for example, on where to look for appropriate reference sources, and they may well also need confidence building and reassurance. A light touch is usually best.

- **Bring in a third party.** It is useful for students' progress, from devising their contracts to final evaluation, to be monitored by a mentor. The mentor need not be a member of staff, and could be a fellow student or friend chosen by the student. Some guidelines or training sessions for mentors are a useful aid.

- **Publish a booklet of learning contracts that worked.** This helps your students formulate realistic learning contracts at appropriate levels. Preferably (with permission) include the names of the original students, who can then be tracked down by your present students for advice.

34. Quality of feedback

If 'assessment is the engine that drives learning' (John Cowan), then the ways in which we give feedback are important in gearing the engine so that maximum effect is achieved from the effort put in by all concerned. This section of the 'Assessment' chapter explores a variety of ways in which feedback can be given to students, and includes many suggestions for optimizing the usefulness of such feedback:

- **Feedback should be targeted to enhance learning.** Feedback should concentrate on what to do to improve. This is better than when feedback is heavily judgmental.

- **Feedback should be timely.** When marked work is returned to students weeks (or even months) after submission, feedback is often totally ignored because it bears little relevance to students' current needs then. Many institutions nowadays specify in their Student Charters that work should be returned within two to three weeks, enabling students to derive greater benefits from feedback. When feedback is received very quickly, it is much more effective, as students can still remember exactly what they were thinking as they addressed each task.

- **Think about how students will feel when they get marked work back.** Students can be in states of heightened emotion at such points. If their scripts are covered with comments in red ink (even when it is all praise) it is rather intimidating for them at first.

- **Try to do more than put ticks.** Tempting as it is to put ticks beside things that are correct or good, ticks don't give much real feedback. It takes a little longer to add short phrases such as 'good point', 'I agree with this', 'yes, this is it', 'spot on', and so on, but such feedback comments do much more to motivate students than just ticks.

■ **Avoid putting crosses if possible.** Students often have negative feelings about crosses on their work, carried forward from schooldays. Short phrases such as 'no', 'not quite', 'but this wouldn't work', and so on can be much better ways of alerting students to things that are wrong.

■ **Try to make your writing legible.** If there is not going to be room to make a detailed comment directly on the script, put code numbers or asterisks, and write your feedback on a separate sheet. A useful compromise is to put feedback comments on post-its stuck to appropriate parts of a script. However, it's worth still using a code, asterisk or some such device so that if students remove the post-its as they read through their work, they can still work out exactly which points your comments apply to.

■ **Try giving some feedback before you start assessing.** For example, when a class hands in a piece of work, you can immediately issue handouts of model answers and discussions of the main things that may have caused problems. Students can read such information while their own efforts are still fresh in their minds, and can derive a great deal of feedback straightaway. You can then concentrate, while assessing, on giving them *additional* feedback individually, without going into detail on things that you have already addressed in your general discussion comments that you have already given them.

■ **Don't forget to give positive feedback.** It is sometimes difficult to find something good to say about a piece of work! Ideally, however, you should start by commenting on a positive aspect before leading into a critique.

■ **Feedback should be efficient.** It has often been found that the time taken over assessment on many courses was much greater than the time devoted to teaching and learning. Assessment systems should be devised to maximize the amount of feedback given to students within the time available. Such methods include the use of assignment return sheets, statement banks, and computer-marked assignments.

■ **Give feedback to groups of students sometimes.** This helps students become aware that they are not alone in making mistakes, and allows them to learn from the successes and failures of others.

■ **Let students argue.** When giving one-to-one feedback, it is often useful to allow students the opportunity to interrogate you and challenge your comments (orally or in writing) so that any issues that are unclear can be resolved.

■ **Feedback should be realistic.** When making suggestions for improvement of student work, consider carefully whether they can be achieved. It may not have been possible (for example) for students to gain access to certain resources or books in the time available.

■ **Feedback should be fair.** Check that you are not giving feedback on the amount of money that was spent on the work you mark, for example when some students can submit work produced by expensive desktop publishing systems, while other students have no access to such facilities.

■ **Feedback should be motivating.** Think carefully about the language you use, so that students are encouraged into doing (even) better next time. The use of 'final' language such as 'excellent' may be rewarding to hear or read, but offers no indication to the best students regarding how they may stretch themselves even further.

■ **Feedback should be honest.** When there are serious problems which students need to be made aware of, feedback comments should not skirt round these or avoid them. It may be best to arrange for individual face-to-face feedback sessions with some students, so you can give any bad news in ways where you can monitor how they are taking it, and provide appropriate comfort at the same time.

■ **Feedback can be given before scores or grades.** Consider whether sometimes it may be worth returning students' work to them with feedback comments but no grades (but having written down your marks in your own records). Then invite students to try to work out what their scores or grade should be, and to report to you in a week's time what they think. This causes students to read all your feedback comments earnestly in their bid to work out how they have done. Most students will make good guesses regarding their grades, and it's worth finding out which students are way out too.

■ **Think about audiotapes for giving feedback.** In some subjects, it is quite hard to write explanatory comments on students' work. For example, in mathematics, it can be quicker and easier to 'talk' individual students through how a problem should be solved, referring to asterisks or code-numbers marked on their work. Such feedback has the advantages of tone of voice for emphasis and explanation. Another advantage is that students can play it again, until they have fully understood all of your feedback.

■ **Consider giving feedback by e-mail.** Some students feel most relaxed when working at a computer terminal on their own. With e-mail, students can receive your feedback when they are ready to think about it. They can read it again later, and even file it. Using e-mail, you can provide feedback synchronously as you work through their scripts, rather than having to wait till you return the whole set to a class.

35. Using computer-generated feedback

Human beings can get bored when giving the same feedback repeatedly to different students; computers don't have this problem! Computer-generated feedback is where you program the feedback messages you wish students to receive in anticipated circumstances, such as replying to options in multiple-choice questions:

- **Occasions where you frequently need to give the same feedback message to different students**. Look for those. Work out exactly what the gist of your feedback message is on such occasions, and consider whether it will be worthwhile packaging up this feedback so that students can get the same help from a computer instead of from you.

- **Listen to yourself giving live feedback to students after they have attempted a task.** It can be worth tape-recording some examples of the way you talk to fellow human beings. The little 'asides' that you slip in to make sure they understand you are very important, and it's worth incorporating such asides in the feedback you get the computer to give them.

- **Devise a task leading towards the planned feedback message.** Normally, the feedback will be reserved for those students who don't get the task right first time. Check out with students in person that the planned feedback is self-sufficient, and that they don't need any further explanation from you in person to get the task right next time.

- **Don't forget to provide feedback to students who get the task *right* first time.** It is just as important to give positive feedback for successful work as it is to give helpful feedback when students encounter problems. Remind them exactly *what* they got right, in case it was a lucky accident.

- **Let students who get things right know about some of the things that might have gone wrong.** Learning from mistakes is useful, and people who don't make any mistakes can miss out on some valuable learning. Students are often quite hooked on finding out more about what they *might* have done wrong, even when they got it all right, and will search for what the computer would have told them if they had got it wrong.

- **Be sympathetic to students who get it wrong.** When you program feedback into a computer-based learning package, it is important that your students feel that the computer is treating them like human beings. Don't include blunt messages such as 'Wrong!' or 'Wrong yet again!'. It is better to come across almost apologetically, with feedback messages starting perhaps as 'Sorry, but this doesn't work out in practice …'.

- **Remind students about *what* they get wrong.** It is important that mistakes can be linked firmly to the task that brought them about. The danger is that when your students read your feedback messages, as programmed into the computer system, they may have forgotten exactly what they were trying to do when things went wrong.

- **Try to devise feedback that explains *why* students may have got something wrong.** It isn't enough just to know *what* was wrong. Whenever you can, devise feedback messages about mistakes along the lines: 'For this to have happened, you may have been thinking that …, but in fact it's like this …'.

■ **Road test your feedback messages with small groups of students.** Ask them if they can think of any better ways of getting the feedback message across. Get them to put into words what *they* might have said to someone sitting next to them who attempted the same task, and got it wrong. If their words are better than your original ones, use theirs!

■ **Explore the possibilities of using e-mail for 'later' feedback.** When you know how well (or badly) students have tackled a computer-based exercise, you may be able to give them feedback through the system of networked computers. This means that only the students concerned see these particular feedback message, and they have the comfort of privacy in which to read the feedback and think about it.

36. Using e-mail and computer-conferencing to give students feedback

Computer communications are very fast and cheap, so they are very useful for providing feedback to students. E-mail is particularly useful as a vehicle for giving students individual feedback on assessed work, whether as stand-alone e-mail communications to students, or alongside or within a computer-conferencing system. Electronic feedback can apply to computer-mediated coursework (where the work is submitted through a computer system), but can also extend usefully to giving students feedback on handwritten or hardcopy work that they have submitted for assessment. The following suggestions may help you to exploit the benefits of communications technology, not least to save your own time and energy in giving students feedback:

■ **Encourage students to send you assessments or samples of work as e-mail attachments.** If work is being produced on a computer, it is easy and quick to attach a saved file to an e-mail message. It will arrive very quickly and it is very cheap to send it.

■ **Make the most of the comfort of privacy.** When students receive feedback by e-mail (as opposed to face to face or in group situations), they have the comfort of being able to read the feedback without anyone (particularly you!) being able to see their reactions to it. This is most useful when you need to give some critical feedback to students.

■ **Remember that you can edit your own feedback before you send it.** For example, you may well want to adjust individual feedback comments in the light of students' overall performance. It is much harder to edit handwritten feedback on students' written work. E-mail feedback allows you to type in immediate feedback to things that you see in each student's work, and to adjust or delete particular parts of your feedback as you go further into marking their work.

■ **Exploit the space.** Inserting handwritten feedback comments into students' written work is limited by the amount of space that there may be for your comments. With e-mail feedback, you don't have to restrict your wording if you need to elaborate on a point.

■ | **Acknowledge receipt of assessments.** Distance students may be worried that their work has not arrived safely, so tell them when it has arrived. An e-mail message is best for this because it is private.

■ | **Provide specific feedback to individuals by e-mail.** As this method of communication is private, it is suitable for giving comments on work to individuals. It is much easier to write this kind of communication by computer than by hand, so use the technology for the whole process.

■ | **Investigate word processing software to help with assessment of written work.** If work is produced by word processing, it is often possible to add comments to it. You can use this to provide comments on the work as part of the feedback process.

■ | **Consider combining e-mail feedback with written feedback.** For example, you can write onto students' work a series of numbers or letters, at the points where you wish to give detailed feedback. The e-mail feedback can then translate these numbers or letters into feedback comments or phrases, so that students can see exactly what each element of feedback is telling them. The fact that students then have to decode each feedback element helps them to think about it more deeply, and learn from it more effectively, than when they can see the feedback directly on their work.

■ | **Spare yourself from repeated typing.** When designing computer-delivered feedback messages, you should only have to type each message once. You can then copy and paste all of the messages where you need to give several students the same feedback information. It can be useful to combine this process with numbers or letters which you write onto students' work, and build up each e-mail to individual students by pasting together the feedback messages that go with each of the numbers or letters.

■ | **Consider the possibilities of 'global' feedback messages.** For example, you may wish to give all of the students in a large group the same feedback message about overall matters arising from a test or exercise. The overall message can be pasted into each e-mail, before the individual comments addressed to each student.

■ | **Check that your e-mail feedback is getting through.** Most e-mail systems can be programmed to send you back a message saying when the e-mail was opened, and by whom. This can help you to identify any students who are not opening their e-mails. It can also be useful to end each e-mail with a question asking the student to reply to you on some point arising from the feedback. This helps to make sure that students don't just open their e-mail feedback messages, but have to read them!

■ | **Keep records of your e-mail feedback.** It is easy to keep copies on disk of all of your feedback to each student, and you can open a folder for each student if you wish. This makes it much easier to keep track of your ongoing feedback to individual students, than when your handwritten feedback is lost to you when you return their work to them.

■ **Make the most of the technology.** For example, many e-mail systems support spell-check facilities, which can allow you to type really fast and ignore most of the resulting errors, until you correct them all just before sending your message. This also causes you to reread each message, which can be very useful for encouraging you to add second thoughts which may have occurred to you as you went further in your assessment of the task.

■ **Use e-mail to gather feedback from your students.** Students are often bolder sitting at a computer terminal than they are face to face. Ask your students questions about how they are finding selected aspects of their studies, but don't turn it into an obvious routine questionnaire. Include some open-ended questions, so that they feel free to let you know how they are feeling about their own progress, and about your teaching too.

■ **Use a computer-conference to provide subtle pressure on students to submit work on time.** Publish lists of work you have received from students, but without names. This will make those who haven't submitted work realize that they could be falling behind.

■ **Create a new conference topic for discussion of each assessment.** Students may want to exchange ideas after they have received feedback on assessed work. If you provide a topic for this, they will know where to discuss this without affecting the structure of the rest of the conference.

■ **Seek permission from participants to use their work to give general feedback to the group.** If the work of one of the students includes something that you could use to illustrate a useful point to the whole group, ask their permission to use it. An e-mail message is the appropriate medium to use for this: the work could remain anonymous. Once you have permission, you can copy the appropriate sections to the conference and discuss it there.

■ **Use the conference system to provide general feedback to groups.** When assessing work, there will be common points that need to be raised for several people. If these are discussed on the group's conference without naming anybody, participants can learn from each other's mistakes.

■ **Consider putting assessment statistics on the conference.** You could make some basic information (such as average scores) available to the group. Some people might find it helpful to see how their performance compared with others in the group. On the other hand, some people might find this demoralizing, so this issue needs careful thought.

37. Keep records carefully

Keeping good records of assessment takes time, but can save time in the long run. The following suggestions may help you organize your record-keeping:

■ **Be meticulous.** However tired you are at the end of a marking session, record all the marks immediately (or indeed continuously as you go along). Then put the marks in a different place to the scripts. Then should any disasters befall you (briefcase stolen, house burned down and so on) there is the chance that you will still have the marks even if you don't have the scripts any longer (or vice versa).

■ **Be systematic.** Use class lists, when available, as the basis of your records. Otherwise make your own class lists as you go along. File all records of assessment in places where you can find them again. It is possible to spend as much time looking for missing mark-sheets as it took to do the original assessment!

■ **Use technology to produce assessment records.** Keep marks on a grid on a computer, or use a spreadsheet, and save by date as a new file every time you add to it, so you are always confident that you are working with the most recent version. Keep paper copies of each list as an insurance against disaster! Keep backup copies of disks or sheets – simply photocopying a handwritten list of marks is a valuable precaution.

■ **Use technology to save you from number-crunching.** The use of computer spreadsheet programs can allow the machine to do all of the sub-totalling, averaging and data handling for you. If you are afraid to set up a system for yourself, a computer-loving colleague or a member of the information systems support staff will be delighted to start you off.

■ **Use other people.** Some universities employ administrative staff to issue and collect in work for assessment, and to make up assessment lists and input the data into computers. Partners, friends and even young children can help you check your addition of marks, and help you record the data.

38. Reduce your burden

More and more lecturers are finding that the burden of assessment is becoming unmanageable. We offer a number of strategies below:

■ **Reduce the number of assignments.** Are all of them strictly necessary, and is it possible to combine some of them, and completely delete others?

■ **Use shorter assignments.** Often we ask for 2,000-, 3,000- or 5,000-word assignments, when a fraction of the length can be just as acceptable. Some essays or long reports could be replaced by shorter reviews, articles, memorandum-reports or summaries. Projects can be assessed by poster-displays instead of reports, and exam papers can include some sections of multiple-choice questions, particularly where these could be marked by optical mark scanners, or using computer-managed assessment directly.

- **Use assignment return sheets.** These can be pro-formas that contain the assessment criteria for an assignment, with spaces for ticks/crosses, grades, marks and brief comments. They enable rapid feedback on 'routine' assessment matters, providing more time for individual comment to students when necessary on deeper aspects of their work.

- **Consider using statement banks.** These are a means whereby your frequently repeated comments can be written once each then printed or e-mailed to students, or put onto transparencies or slides for discussion in a subsequent lecture.

- **Involve students in self- or peer-assessment.** Start small, and explain what you are doing and why. Involving students in some of their assessment can provide them with very positive learning experiences.

- **Mark some exercises in class time, using self-or peer-marking.** This is sometimes useful when students have prepared work, expecting tutor-assessment, to the standard that they wish to be seen by you.

- **Don't count all assessments.** For example, give students the option that their best five out of eight assignments will count as their coursework mark. Students satisfied with their *first* five then need not undertake the other three at all.

39. And when you still find yourself overloaded ...

No one wants to have to cope with huge piles of coursework scripts or exam papers. However, not all factors may be within your control, and you may still end up overloaded. The following wrinkles may be somewhat soothing at such times!

- **Put the great unmarked pile *under* your desk.** It is very discouraging to be continually reminded of the magnitude of the overall task. Put only a handful of scripts or assignments in sight – about as many as you might expect to deal with in about an hour.

- **Set yourself progressive targets.** Plan to accomplish a bit more at each stage than you need to. Build in safety margins. This allows you some insurance against unforeseen disasters (and children), and can allow you to gradually earn some time off as a bonus.

- **Make an even better marking scheme.** Often, it only becomes possible to make a really good marking scheme after you've found out the ways that candidates are actually answering the questions. Put the marking scheme where you can see it easily. It can be useful to paste it up with Blu-tack above your desk or table, so you don't have to rummage through your papers looking for it every time you need it.

■ **Mark in different places!** Mark at work, at home, and anywhere else that's not public. This means, of course, carrying scripts around as well as your marking scheme (or a copy of it). It does, however, avoid one place becoming so associated with doom and depression that you develop place-avoidance strategies for it!

■ **Mark one question at a time through all the scripts, at first.** This allows you to become quickly skilled at marking that question, without the agenda of all the rest of the questions on your mind. It also helps ensure reliability and objectivity of marking. When you've completely mastered your marking scheme for all questions, start marking whole scripts.

40. What lends itself to peer-assessment?

■ **Student presentations.** Peer-assessment is particularly useful for the style and process dimensions of student presentations. It can also be used for the content side of presentations, when the topics are sufficiently shared so that students are well informed enough to make judgements on the content of each other's presentations.

■ **Reports.** Peer-assessment helps to alert students to good and bad practice in report writing, and helps them develop awareness of the importance of structure, coherence and layout in reports.

■ **Essay plans.** Peer-assessment of essay plans can widen students' horizons about different ways of brainstorming the content and structure of essays. It takes almost as much creative thinking to design the content of an essay plan as it would to produce the final essay, so peer-assessing such plans helps students to cover a lot of sharing of ideas in a relatively short time.

■ **Calculations.** Peer-assessing correct answers is simple and quick. Peer-assessment allows students to identify exactly where things went wrong when marking incorrect answers, and alerts students to potential trouble spots to avoid in the future.

■ **Interviews.** Peer-assessment allows students to exchange a range of opinions, attitudes and reactions to each other's interview performance, in a less threatening way than can be the case when such performance is lecturer-assessed.

■ **Annotated bibliographies.** Peer-assessment of bibliographies can be a fast and effective way of alerting students to *other* sources of reference, which students working on their own might otherwise have overlooked.

■ **Practical work.** Peer-assessment of experimental work can allow students to receive feedback on their practical skills, when lecturer-assessment of such skills may be threatening – or not possible, for example due to limited lecturer availability when large groups of students are involved.

- **Poster-displays.** Peer-assessment of poster-displays can be a rapid way of alerting students to a wide range of approaches to the visual presentation of ideas.

- **Portfolios.** Where students are familiar with all the requirements for the successful demonstration of their achievements through portfolios, students are often highly competent in assessing each other's work, particularly if they themselves have recently undertaken a similar preparation task.

- **Exhibitions and artefacts.** Art students in particular have a long tradition of participating in critiques of each other's paintings, plans, models, garments, sculptures and so on. Students participating in 'crits' learn a lot about the level of work required, and the ways in which aesthetic judgements of work are formed within their own particular subject contexts.

41. Getting started with peer-assessment

- **Take it a bit at a time.** Some people (students and lecturers) find the use of peer-assessment very radical, so it is a good idea to introduce it gradually, on a small scale, until you, your colleagues and students are confident about how it will work best.

- **Keep everyone in the picture.** Tell everyone what you are doing and why. Students and colleagues need to understand the thinking behind what you are doing, to avoid them perceiving it as a soft option or abdication of responsibility. If they understand that peer-assessment is actually part of the learning process, they may find it more acceptable.

- **Provide mark-free rehearsal opportunities.** This helps students get the hang of what is required of them, and also builds in an opportunity for students to get interim feedback at a stage where there is time to bring about improvements.

- **Provide, or negotiate, really clear assessment criteria.** Students should not be able of over-mark friends or penalize enemies if the criteria are unambiguous and explicit. All marks should be justifiable by reference to the criteria, and to the evidence of achievement of them.

- **Make peer-assessment marks meaningful.** Some argue that peer review is really only suitable for feedback purposes. However, if students are to take peer-assessment seriously, it should count for something, even if it is only a small proportion of the final grade. You may prefer to parallel-mark, with lecturer grades counting as well as averaged peer-grades if this is appropriate.

- **Moderate peer-assessment.** To ensure that the students see peer-assessment as fair, lecturers must overview the marks awarded and provide a 'court of appeal' if students feel justice has not been done. This may mean offering vivas to any dissatisfied candidates.

- **Keep the system simple.** Try not to give yourself really complicated addition and averaging tasks to do after peer-assessment has taken place. Too many separate components make it laborious to arrive at final marks. If the numerical side can't be simplified, it is worth using computer programs to do the donkey work!

- **Involve students in the assessment criteria.** You can do this by letting students participate in the generation of assessment criteria, and the weighting to be given to each criterion. Alternatively, you can provide the criteria in the first instance, and give students lots of opportunities to ask questions about what they really mean.

- **Allow plenty of time.** Just because *you* can assess a poster-display or an essay fairly quickly doesn't mean that students will be able to do so too, especially if groups are assessing other groups and are required to provide a mark by consensus. Presentations *always* over-run, and students will tend to make snap conclusions and 'guesstimates' when under pressure regarding time.

- **Monitor student achievement.** It's a good idea to review how well students are peer-assessing, by the same kinds of methods you may use to review your own assessment, to ensure reliability and validity of marking. It is often reassuring for students (and colleagues) to see that peer-assessment using explicit criteria, and based on the production of clearly specified evidence, produces data that are very similar to marks produced by lecturers themselves.

42. Using student self-assessment to enhance their learning

There are many levels on which student self-assessment may be used, ranging from activities intended simply to promote reflective learning, to formal strategies which allow student self-assessment to count in their overall marks. The following suggestions may help you decide when to introduce elements of student self-assessment into your courses:

- **Make self-assessment an integral element of learning.** Help students to become lifelong learners who can evaluate their own performance after they have finished formal study. This is a valuable skill, which will help them in their professional careers.

- **Think of some things that no one but students can really assess.** For example, students alone can give a rating to how much effort they put into a task, how strong their motivation is in a particular subject, or how much they believe they have improved something over a period of time.

- **Give students practice at positively evaluating themselves.** For example, give them nine post-its and ask them to list nine qualities or skills they have, and get them to prioritize them in a ranking order one to nine.

■ **Emphasize the crucial relationship between criteria, evidence and self-evaluation.** Help students to learn to make balanced judgements about themselves that relate directly to the assessment criteria, by providing clear evidence of what has been achieved.

■ **Encourage the use of reflective accounts and journals, to promote self-evaluation.** By encouraging students to review their own performance regularly through journalling, they can build up a picture of their own work over a period of time.

■ **Support students in self-assessment.** Give them lots of guidance at the outset, then progressively let them take a greater degree of responsibility for their assessment as their understanding of the process matures.

■ **Help students to get to grips with assessment criteria.** Let them discuss what the criteria will mean in practice, and get them to describe exactly what sorts of performance or evidence will demonstrate achievement of the criteria.

■ **Help students to prepare for self-assessment by assessing peers.** It is often easier to make judgements about their own work when they have participated in looking critically at what others have done.

■ **Include self-assessment when assessing group process.** Frequently students are asked to peer-assess each other's contribution to group tasks. It is also feasible for them to assess realistically what they have added themselves to the process, applying the same notions of criteria and evidence as they did to their peers.

■ **Use flexible learning materials.** Most such materials include a lot of self-assessment exercises in one way or another. Usually, the primary benefit of these is not strictly self-assessment, but the delivery of feedback to students who have had a try at the exercises. However, flexible learning continuously develops students' own picture of their progress.

■ **Provide computer-based self-assessment opportunities for students.** It can help students find out a lot about how their learning is going when computer-based packages are available in a library or resource room, where they can check their knowledge in the comfort of privacy. Check out Web sites that could serve a similar purpose for your students. Such packages can also provide feedback and direction, as well as giving students a quantitative indication of the state of their learning.

■ **Provide self-assessment opportunities as diagnostic aids.** Open-learning or computer-based packages can include sets of questions designed to help students identify which sections of their work may need particular attention. The packages can also include remedial 'loops' through which students experiencing particular difficulties can be routed.

■ **Use self-assessment to establish existing competence.** Self-assessment exercises and tests can be a quick way of enabling students to establish how much of their prior learning is relevant to the prerequisite knowledge for their next course or module. This can help students avoid wasting time studying things they have already achieved well enough.

■ **Use self-assessment sometimes in lectures and tutorials.** For example, when students have brought along coursework expecting to hand it in for tutor-marking, it can be useful to lead the whole group through self-assessment against clear marking guidelines. The work can still be handed in, and it is usually much faster and easier to moderate students' own assessments than to mark the work from scratch.

■ **Use self-assessment as part of learning contracts.** When students are producing evidence specifically relating to their own learning contracts, it can be useful to ask them to self-assess how well they have demonstrated their achievement of some of their intended outcomes. One way of firming this up is to allocate some tutor-assessed marks for the quality of their own self-assessment; this also allows students to be given feedback on this.

■ **Suggest that students use video to self-assess their presentation skills informally.** Watching videotapes of their own presentations in the comfort of privacy can allow students to reflect very deeply on their skills. In fact, it is sometimes useful to suggest that students view each other's videos informally after self-assessing, to put the self-critical evaluations some students may have made of themselves into more comfortable perspective.

■ **Include self-assessment with student portfolios.** Ask students to include in their portfolios self-evaluations of their work. Reserve some of the marks for portfolios for the quality and depth of students' self-appraisal.

■ **Experiment with non-print media for self-assessment.** For example, when art students are preparing an exhibition or display, ask them to provide an interim self-critique on audiotape.

■ **Get students to self-assess added value.** Getting students to self-appraise the added value that a course or module has given them can be a useful adjunct to student feedback procedures, and helps students to put their learning into perspective in the overall context of their development.

43. Self- and peer-marking

This is the most straightforward way of involving students in their own, and each other's, assessment. Usually it does not involve a high level of moderation, since it often relies on tutor-provided correct answers, or model answers. The following suggestions may be useful:

■ **Don't give the solutions out too early.** Get students in pairs and in groups to look at their own and each other's work, and discuss among themselves what they think is right or wrong with it. Only then let them see the solutions you have provided, by which stage much learning will have taken place in the dialogue.

■ **Provide 'surgery' opportunities.** Students may well wish to interrogate your 'correct' answers. Check up on any 'almost right' solutions, and take the chance to participate in 'yes, but …' discussions. These sessions also provide chances for learning to take place.

■ **Make sure that the students can't get their hands on the answers before they have attempted the tasks.** When the answers are too easily available, it tends to demotivate students from making real attempts at finding solutions for themselves. Of course, in some contexts such as when using flexible learning materials, it may not always be possible to control the availability of answers. Then, it's worth appealing to students' better nature, saying 'You can of course cheat, but it won't help you very much in the long run.'

■ **Give students the chance to find out** *why* **they were right, as well as why they were wrong.** This multiplies the ways in which students can benefit from self- and peer-marking.

■ **Use self- or peer-marking as a rehearsal opportunity for summative assessment.** Let the students see what kinds of performance are expected of them, by giving them a practice assessment task (such as assessing answers to last year's exam papers). Let students mark themselves against the tutor-provided marking guide.

■ **Let one group of students help you to develop model answers for the next cohort.** Suitably anonymized extracts of excellent examples from the first run of an assignment can be used (with student permission) to provide varied and appropriate models against which students can measure their own achievement. (This, after all, is a process that happens informally in many cases.)

■ **Let students practise making 'standards' decisions on examples of past students' work.** Alternatively, specially composed 'examples' can be prepared for this. Ask students in groups to assign 'Pass, Merit or Distinction' (or '1st, 2:1. 2:2, 3rd) to some examples of work. Ask each group to write a short statement defending *why* each decision was reached.

■ **Allow student self-assessment before lecturer assessment sometimes.** Produce a short attachment sheet for students to fill in just before handing in some work to be tutor-marked. Ask, for example, what mark or grade they believe their work deserves, what improvements they would attempt to make if doing it again, and what they think is the best aspect of the work they are submitting.

■ **Sometimes, return tutor-marked work with feedback comments, but no marks or grades.** Write down your own mark or grade in your own records. Ask students to self-assess their work in the light of your feedback comments, and hand it in again a week later with their own marks or grades on it. Expect nine out of ten students normally to more or less agree with you! Write on your own marks at this point, and arrange one-to-one discussions with the few students where there is a significant difference between their self-assessment and your own judgement.

Feedback, evaluation and external scrutiny

This relatively short chapter addresses ways of finding out, from students themselves, how their learning experience is going.

The thrust of the first part of the chapter is to discourage undue reliance on the results derived from endless **questionnaires**!

Other ways of gathering good-quality feedback from students may be more time-consuming, but well worth the effort needed.

The chapter concludes with some thoughts on another variety of feedback on our work as lecturers – that associated with one or other forms of 'inspection' or **external scrutiny**! Some strategic suggestions are offered, and it is hoped that these will be found useful by colleagues.

Quality assurance has different names and different processes in different countries. In higher education in the UK the process is currently called 'subject review'. It uses a peer review system based on a Self-Assessment Document in which the subject team identify the aims and objectives against which their provision will be judged under six key headings:

- Curriculum Design Content and Organization,
- Teaching, Learning and Assessment,
- Student Support and Guidance,
- Student Progression and Achievement,
- Learning Resources and
- Quality Management and Enhancement.

In further education in the UK a comparable system is used, again making use of self-assessment and peer review. There are many elements of common ground between the different external scrutiny systems, and the processes that can be used to maximize the chance that such reviews will produce successful outcomes. The sections that follow give some practical suggestions based on UK experience, to help prepare for quality reviews of various kinds, the self-assessment process (upon which the quality review will be strongly based), and offer some tips for ensuring that quality is evident during the review visit.

1. Some problems with questionnaires

Decide whether or not each of the following potential problems may exist in the processes and instruments you currently use for gathering student feedback:

■ **The 'tick-box' syndrome.** People become conditioned to make instant responses to questions. Getting through the questionnaire quickly becomes a virtue. Responses are made on a surface level of thinking rather than as a result of reflection and critical thinking. (This is not a problem on those occasions where instant reaction is what is *wanted*, but the feedback we gather is not usually analyzed on that basis.)

■ **'Performing dogs' syndrome.** Many people filling in questionnaires tend to want to please! They can usually tell which responses will please the people giving them the questionnaire, and the people whose work is involved in the issues covered by the questionnaire. If they like the people, they are likely to comment favourably on things, rather than use questionnaires to show their real views.

- **Lost learning opportunities.** Questionnaires are often used after an event rather than during it. This tends to minimize any real learning outcomes of the process of completing questionnaires. The sense of ownership is reduced, when students don't see how their responses will be of any direct benefit to themselves, and may only help their successors.

- **The 'WYSIWYG' syndrome** (what you see is what you get). Questionnaires produce feedback on the particular issues covered – but often not on other important issues. There is a tendency to design questionnaires that will give positive feedback, and to avoid asking those questions where there is every possibility of critical replies.

- **'Blue, rosy and purple' questionnaires.** A major limitation of most questionnaires is that responses are coloured by how people feel at the moment of filling them in. If the same questionnaire were used a few days later, some responses might be completely different. Yet the results are often statistically analysed as though they reflected permanent, considered reactions to questions and issues, rather than fleeting, transient reactions.

- **'Conditioned response' questionnaires.** When the same questionnaire format is used repeatedly, students can become very bored, and may revert to answering many of the questions in the same way as they have often done previously. Feedback then is not specific to the particular occasion when the questionnaire is being used, and at best represents overall feelings rather than specific responses.

- **'Death by questionnaire'.** This is caused by using too many questionnaires, too often, badly designed, and with nothing ever happening as a result of the feedback that is given.

2. Some kinds of structured questions

- **Experiment with ticking boxes or putting marks on scales.** This can be done with contrasting dimensions at opposite sides of a form, such as:

  interesting .... boring
  too fast .... too slow
  approachable .... unapproachable

- **Try out 'Usefulness' measures.** Various dimensions can be mentioned at the left-hand side, with boxes for 'very useful' 'quite useful', 'not useful' to tick. The dimensions can include such things as handout materials, visual aids and worked examples done in class.

■ | **Explore 'agreement' measures.** A series of statements can be checked against boxes such as 'strongly agree', 'more or less agree', 'disagree', 'strongly disagree', for example. The statements can usefully be both positive and negative, to ensure that respondents don't fall into the pattern of agreeing (or disagreeing) with everything they see. Typical statements can be along the lines:

  - 'I find your lectures usually stimulate me to further work'
  - 'I remain switched off for most of my time in your lectures'
  - 'I am clear about the intended learning outcomes of each part of this module'
  - 'I don't really know what is expected of me in this subject'

■ | **Try out number-gradings.** Here students can be asked to enter numbers to indicate their feelings with regard to a statement or an issue, for example: 5 = most useful, 4 = very useful, 3 = quite useful, 2 = of limited use, 1 = of little use, 0 = of no use.

■ | **Explore 'More', 'Just right', 'Less' boxes.** These could be used (for example) for students to record their feelings about the things they do in tutorials, for example:

  - practising problem solving;
  - seeing worked examples done;
  - working through case study materials;
  - asking questions of the lecturer;
  - being asked questions by the lecturer;
  - having marked homework discussed individually;
  - having marked practical work returned and discussed;
  - seeing examples of assessment criteria;
  - using assessment criteria directly to mark own (or others') work;
  - practising addressing previous exam questions.

■ | **Get students prioritizing.** This sort of structure helps overcome the 'tick-box' syndrome, as it causes students to think more deeply about issues. For example, they can be asked to enter '1' against the best feature of Dr Smith's classes, '2' against the next-best, and so on... Questions and choices need to be clear and unambiguous.

3. Some ideas for open questions

Open questions allow each student to respond freely to set areas. While such questions can overcome some of the limitations we have mentioned regarding structured questions, the fact that students are entering their responses in their own handwriting can be a deterrent against them expressing negative or critical views, where they may feel that they could be traced and maybe even penalized as a result. The following examples illustrate open questions most often used in questionnaires.

The two most useful features of your lectures are:

1:

2:

The two least useful features of your lectures are:

1:

2:

Suggestions for improvement:

The three topics I found most difficult to make sense of in this module are:

1:

2:

3:

4. Some ways of using questionnaires

■ **Consider making the use of questionnaires private to individual members of staff.** For feedback about lectures (or tutorials, or lab work) we think it best that each lecturer designs and uses his or her individual questionnaire, and obtains feedback for his or her own use privately. This doesn't mean, however, that the forms are to be filled in 'privately' by students – it may well be better to use them as an agenda for group feedback.

■ **Make questionnaires 'short and often, not long and once'.** Any feedback form should be short enough not to bore or alienate students. A good guide may be that it should be possible for a group to complete the form in a few minutes or so. This means separate forms for lectures, tutorials and so on.

- **Use questionnaires for formative rather than summative feedback whenever possible.** Seek feedback during a programme, so that something can still be done about matters emerging. Feedback after completion of a programme is still useful, but is not seen by students as so valuable as when they have the chance to suggest changes they themselves will benefit from directly.

- **Employ questionnaires for a wide range of matters to do with our presentation, style and approachability.** These aspects of, for example, lecturing can be gathered in the private mode suggested above. Individual questionnaire components can be selected/composed by each staff member to search for comment about issues that may be of particular concern to the lecturer concerned.

- **Consider 'more public' questionnaires for general issues, and for summative feedback.** These can be used to measure feedback relating to non-personal variables, for example:

  - relative workload of different topics or modules;
  - perceived relevance of topics, as seen by students;
  - relevance of practical work to theory, as seen by students;
  - balance of lectures, tutorials, and other teaching/learning situations.

  The 'more public' sort of questionnaire is more likely to have value when used towards the end of a course or module, and to gather summative feedback, which can be used in reviewing the course or module prior to the next time it will be delivered.

- **Structured questionnaires can have the advantage of anonymity.** Even if using a mixed questionnaire containing open-ended questions as well, you may decide to issue the structured and open-ended parts separately because of this factor.

- **Try to avoid surface thinking.** Students – and anyone else involved – get bored if they have long questionnaires to complete, and the decisions or comments they make become 'surface' rather than considered ones. Even though students may be able to respond to a structured questionnaire of several pages in relatively few minutes, the fact that a questionnaire *looks* long can induce surface response behaviour.

- **Consider the visual appearance of your questionnaires.** Go for a varied layout, with plenty of white space, so that it does not look like a solid list of questions. Use a mixture of response formats, such as deletions or selections from lists of options, yes/no choices, tick-boxes, graduated scales, and so on – make it *look* interesting to complete.

- **For every part of the questionnaire, have definite purposes, including positive ones.** Don't ask anything that could prove to be superfluous or of passing interest only. Ask about positive experiences as well as searching for weaknesses.

- **Plan your evaluation report before you design your feedback questionnaire.** It helps a great deal if you know exactly how you plan to collate and use the responses you will get from your questionnaires. Working out the things you hope to include in your report often alerts you to additional questions you may need to include, and (particularly) to superfluous questions which would not actually generate any information of practical use to you.

- **Make each question simple and unambiguous.** If students' interpretations of the questions vary, the results of a survey are not valid enough to warrant statistical analysis of any sort. In particular, it's worth ensuring that in structured questions, students are only required to make decisions involving a single factor.

- **Ask yourself 'what does this question really mean?'.** Sometimes, your reply to yourself will contain wording that will work better in your questionnaire than the original idea you started with.

- **Avoid safe middle ground in scales.** For example, the scale 'strongly agree, agree, undecided, disagree, strongly disagree' may give better results if the 'undecided' option is omitted, forcing respondents to make a decision one way or the other (or to *write* 'can't tell' on the questionnaire, which then has the validity of a conscious decision).

- **Be aware that some respondents will make choices on the basis of those they think they are expected to make.** Many respondents set out to 'please' the person gathering the feedback, possibly thinking of possible recriminations if critical selections may be traced back to their authors.

- **Keep prioritizing questions short and simple.** For example, if students are asked to rank seven factors in order of value (or importance), it may be easy enough to analyse the best and worst choices, but difficult to make a meaningful analysis of 'middle ground'.

- **Pilot your draft questionnaire.** There is no better way to improve a structured questionnaire than to find out what students actually do with it! Use short print runs for questionnaires, and edit between each use.

- **Feed back the results to your respondents.** Tell them about the changes that are proposed on the basis of the results from the questionnaire. Otherwise people are likely to become disillusioned about the whole process of giving feedback.

5. Designing open feedback questionnaires

Most questionnaires use a balance of structured and open-ended questions. The suggestions below may help you get the most from students' responses to open-ended questions in questionnaires:

■ **Include some questions that aren't too open!** For example, when seeking feedback about the most successful and least successful features of a course, make your forthcoming evaluation of students' responses simpler by making each question already relate to particular aspects of the course.

■ **Remember that students' responses can be influenced by their mood at the moment of answering the question.** Ideally, you may wish to balance this source of variation out in one way or another, for example by issuing a similar questionnaire at another time, and comparing responses, or by including some alternative questions in other parts of your questionnaire which 'test' the same agenda, so you can be alerted to inconsistency in responses due to swings of mood.

■ **Don't leave big spaces for students to fill in their replies.** You can compensate for this restriction later with 'any other comments?' space. If students' responses are necessarily short, you are more likely to get easily interpreted answers to your questions, which helps make statistical analysis more fruitful.

■ **Decide whether you want the questionnaire to be anonymous, optional, or respondent-known.** With responses involving handwriting, there is always the possibility of tracing respondents, and students may respond differently with this possibility in mind. With computer-based open-ended questionnaires, this dimension is simplified, but not entirely overcome if log-in data could be used to trace respondents.

■ **Resist pressures to overuse standard questionnaires.** This applies equally to structured or open-ended versions or mixed-mode questionnaires. Students quickly get bored with identical questionnaires, and are likely to fall into a standard mode of response, where there is considerable 'echo effect' carried forward from previous decisions and responses. The most useful feedback data is normally generated by specially produced questionnaires relating to a specific course or subject, or a particular aspect of the teaching and learning in that subject.

■ **Try to get a good response rate.** When questionnaires are filled in during contact time, you are more likely to get everyone's views. If questionnaires are taken away by students to be sent back later, there is a tendency to get lower response rates, and the students who actually go to the trouble of responding may not be representative of the whole group.

■ **Give students some free-ranging questions.** For example, it's worth considering asking them 'What other questions should be included in future editions of this questionnaire?' and inviting them to supply their own answers to the questions they think of. Such data is unsuitable for any statistical purposes, but is valuable in qualitative analysis of feedback from students.

■ **If doing a survey by post, supply a stamped, addressed envelope.** This is a significant 'psychological persuader' in encouraging people to respond to questionnaires. It is a way of indicating that responses are indeed valued. Even where internal mail facilities can be used, an addressed reply envelope helps in this respect.

■ **Work out how you are going to analyse the data from open-ended questions.** Sometimes a transcript collecting all responses to a question is necessary before the gist of the feedback can be discerned accurately. In other circumstances, counting the number of times something is mentioned in students' responses can be a valuable process.

■ **Don't accumulate piles of uninterpreted questionnaire data!** It's best to make a deliberate effort to produce a summary report (even if only for your own private use) for each set of data. A pile of feedback responses quickly becomes out of date as new developments are implemented in courses. Also, it is worth showing the respondents that you take the data seriously enough to analyse it straightaway.

6. Feedback from interviews with students

Interviews with students can be a valuable source of feedback. However, interviewing students is costly in terms of time and effort; the following suggestions may help you to make it a cost-effective process:

■ **Prepare your agenda carefully.** To enable you to analyse and collate the feedback you get from students, it is important that they are all asked the same questions in the same way. It is all too tempting to develop the agenda on the basis of the replies of the first few students, so it is usually worth piloting your question list on a few students (not necessarily from the group to be targeted) before starting on a set of 'real' interviews'

■ **Link interviews with other means of getting feedback from students.** If you are already using (or planning to use) structured or open-ended questionnaires, you may find it worthwhile to work out what *else* you will be particularly looking for in feedback from interviews.

■ **Consider the merits of using interviews to follow up questionnaire feedback.** When you have already analysed questionnaire responses by students, you may be able to pinpoint a few issues where you want to ask students more detailed or more personal questions about their experiences with a subject or a course.

■ **Consider the alternative possibility of using preliminary interviews to establish the agenda for feedback questionnaires.** This would probably not take the form of interviews with the whole group, but with a representative selection of students.

■ **You may not be able to interview the whole group.** Decide how you are going to select the students you choose to interview. There are many possibilities, each with its own advantages and drawbacks. For example, you could select randomly by name or student number, or you could make a representative selection including high-performers, middle-range performers and low-achievers in related assessments, or you could ask for volunteers (not, however, the most representative of the possibilities).

■ **Remember that students may be anxious.** Any kind of interview may feel to students as if there is an assessment dimension present, and this may cause them to be restrained, especially when it comes to expressing dissatisfaction.

■ **Ask questions that lead students to answer rather than to refrain from comment.** For example, asking students 'Was there anything you found unsatisfactory?' may be less fruitful than asking 'What was the thing you liked least about the way this module was taught?'.

■ **Don't lead your witnesses!** It is one thing to ensure that students feel free to answer questions, but another to lead them towards the answers you want, or the answers they may think you want. 'Do you like the way I used coloured overheads in my lectures?' is an obvious example of a leading question!

■ **It's essential to make good notes!** After four or five interviews, you may have a good idea of the general nature of responses to your questions, but you could have lost a lot of the specific detail. More recent interview happenings tend to 'drown' earlier ones in one's memory.

7. Feedback from groups of students

Students may be more forthcoming in a group, and you could consider posing the questions (maybe as a handout), leaving the group to come to decisions about how the students wished to answer them, then return to hear their answers. Students have the safety of being able to report minority views or controversial views, without the student who actually speaks such responses having to 'own' the view reported. Group interviews can actually save a considerable amount of time compared to solo interviews, and allow students to compare and contrast their own perspectives. Students in groups can also be helped to prioritize or sequence in order of importance their responses, making their feedback even more valuable. Group interviews can also be used to get students to clarify or explain issues or responses that at first may be unclear.

This can be more useful than feedback from individuals, for the following reasons:

■ **Feedback from groups captures discussion, reflection and debate.** This is more useful than only having the reactions of individual students.

■ **A group can present negative feedback with less embarrassment than an individual.** Individuals can be more forthcoming in making inputs in a group, when their feedback is then rendered more or less anonymous within the group.

■ **Group feedback is likely to range more widely.** Where a questionnaire is used as an agenda for group feedback, the group is more likely to be willing to go beyond the agenda.

8. Using the nominal group technique to elicit feedback

This is essentially a process for surveying the views of a group of students. The following account is modified with permission from work by Tony Claydon of the University of Northumbria at Newcastle. The technique:

> provides a means of collecting quickly a lot of information from students;
> is tightly structured and controlled by the facilitator, and limits student–student interaction;
> provides students with equal opportunities to participate.

Some of the advantages claimed for the nominal group technique are that it:

> enables a wide range and large number of issues to emerge;
> enables individual students to make their views public within the group, and so build upon each other's ideas. It is important that the facilitator guarantees anonymity of responses from the group, so that whatever is said there by any individual is not revealed outside;
> provides equal opportunities for students regardless of their relative status or tendency to dominate discussion elsewhere;
> enables a clear overview of responses to be provided without one or two individuals skewing the outcomes.

The technique can be structured into a series of steps as presented below. However, it is worth exploring in advance the implications of each of the steps before deciding on the exact way you may employ the technique:

- **Introduce the technique to students.** Outline its purpose in the specific context, and its structure.

- **Set the task to be undertaken, or the issue to be addressed.** This technique particularly lends itself to the making of decisions about courses and programmes, and the acquisition of feedback from students. In the first case, students may be invited to state which subjects from a number of possibilities they would like to see included in part of a course or programme. In the second case, they may be asked to identify the strengths and weaknesses of the course or programme as they perceive it.

- **Give individuals time to think, and to write down their views.** For example, when evaluating a programme, students might be asked individually to write down five strengths and five weaknesses in around 10–15 minutes. Views are best expressed in short pithy phrases. Students at this stage are asked not to discuss their views.

- **Collect students' views, and display them, preferably on flipchart paper.** In order to give students equal opportunities to participate, their views can be obtained in a series of rounds in which each student is asked in turn for an opinion or a brief statement. This is then written up and displayed by the facilitator. Students' own words should be used as far as is practicable. Each item written up should be numbered for ease of reference later. No evaluative comments should be allowed to enter at this stage.

- **Continue rounds until all student views have been recorded.** This stage typically takes between 30 and 45 minutes. The facilitator should not add any items to the list, nor fail to record any item unless the ground rules on which the group is working specifically include a decision not to record sexist or racist views.

- **Be careful about naming names.** If views are being collected regarding a programme, the facilitator should clarify at the outset whether the ground rules will permit students to name any particular teachers about whom they have any comments, or whether they should restrict themselves to more general terms.

- **Check each statement for clarity.** Students are invited to ask for clarification of each other's statements, and where there is any doubt, the proposer of any statement should be aided to express it more clearly.

- **Scrutinize the list for overlap or duplication.** Some items may be obvious duplicates, in which case all but one may be eliminated. Other items may overlap, in which case a more precise form of words might be sought, to distinguish one view from another. It is possible that students will have conflicting views as to whether items overlap or not. If this is the case, it is probably advisable to leave the original words intact if a consensus is not readily obtainable.

- **Invite the students to express their preferences.** Each student is asked to select from the main list perhaps five or six items that seem to be most important or convincing, and to record them. Students should be able to use the numbering system as a kind of shorthand. Once they have done this, students are then asked to hand in their preference lists for analysis.

- **Summarize students' views, and provide time for them to be discussed.** If views have been collected on the strengths and weaknesses of a programme, later discussion might appropriately centre on ways of building on the strengths, and minimizing the weaknesses.

- **Consider how the resulting information might be used, and to whom it might be distributed.** Student feedback on programmes might be highly sensitive, and individual members of staff whose work has been criticized by students may feel hurt and unjustly treated, especially since the technique provides them with no opportunities to respond.

- **Consider whether an outsider may be needed.** It is frequently the case that, although individual teachers may be criticized directly or otherwise by some members of student groups, such views do not figure significantly in the final list, reflecting more accurately the common views of the group. Even so, it is advisable to use a neutral colleague, perhaps from another department, to conduct a nominal group technique in your department if the aim is to have students evaluate your programme.

■ **Review whether the technique is entirely appropriate to the feedback that emerges.** Clearly, the nominal group technique is not suitable when students need to debate issues, critically analyse arguments, and justify their opinions. Also, the nominal group technique is best used sparingly, since its tight structure, although initially attractive to students, might become frustrating with repetition.

9. Establishing a culture of student feedback

'Not another questionnaire', we often hear students groan! With the fragmentation produced by modularization and semesterization, there is the danger that students become snowed under by a plethora of separate questionnaires on each and every aspect of their experience. The following suggestions may help the right balance to be achieved:

■ **Contribute to an institutional strategy for student feedback.** This does not mean that there should be uniformity in every department; appropriate feedback devices may be very different in programmes as diverse or distinctive as humanities and engineering. However, an institutional strategy does mean that someone has thought about the overall implications of the various possible options.

■ **Obtain the big picture first.** It is dangerously easy for feedback to be collected about the nuts and bolts, but not about the whole engine. The following questions should be asked: 'For what overall purposes are we seeking student feedback?' and 'How do we intend to use the overall data?'

■ **Undertake an audit of current feedback practice.** In our increasingly busy institutions, it is often difficult to know what someone is doing in the next office. Finding out what is happening at local and institutional level can help to clarify thinking, and be the basis for disseminating best practice.

■ **Involve everyone in the design of student feedback processes and instruments.** Colleagues may have employed successfully their own feedback mechanisms for many years, and it is important to value their experience, and avoid replacing something that was going well with something less effective.

■ **Involve students in discussions about a culture for gathering and addressing their feedback.** Students know what works for them, and what causes them problems. Sometimes staff may not be aware of the 'big picture' problems, while students can be very good at suggesting ways to identify and quantify such issues.

■ **Work closely with the Students' Union.** Officers of the Union have a wealth of experience of working with, and listening to, students. Joint meetings about feedback processes and instruments can help to focus on important issues, and can lead to Union encouragement to students to participate fully in giving feedback.

■ **Variety is the spice of life!** Each of the many methods available for collecting student feedback has its advantages and disadvantages. Using a variety of methods can help to ensure that a much fuller picture is obtained, and that students don't become irritated by the monotony of giving the same sorts of feedback again and again.

■ **Close the feedback-quality loop.** Students want to know what has happened as a result of their comments, and the reasons for any decisions that result. Create ways of reporting back to staff and students changes that are being implemented as a result of feedback.

■ **Evaluate your institution's feedback systems.** It is useful to triangulate information about how well feedback is working, by comparing findings about it from teaching staff, students and support staff.

■ **Don't forget the good points!** It is very easy to focus actions on the negative feedback that may be gathered, and the 'could do better' agendas. The 'well done' agenda is just as important, and it helps to recognize and celebrate those responsible for positive feedback, and build on such strengths.

10. Feedback from student representatives

Most institutions have policies on student representation on decision-making committees and boards. Student representation is, however, not without its problems. The following suggestions may help you to make the most of having student reps on committees:

■ **Try to ensure that the right person is chosen to represent student views.** Too often, the duty is thrust upon the first student who shows interest, or who is too polite to refuse! It can be worth allowing a class a period of time in which to choose who will represent them, and providing some contact time to discuss what is involved, and maybe to facilitate a ballot or election.

■ **Remember that the student(s) chosen may be somewhat in awe of the Committee.** Students can feel uncomfortable in a gathering of so many highly qualified academics, and this can lead them to be observers rather than true participants in the processes of meetings.

■ **Take care when putting student representatives 'on the spot'.** They won't necessarily be able to speak at once on behalf of their classmates. They may be able to give their own personal views (which of course are valuable in their own right), but you may need to allow them time to find out the opinion of their colleagues before reporting back to a future meeting of the Committee or Board.

■ **Allow student representatives to contribute to the agenda-forming process.** When they are given time to supply suggestions for the agenda of a future meeting, they have the chance to discuss the matter with fellow students, and the ownership of the representation is duly enhanced.

■ **Be prepared to give student representatives responsibilities for researching particular views of their classmates.** It is important that this does not become burdensome to them. It helps, however, when they have definite purposes underpinning each stage of their liaison with their fellow students. Student reps can, for example, have more success at getting a good response rate from a questionnaire to the class, especially if entrusted and briefed to make their own preliminary analysis of the findings *before* giving in the completed questionnaires.

■ **Treat student representatives as full committee members.** This means (for example) ensuring that they receive 'Notice of Meetings', agendas, and minutes in the same ways as academic members of the committee. They should also feel at liberty to show any of the documentation to fellow students.

■ **Make sure student reps' comments and contributions are minuted accurately.** Even if they make controversial comments, the fact that they *are* being minuted acts as an appropriate restraining process. Also, this helps the student reps themselves prove to the students they are representing that they have indeed followed through matters at the Committee.

■ **Don't cut student reps off in mid-flow!** It may have taken them considerable courage (maybe backed by substantial preparation or research) before they make an impassioned plea or complaint or suggestion. Courtesy demands that they are given at least as much chance to have their say as anyone else.

■ **Don't let student reps become overburdened with duties and commitments.** Remember that they are also studying, and it is tragic if their studies suffer significantly as a result of the energies and time they put into representing fellow students.

■ **Consider ways in which student reps may gain academic credit for their role.** For example, this could be done as a project module in an independent studies pathway. Many Student Union branches are looking at accreditation of the student representative role. Alternatively, consider finding ways of including the service of student reps in student profiles or records of achievement.

■ **Remember to thank student representatives for their time and their work.** It is important that they feel that their role is valued, and not just a ritual for appearance's sake. As well as verbal appreciation at meetings, it is worth sending each student representative an official 'thank you' letter when terms of office are completed.

11. Preparing for quality visits

■ | **Recognize the importance of making sufficient time available for preparation.** It's all too easy to be so busy with everyday matters that it's tempting to take the attitude 'They'll just have to take us as they find us.' Sound preparation pays dividends in terms of both staff confidence and good outcomes.

■ | **Prepare well in advance.** It's never too early to start. As soon as you get advance warning of your dates, devise a strategy and action plans, working out target dates for each major task, and spreading responsibilities in ways that help to ensure that staff take on ownership of the processes.

■ | **Don't grumble about 'waste of time'.** Try instead to see review as a chance to overhaul your teaching programmes. While it is natural (and often justified) to complain about valuable time being taken away from teaching and research, both could be damaged even more by the effects of quality being found to be lacking. Various studies on QAA review have emphasized the long-term benefits that have accrued to involvement in a process that foregrounds teaching, learning and assessment.

■ | **Regard review as an ongoing process, not a one-off event!** When the sorts of actions that are involved in preparing for quality visits are not special, but are part of the normal day-to-day life of an institution, the distance between 'where you are' and 'where you want to be seen to have reached' is narrowed continuously, and the anxiety that can be caused by an impending spotlight is reduced.

■ | **Raise consciousness of all categories of staff about the process.** Don't assume review only involves academic staff. It requires a team effort right from the start, including everyone from porters to senior management. Different kinds of briefing may be appropriate, so everyone knows what is expected of them. Don't forget to keep people informed and updated throughout the process.

■ | **Work from the outset at getting the statistical information as accurate as possible.** In most institutions, you will not just be able to rely on centrally collected data, which is rarely completely accurate at a local level. Use standard procedures to provide statistical information where these exist, but check and double check these against staff perceptions. Remember too that it is normally possible to provide statistical updates close to the visit, so you can present the most accurate picture possible based on live data.

■ | **Think about how best to present your statistical information.** UK systems with tight word counts and restrictions on available pages mean that statistics need to be accurate, self-explanatory and well presented. Flow diagrams and charts can be more effectively used to represent student progression data, for example, than mere description.

■ **Promote peer observation and review well in advance of the visit.** Teaching staff may feel very apprehensive about being observed teaching and may need practice if they are to be confident under external scrutiny. Set up support groups and encourage discussion of the advantages of peer observation. Instituting peer-observation cells can be really beneficial, particularly if staff involved are trained to make it part of routine enhancement activities, not something just set up prior to the visit.

■ **Make full use of people with experience of your kind of external review.** In large universities and colleges, there are likely to be colleagues who have been involved in previous subject reviews, or who are trained assessors with experience of review elsewhere. They are far too valuable to waste and can be co-opted to comment on draft Self-Assessment Documents, take part in staff briefing sessions and to help run rehearsals, all aimed at helping teams present themselves in the best possible light.

■ **Nominate your own staff to be involved in the review process nationally**. Many have reported that subject groups which have the benefit of having trained assessors among their number tend to have a better understanding of the process and tend to do better than those in which staff stand aloof from the process. It's a good idea to get insider knowledge by participation.

■ **Make use of external expertise**. In institutions where there is no experience of external scrutiny, for example mono-disciplinary colleges, or where there are no trained reviewers on the staff, bring in outsiders to brief staff and help to prepare for review.

■ **Avoid complacency based on past success.** Even if past reviews in your subject or institution have resulted in very positive outcomes, the next round will almost certainly involve different people and a new process, since the way in which review is undertaken is being continuously modified.

■ **Avoid despair based on previous failures!** Even when a previous review has been traumatic, this does not necessarily mean that the next one will be a disaster. Many things are likely to have improved since that time, and because this can happen gradually, the home team may not be aware of the scale of the advances made.

■ **Work with your team on developing a collaborative approach.** When colleagues are pulling together constructively, the impression they create is always much more favourable than when there are conflicting attitudes and approaches in an institution. It is important that everyone feels part of the team, and that there isn't a top-down ethos where colleagues may lose any sense of ownership of their responsibility for ensuring that the outcomes are favourable.

■ **Involve students in preparations at a very early stage**. They are important partners and need to be consulted on the self-assessment documentation, for example. If students don't recognize the subject provision as described in the paperwork, they may not support staff with the right kinds of comments when reviewers talk to them. That is not to say they need coaching before a visit, but they do need careful briefing.

■ **Use external scrutiny as a lever to ensure improvement to the learning environment.** In some institutions, Estates Services departments target funding on areas about to undergo external scrutiny and this is often a good chance for teams to negotiate to upgrade the teaching accommodation. In addition, teams can do a lot themselves to produce a good impression. Clutter can be disposed of in classrooms and staff work-rooms, student work can be displayed on walls and in corridors and relevant posters and pictures can be hung to soften the atmosphere.

■ **Make use of the documentation provided for you about the external scrutiny process.** Make sure you and all staff have access to the relevant and up-to-date handbook and analyse it carefully to make sure you have all bases covered.

■ **Do your research on the process.** Read past overview reports, which are available for example in the UK on the World Wide Web. Look for areas that have excited comment in previous review rounds and make sure that any gaps and problems identified do not recur in your own subject provision.

■ **Do your research on your external scrutineers.** Once you have the names of the team who will visit you, check out their CVs so you have an idea of their areas of interest. It's not a bad idea, if they have publications themselves on areas you teach, to make sure these are available and prominently displayed in the library and on reading lists if they are relevant to your students.

■ **Don't get the whole process out of proportion.** It is unwise to have endless, long meetings about preparing for a visit so far in advance of the visit that staff get sick of the process before it looms close. Frequent very short meetings at regular intervals throughout the preparation period work better, especially when they identify responsibility and lead to action. Make sure each meeting has a small but definite purpose, rather than having meetings with so much on the agenda that nothing actually gets achieved.

■ **Distinguish between the 'urgent' and the 'important'.** Not everything that seems urgent is important, and not everything that is important is urgent! When creating the agenda for decisions to be made in preparation for the visit, make sure that the important issues get a fair hearing.

■ **Don't try to solve every problem overnight!** External scrutineers expect there to be some problematic areas and get suspicious if none are apparent. It is far better, once problems have been identified, to be relatively open about them, but to be able to demonstrate that an action plan has been devised to address it.

■ **Make good use of briefings and rehearsals.** It is said that 75 per cent of the success of an event is achieved before the arrival of the visiting reviewers. Brief students, former students, employers, and all categories of staff who are likely to come into contact with the externals. Don't give them a pre-prepared script, but do provide guidance on the importance of the visit, and use briefings to try to identify in advance what issues are likely to arise, so that you can have in place strategies to combat difficulties.

12. Writing a Self-Assessment Document

The UK system of quality assessment requires subject groups which are to have the quality of their teaching and learning reviewed to produce a Self-Assessment Document (SAD) outlining the nature of the curriculum provision. This provides the basis for a quality assessment visit by a team of reviewers, who judge the provision against what is claimed in the SAD. The following tips are designed to help departments about to be reviewed to write such a document effectively:

- **Think carefully about the picture you want to paint of your department.** The Self-Assessment Document provides an opportunity for departments to make a case for what they do. In a strictly prescribed format, it enables those who know best the courses and modules being assessed to provide a basis for evaluation. Assessment is made against the institution's own aims and objectives.

- **Remember that the Self-Assessment Document will set the agenda for the visit.** Whatever you claim will provide the framework of what quality reviewers will review. They are likely to look for gaps, inconsistencies, problems and places where key issues are raised.

- **Self-assessment should be analytical.** The aim is not just to provide a narrative account of a department's achievements, but to portray an actively self-critical and self-improving process rather than one that is complacent, static or unaware. A self-assessment that implies there are no problems will not look credible.

- **Start data collection early.** Writing the necessary documentation can be a gruelling task and one of the biggest jobs can be actually locating all the figures and information needed. Use existing data wherever possible as a basis for the document, but don't assume that centrally provided figures will be accurate at a local level.

- **Aim to write very concisely**. Be prepared to be very selective about what you include and use tables and graphs in the annexes where possible, to cover detail that cannot be fitted into the word count.

- **Stick to the guidelines.** Do not exceed (or undershoot) the word length as the documentation will be sent back for revision if you do not adhere strictly to the guidelines.

- **Make sure aims and objectives are really clear.** If objectives are not written in terms of what students will achieve by the end of a programme, they will be rejected.

- **Consider getting help before starting to assemble the paperwork.** Your own institution's Quality Enhancement Unit, or Educational Development Service (or equivalent) may have considerable experience in helping people prepare for quality assessment. Alternatively, it can be well worth bringing in people with relevant experience from outside the institution.

■ **Don't give the task of preparing the Self-Assessment Document to one person alone.** An individual is likely to be too close to the task and may not be able to have a clear overview. A working group with shared responsibilities and duties is best suited to the task.

■ **Get feedback on the document throughout its development.** The more people you can involve in polishing and tuning (but not lengthening!) the Self-Assessment Document, the less likely it is that you will be surprised or dismayed by the reactions of the document's intended recipients in due course. Seek feedback from colleagues, student reps, and employers where relevant.

■ **Let one person have final responsibility for the ultimate version of the document.** One person needs to ensure a single authorial voice throughout the document.

■ **Use someone outside the preparation process to review your documentation once it is written.** Brief this person to look for areas that are not fully explained or documented. Remedy them if possible within the limits of space in the documentation or note them carefully to help you prepare for questioning on the day of the visit.

■ **Make sure that the documentation is impeccably produced.** Typographical errors, poor layout and discontinuities will all give a poor impression of the department even before the quality reviewers visit.

■ **Be aware that reviewers will have available to them documentation other than the self-assessment.** All data published by the institution is likely to be scrutinized by the reviewers. It is therefore important that they are not faced with contradictory claims.

■ **Start with the mission statement of your institution.** Whatever your institution claims to be and do should be reflected in your Self-Assessment Document. This can provide difficulties when there is a published mission statement that is unwieldy or imprecise, but it should provide your starting point. Quality reviewers are not in the business of judging mission statements: their task is to judge how well these have been interpreted locally into teaching and learning provision.

■ **Make clear links between the different elements of the documentation.** It should be possible to see how the institution's mission statement, subject rationale, subject aims, subject objectives, course aims and course objectives all link together. These in turn should link to session aims and learning outcomes when individual classes are observed.

■ **Define your subject rationale.** This is likely to be fairly brief and should clearly articulate the reasons why the subject is being taught here and in this particular context. If the rationale doesn't address all aspects of the mission (as, indeed, it often would not be expected to do) you should clarify why this is the case.

■ **Define your subject aims.** These should be a statement of the broad direction to be taken in the teaching and learning process which is directly linked into the module/course/programme rationale. Aims are usually expressed in terms of the sorts of abilities, knowledge and attitudes that can normally be expected of a student who successfully completes a course of study in this area.

■ **Outline your subject learning outcomes.** These tend to be more specific and tend to be closely linked to separate components of the teaching and learning experience. They relate to the acquisition of knowledge, development of understanding, conceptual, intellectual and subject-specific skills, the development of generic transferable skills, the development of values, of motivation and positive attitudes to learning.

■ **Link these to your course aims and outcomes.** It should be evident in your documentation that the mission, rationale, aims and objectives of the institution and department are clearly translated into what you actually teach and assess. Inevitably there will be overlap between course and subject aims and objectives, so care will be needed in the writing of them so that there isn't repetition.

■ **Draw clear links between learning outcomes and assessment processes and instruments.** Quality reviewers will need to be able to see clearly how you assess whether students have achieved what you claim they will. Discrepancies between the teaching and learning processes and the ways in which they are assessed will be unhelpful to your case.

■ **Identify and assess what is distinctive about your subject.** If you claim in your documentation, for example, that you have a distinctive international focus for your teaching, this should be clearly evidenced in the curriculum as well as the prospectus.

■ **Provide profiles of staff and students and information about learning resources available.** These can be supported by tables, graphs and other data in the annexes at the end of the document.

■ **Evaluate the quality of your educational provision.** The six aspects of provision that the UK higher education system requires to be covered are:

    Curriculum Design Content and Organization,
    Teaching, Learning and Assessment,
    Student Support and Guidance,
    Student Progression and Achievement,
    Learning Resources,
    Quality Management and Enhancement.

■ **Provide documentary evidence of your achievements.** It isn't enough merely to claim that your teaching in the department is underpinned by world-class research. Evidence for this should be provided in the form of specific examples. You can also provide employment statistics, student and employer feedback and so on.

■ **Provide in annexes additional material required.** Guidance on these is also given in the QAA Handbook. Annexes are likely to include statistical indicators, the structure of the provision, details of modular schemes where applicable, information about partnerships of various kinds and so on. Don't send extraneous material that is not asked for.

■ **Don't try to hide the problems.** By the time quality reviewers have read all your documentation and talked to staff and students they are likely to have a clear idea of anything that might be going wrong in your department, so it is futile to pretend problems don't exist.

■ **State clearly what you plan to do about any areas of difficulty.** Quality reviewers are likely to be more impressed by proposals of action to be taken on problem issues and areas of difficulty than by head in the sand attitudes that ignore difficult areas.

13. Preparing for the week of the visit

The following suggestions may help make a quality visit go that little bit more smoothly, and can certainly make the visitors feel more welcome:

■ **Prepare the base rooms.** A welcoming, well-equipped base room for the reviewers will certainly help. It needs to be private, well stocked with drinks (hot and cold) and snacks. Such a room needs a telephone, computer, e-mail facilities, printer, photocopier, surfaces to write on, boxes with the information to peruse, and space to lay out samples of students' work.

■ **Look after creature comforts.** Make sure their base room is warm enough in winter or well ventilated (or air-conditioned) in summer. Make sure their travel arrangements home are catered for (have timetables and taxi numbers to hand).

■ **Plan for emergencies.** Such things as train strikes, go-slows, broken lifts, ill relatives and headaches can all disrupt a visit. All these are traumatic – almost as much as a photocopier that breaks down! Check whether any other special events are happening on the day. Make arrangements to cover equipment failures and so on.

■ **Keep the channels of communication going.** Events can change suddenly – be prepared for this. You may need to reschedule staff because of changing circumstances. The reviewers may realize that they have sufficient information on a topic and wish to change the focus. Additional paper information may be sought, or a request made to interview a particular member of staff.

■ **Offer a support mechanism.** Occasionally things may not go according to plan. Someone may feel unwell but struggle on. A lecture may go badly or students may be unusually quiet. A sympathetic ear and a strong cup of tea may do the trick.

■ **Make sure that internal visits run smoothly.** Plan so that subject reviewers' visits to the library, IT centre, educational development service and other venues run smoothly as part of the quality appraisal event. Involve staff from Central Services (for example Student Services, Library, IT Department) in your preparations. They often have valuable experience from previous visits to other subject areas.

■ **Make good use of your institutional facilitator.** This person is trained to make good links between the visiting panel and the subject team. Listen to the institutional facilitator's advice and act upon it.

■ **Keep an eye on loose cannons.** If you feel you have people who are likely to be destructive on the day, don't try to hide them or over-compensate for their actions or views, or send them off on a field trip! Quality reviewers are not fools and will be able to tell the difference between those with a genuine grievance or problem, and troublemakers.

Chapter 7

Looking after yourself

While other chapters in this book have been about looking after your students, this one is about ensuring that *you* survive! We are only too aware of the levels of stress that are experienced by many lecturers, due to all manner of causes, many of which are beyond their control. We hope that the suggestions in this chapter will contain something for everyone, and help to reduce some of the causes and effects of stress.

1. Time management

How much time there is to be managed is open to question! Often lecturers have much of their time predetermined by teaching timetables and research commitments. But even if only a quarter or third of your working time is under your control, we feel the following tips will help you to make it more productive:

- **Budget your time.** Your 'budget' is that time in your working day that is not predetermined by your teaching timetable, research commitments and other duties. If your immediate reaction is 'what's left!', read on. To budget effectively, you will need to tackle tasks systematically rather than trying to do everything at once.

- **Keep a list of the work you need to do under a series of headings.** These headings could make up a priority list of: *must do immediately*; *should do soon*; *may be put on the back-burner*; or reflect a four-way split of each item of work as *urgent and important*; *urgent but routine*; *important but not urgent*; *routine and not urgent*. This task list is best drawn up on a daily basis, crossing out or carrying forward items as you tackle them.

- **Avoid the temptation to do the routine and not urgent tasks first!** They tempt because they can be simple, distracting or even fun. But keep a note of them; they can be done in the quieter patches. However, there are benefits to be gained from spending no more than half an hour on a non-urgent task before starting on an urgent one.

- **Whichever list you use, remember it is dynamic and will need to be reviewed daily.** Time has a nasty habit of moving things on and what was once not urgent emerges suddenly as something needed yesterday. Remember too that you may be better off by doing three things from your list in part than spending all your time budget on just one of them.

- **Use a wall chart or a 'What I am doing?' grid.** Such devices provide you with a means to plan ahead and schedule your known commitments. They also tell other people about your current activities. It's useful for your colleagues if you also include a location and a note of how you may be contacted.

- **Keep your paperwork well filed**. It's a temptation just to fill the in, out and pending trays! Do this and you'll inevitably spend ages looking for that vital piece of information or in despair assume that it's been lost (or not received). Use a relatively quiet time to set up, maintain and update your filing system.

- **Is your journey really necessary?** Avoid multiple trips to the photocopier or mail point. Ask yourself: 'Rather than see someone, would it be quicker to phone, e-mail or write?', 'Do I really need to go to such-and-such meeting?', 'Do I actually need to go to the *whole* of that meeting?'

- **Work out which tasks you can delegate and do so**. Even with tight staffing levels, there will be clerical and technical support staff. Often such staff are better able than you to do the routine jobs like typing, filing or photocopying. They can be quicker too! Junior colleagues may be pleased to help as a way to help them develop their skills or 'visibility' in your organization.

- **Each day schedule particular times to make your phone calls and to check your e-mail**. Making and receiving calls and e-mails *ad hoc* across the working day can be time wasting and distracting from other tasks. Invest in an 'ansaphone' or 'voice mail' as a way to control but not lose calls. Encourage those you phone, but never seem to be available, to invest in similar technology!

- **Try the *do it now* technique**. Don't be put off if you can't do the whole task in one bite. Break it up into smaller components that you can and will do straight away.

- **In the end you must decide what kinds of activity have a high payoff or a low payoff for you in terms of your time investment**. You may find that, for you, doing your paperwork by e-mail and phoning rather than writing will have high payoffs. And you might find that attending meetings has a low payoff, as may have writing jobs-to-do lists!

2. Workload management

Heavier workloads have become a fact of life for most lecturers. It seems highly unlikely that this situation will change. Most countries are spending less on education and training than the UK, and the trend remains towards students themselves finding the money to fund their own education. While we in no way believe that spending on education should be downgraded, we would like to offer readers some suggestions on how they may accommodate some of the effects of the changes:

- **Don't waste energy on trying to turn the clock back!** What some people affectionately refer to as 'the good old days' are very unlikely to return. One danger is that we spend so much time talking about how much better things once were, that we put even more pressure on the time and energy we have to face today and plan for tomorrow.

- **Prioritize your own workload.** It is useful to go through all the tasks and roles that you undertake, asking yourself which are the *really* important ones, and which are the ones that would not have significant effects on your students if you were to prune them or abandon them.

- **Manage your time.** When snowed under with work, the danger is that time seems to manage you. It can be worthwhile spending a couple of hours on a time-management training programme. Look for that one good idea that will save you a couple of hours, again and again.

- **Cut your assessment workload.** This does not mean reduce the quality of your assessment. It is widely recognized that over-assessment is bad for students, and in former times it was all too easy for such patterns of over-assessment to be established. Now may be the time to think again about how much assessment your students really need, and to improve the quality of this, but at the same time significantly reduce its volume.

■ **Make good use of learning resource materials.** Students nowadays learn a great deal more from computer-based and print-based materials than once was the case. The quality of learning resource materials is improving all the time, and such materials are getting steadily better at giving students opportunities to learn-by-doing, and to learn from healthy trial and error. Materials are getting much better at providing students with feedback on their individual progress and performance. Making the most of such materials can free up valuable face-to-face time with students, so you can deal with their questions and problems rather than merely imparting information to them.

■ **Make better use of your learning centres.** Arranging for your students to do relevant parts of their learning in such centres can bring variety to their learning environment, and can relieve you of some of the responsibility for looking after them.

■ **Make good use of your administrative and support staff.** It is easy for us to find ourselves doing tasks which they could have done just as well, and often they could have done them more efficiently than ourselves.

■ **Make better use of feedback from students.** Listen to their concerns, and focus on them, making your own work more useful to them at the same time. They know better than anyone else where their problems lie, so it is worth making sure that your valuable time is spent addressing the right problems.

■ **Cut your administrative workload.** Life may seem to be full of meetings and paperwork, but is it all really necessary? A well-chaired one-hour meeting can usually achieve as much as a much longer one.

■ **Don't carry your entire workload in your mind.** We can only do one thing at a time, so when doing important work such as teaching and assessing students, don't get sidetracked into worrying about the numerous other tasks jostling for your attention.

■ **Give yourself a break!** One of the symptoms displayed by people under pressure of work is that they seem to forget that we all need time off, and the world won't grind to a halt if we don't do everything on our 'to-do' lists. Having a break, and switching your mind away entirely from the pressures, will mean you can return to the fray re-energized and strengthened.

3. Stress management

The lecturer's job can be extremely stressful as staff are put under increasing pressure to teach longer hours and in possibly unfamiliar ways, and to spend longer hours on assessment and record keeping as well as research. At the same time, students are becoming more diverse and have an ever-widening range of requirements and expectations. These tips cannot eliminate your stress, but may suggest some strategies to help you deal with it:

■ **Get better at recognizing the physical signs of stress.** These include raised heart rate, increased sweating, headaches, dizziness, blurred vision, aching neck and shoulders, skin rashes, and lowered resistance to infection. When people are aware that such symptoms may be caused by stress, it helps them to look to their approaches to work to see if the causes may arise from stress.

■ **Get better at recognizing the behavioural effects of stress.** These include increased anxiety, irritability, increased consumption of tobacco or alcohol, sleep disturbance, lack of concentration, and inability to deal calmly and efficiently with everyday tasks and situations.

■ **Increase awareness of how the human body reacts to stress.** Essentially this happens in three distinct stages. 'The alarm reaction stage' causes defences to be set up and increased release of adrenaline. 'The resistance stage' is when the body will resist the stressor, or adapt to the stress conditions. 'The exhaustion stage' results when attempts by the body to adapt have failed, and the body succumbs to the effects of stress.

■ **Don't ignore stress.** There are no prizes for struggling to the point of collapse: indeed, this is the last thing you should be doing. As the symptoms of stress become apparent to you, try to identify the causes of your stress and do something about it.

■ **Get over the myths surrounding stress.** Research has shown that stress should not be regarded as being the same as nervous tension, and is not always a negative response, and that some people do indeed survive well and thrive on stress. In an education organization, it is more important to manage stress than to try to eliminate it.

■ **Look to the environmental causes of stress.** These include working or living under extremes of temperature, excessive noise, unsuitable lighting, poor ventilation or air quality, poorly laid out work areas, and even the presence of vibration. In your own institution, finding out what people think of such environmental conditions is a good first step towards adjusting them.

■ **Look to the social causes of stress.** These can include insufficient social contact at work, sexual harassment, racial discrimination, ageism, inappropriate management approaches, unhealthy levels of competition, and conflict between colleagues. Any or all of these, when present, can be discovered and identified by asking people about them.

■ **Look to the organizational causes of stress.** These include inappropriately heavy workloads, ineffective communication, excessive supervision or inadequate supervision, lack of relevant training provision, undue concern about promotion or reward systems, and unsatisfactory role perceptions. Once identified, all of these causes can be remedied.

■ **Cultivate the right to feel stress, and to talk about it.** Stress is at its worst when it is bottled up and unresolved. It should be regarded as perfectly natural for people's stress levels to vary in the normal course of their work. When stress is something that can be discussed, it is much more likely that the causes will be addressed.

■ **Allow yourself to feel anger.** It isn't surprising that people under stress often feel full of rage, which is often not specifically directed. People often become very frustrated when they feel powerless, so it may be worth taking stock of what is and what is not within your control. Anger, once generated, can be directed in many directions, and the most harmful of these is inwards. All the same, it is unwise as well as unprofessional to vent your rage on others, especially innocent bystanders who are caught in the cross-fire. Find ways to let off steam that are not destructive to yourself and others.

■ **Write it out of your system.** Some people find it very helpful to write about the issues that stress them and make them angry. This can take the form of a diary in which you record your feelings and analyse the situation, or letters you would like to send to the people who are causing you stress, or other forms of writing to take your mind off the current situation.

■ **Have some fun.** Look for ways in which you can de-stress yourself by doing things that make you happy. A little hedonism goes a long way. Think about the things that give you pleasure, like cooking, reading for pleasure, going to concerts or having a day of total sloth. Regard these as part of a programme of active stress management rather as a guilt-inducing interference with your work. You deserve some time for yourself and you shouldn't regard it as a luxury.

■ **Don't be afraid to go to the doctor.** The worst excesses of stress can be helped by short-term medication and medical intervention of some kind. People are often unwilling to resort to a visit to their GP for matters of stress when they wouldn't hesitate to seek help for a physical ailment. Don't let such feelings get in the way of finding the kind of support you need.

■ **Try not to worry about not sleeping.** Sleep disturbance is one of the most common features of stress and worrying about it makes it worse. Try to ensure that you are warm and comfortable at bedtime, avoid working for at least an hour before you retire and use music or reading to help get you into a relaxed state. If sleep doesn't come, try to use the rest period to recoup some energy and try not to go over and over in your mind what is troubling you. Taking exercise and cutting down on your caffeine intake can help.

■ **Use relaxation techniques.** There are innumerable methods that can be used to help you unwind, including deep breathing, massage, aromatherapy and meditation. It might be worth your while to explore the techniques that sound most attractive to you and try to use them to help you cope with stress.

■ **Work it out in the gym.** It may feel like the last thing on earth you want to do, to take physical exercise at the end of a long stressful day, but lots of people find it helps them relax. Join a gym, take the dog for long walks, swim, take up golf, play a mean game of squash or just do aerobics at home to help your body to become as tired physically as your mind is mentally. Find out what kinds of exercise works best for you and try to use it as a bridge between your working life and your own time. Try not to let your exercise requirement end up feeling like another kind of work you have to do!

■ **Get a life outside college.** Family and friends still deserve your attention, even if work is very busy, and we all need to learn to keep a sense of proportion to our lives. Try not to neglect hobbies and interests, even if you sleep through the film or nod off after the sweet course. Let your pets help you to remember how to be a human, too!

■ **Take a break.** Often our panics over time management are caused not so much by how much we have to do as much as whether we feel we have sufficient time to do it in. Try to take a real break from time to time, so as to help you get your workload into proportion. A little holiday or a whole weekend without college work occasionally can make you better able to cope with the onslaught on your return.

■ **Overcome powerlessness with action.** When you are stressed out, it is often because you feel totally powerless in the situation. It can be useful to look at the areas you do have some control over and try to do something about them, however minor. This may not change the overall picture very much, but will probably make you feel better.

■ **Talk about your problems.** Actually voicing what is stressing you to a colleague, a line manager, the person you are closest too or even your cat can sometimes improve the situation. Bottling it all up through some misplaced sense of fortitude can be dangerous.

■ **Try counselling.** Many colleges have someone to whom staff can turn for trained counselling in times of great stress. Otherwise you could look elsewhere, through your GP, or in the phone book under therapeutic practice or alternative medicine, to find someone who can guide and support you through the worst patches. This is often more productive than piling all your stress onto your nearest and dearest who usually have problems of their own!

■ **Try not to personalize a situation into hatred and blame.** It is easy to fall into the trap of seeing all your stress as being caused by an individual or group of people who have it in for you. Of course, it may be the case but usually high-stress situations are caused by cock-up rather than conspiracy!

■ **Avoid compounding the problem.** If things are pretty stressful at work, try to avoid making important life changes at the same time, such as moving to a larger house or starting a family, if these can be deferred for a while.

■ **Audit your intake of stimulants.** For those whose culture allows alcohol, a little can be felt to be a wonderful relaxant, but excessive intakes can be problematic. It's natural to drink a lot of beverages containing caffeine when trying to get through a lot of work, but it can interfere with your metabolism and sleep patterns. Eating rich food too late at night and smoking too much can also get in the way of being calm. Moderation is boring but a good policy for those under stress.

■ **Try to adopt a long-term perspective.** It can be really hard to project into the future and to review current stress as part of a much larger pattern, but if you can do it, it helps. Much of what seems really important now will pale into insignificance in a few weeks', months' or years' time.

- **A problem shared is a problem doubled!** Stressed people meeting in groups can reinforce each other's stress by constantly rehearsing the problems. Encourage the group to agree a moratorium from time to time on chewing over the same old issues. Maybe have a meal out as a group together or go to the races together instead. It won't take away the stress, but it might help you forget about it for a while.

4. Working well with academic colleagues

Working in an educational institution can be really miserable if the people around you aren't supportive and helpful. Try to start by ensuring that the people around you find *you* a helpful and supportive colleague, and you may be delighted at how the condition can spread:

- **Help out when the going gets tough.** If someone in your team is struggling, it makes a big difference if you are prepared to roll up your sleeves and lend a hand, whether it is in collating marks, stuffing envelopes or preparing for an important event. With luck they will reciprocate when you are having a tough time too.

- **Don't spring surprises on colleagues unnecessarily.** If you know you are going to be away for an extended period, or if you can't fulfil your obligations, try to give as much advance notice as possible. This will enable colleagues who have to fill in gaps for you to build it into their own schedules.

- **Keep to deadlines, especially when they impact on others.** If you are late doing your own marking, for example, or in putting together your section of a report, it will often affect others whose own time management will be thrown out of kilter. Try as far as humanly possible to do what you have said you will within the time available.

- **Keep track of what your colleagues really appreciate in what you do.** Try to do more of these things whenever you can. It can also be worth working out what a 'terrible colleague' might be like, maybe by making a word-picture of a hypothetical case, and avoiding doing the sorts of things that may be brought to mind by such a picture.

- **Find out how colleagues feel.** Don't just wait for them to tell you how they feel, and don't keep informal conversations to work-based topics. Simply asking 'How are you feeling today?' or 'What's on top for you just now?' can be open-ended questions which allow colleagues to share with you things that are important to them at the time, but which would just not have arisen in normal work-oriented discussions.

- **Be considerate when sharing an office.** Often staff workrooms are extremely cramped for space, and colleagues who leave papers all over a shared desk and who hog all available storage space make life difficult for others. Don't leave dirty cups around, clear up your own mess and be thoughtful about noise. If students need to be seen privately, try to agree times when fellow tutors can have uninterrupted use of the space.

■ **Be punctual for meetings.** Everyone slips sometimes, for very good reasons, but as a rule, try to ensure you are always spot on time for meetings, so other people aren't kept waiting for you while you make a last-minute phone call or a cup of tea.

■ **Keep colleagues informed about what you are doing.** People need to know what you are up to when this impacts on their work. If, for example, you know you will be filling the office with a lot of bulky portfolios to mark, it might be a good idea to tell colleagues before they fall over the boxes coming into the room. Tell them also when you will have visitors, when you will be away and when you expect to have a lot of students visiting you.

■ **Be gracious when rooms are double booked.** This inevitably happens from time to time and can be the cause of much disagreement. Colleagues with two or more groups of students needing to use the same room should tackle the problem together, rather than having a slanging match over who had booked the room first. It makes sense for the group *in situ* or the largest group to occupy the available room with their tutor, while the other group is asked to wait somewhere like the refectory or quietly in the corridor until another room is found.

■ **Leave teaching spaces as you found them (or better!).** If you move furniture or use the walls for display, try to leave the room fit for use by others when you leave. Encourage students to clear their own litter and leave the space tidy.

5. Working well with administrative and support colleagues

In an ideal world, we would not be differentiating between any of the people who contribute to the running of an educational institution on any basis founded upon job title or job description. However, it is still common to think of distinctions between staff who mainly teach, and those who mainly do other things! Therefore in this set of suggestions such distinctions have been reluctantly retained, while at the same time offering advice to blur or remove such differentiation:

■ **Never neglect the courtesies.** Individual support staff sometimes over-inflate their importance and may seem to you to be overly bureaucratic or inflexible. Nevertheless, you will find it useful to gain their respect and cooperation. Ask, rather than instruct, and offer genuine thanks for the work done.

■ **Get feedback from support staff on the way you work with them.** Get them to say what actions you take are helpful to them and what causes them concern. Apart from improving the effectiveness of the relationship, it can help you with your own self-evaluation of your performance.

■ **If you are responsible for any support staff, encourage them to network with others.** This could be within your own college, regionally or nationally. Support networks exist for library, audio-visual and specific areas of technical expertise. Remember their own professional updating and exposure to 'best practice' is as important as your own.

■ **Don't expect disorganization on your part to constitute an emergency on theirs!** Try to give fair notice of tasks you want them to do. Provide a clear statement of what you need doing. Check they understand and that the task is achievable in the time you've given.

■ **Help them to get credit for what they do.** Praise is always a great motivation, but don't just keep it private. If their contribution has been particularly good or critical, give them public acknowledgement and credit. If the particular member of staff is working towards a professional qualification or NVQ, such public backing can used by them as portfolio evidence.

■ **Describe the precise nature and the priority of each task you ask them to do.** Photo-copying and typing requests can often be accompanied by a pre-printed request pro-forma. Sometimes, where there are cost implications, you will need a budget code and the signature of the budget holder. Let them advise you too, as they will be able to bring their experience to bear on the best way to do the job.

■ **Treat your support staff as equal partners.** If there are cultural or status barriers between academic and non-academic staff, do what you can to break them down. Remember that effective teamwork includes everyone, regardless of job description or remuneration levels.

■ **Help them to do a decent job.** Give them all the information and paperwork they need. Help them by providing full addresses, references or other data. The art of effective delegation is to give people responsibility for what they do, but also to provide support and inspiration to help them do tasks well.

■ **Use their strengths.** For example, they may be far better keyboard operators or video technicians than you! Find out what they are best at, and play to their strengths, as well as helping them to develop new areas of competence.

■ **Include them in social and morale-building events.** It's easy to forget that achievements and successes are usually the result of team effort. Such events don't always have to be expensive, externally facilitated away-days. Home-produced activities can often help a group to meld as well as anything more elaborate.

6. Managing your meetings

Committee work and meetings can take many different forms, ranging from course boards, exam boards, and a host of other kinds of meetings. Most of the suggestions below are aimed at colleagues who are relatively new to participation in committee work, and who may find their first experiences of such work daunting, impenetrable, frustrating or confusing:

- **Decide whether you are sure you need to attend.** Life is too busy to attend irrelevant meetings. If you find that you do not participate at a meeting, you probably should not have gone to it.

- **If chairing the meeting, ensure that the agenda has timings on it.** People need to be able to plan when to start the next thing they will do after your meeting, so a realistic finishing time should be worked out and published. Also, separate agenda items should be timed appropriately, so that all can be discussed adequately and fairly in the time available, and so that it can be clear to everyone when the time available for a particular item is about to be used up.

- **Take the right paperwork with you.** It is also useful to find time before the meeting to read the paperwork – or at least to scan it – highlighting points where you may wish to make a contribution, and jotting down keywords that will help you to remember what you want to say.

- **File your papers appropriately.** It helps you to keep on top of the paperwork and enables you to find what you need for the next meeting without stress.

- **Read the last set(s) of minutes.** This is especially important if you are new to a group, as it helps you to get a feel for what is going on. It also helps you to feel clued-up, even if you have met the group several times before.

- **Try to provide documentation in advance of the meeting.** Do this for key issues you wish to raise. What you have to say is likely to be taken more seriously if it is available on paper. It also means that there is less chance of your points being left until 'any other business' when they are more likely to be ignored.

- **Make supporting papers short, precise and readable.** Try making an A4 summary if the information is detailed or contains support data or statistical information. List action points. It helps considerably if it is clear at the meeting exactly what decisions are intended to be taken, and spelling these out boldly and concisely in committee papers can facilitate these decisions being addressed.

- **Work out who is at the meeting, and make yourself a seating diagram so that you know who is saying what.** When names are not displayed on the table already, and if new to a committee, it can help you to pick up the threads of the different contexts and positions of contributors. Having people's names helps you to put names to faces in the future, and connecting what you've already heard about people to their behaviour and interests as seen at the meeting.

- **Carefully note any action points down to you, and act on them.** You can wait to see the minutes to check what exactly your action points are, but make sure that you can be seen to have taken action before the next meeting. If you're unsure about what you're expected to do, or do not think it will be feasible, make sure that you speak about it at the time during the meeting, or approach the Chair as soon as you see what the minutes have listed for you to do.

■ **Jot down your own notes at the meeting.** The minutes of a meeting may be minimal and focused on decisions rather than discussions, and may not cover all the detail that you may need to remember.

■ **Watch out for hidden agendas.** An astute meetings-watcher may be able to discern all kinds of hidden currents and covert politics, which may influence outcomes more significantly than the actual contributions to the meeting. You may need to keep your eyes and ears open, particularly for subtle nuances.

■ **Don't let conflict in meetings rattle you.** Often you will find that postures are adopted and sabres are rattled, while the participants themselves often emerge from the meeting seemingly as the best of friends. Remember that behaviour in meetings can often be strategic and theatrical.

■ **If a meeting is irrelevant to you, consider leaving.** There is little point storming out, simply slip away quietly and with minimum disruption at a natural pause, so long as the conventions of the context don't make this seem hopelessly discourteous.

■ **Consider attending only parts of a meeting.** This is especially possible when there is timed business, and you can judge when to arrive and depart from the meeting according to when the items you need to attend for are timed. However, it is a fair assumption to expect most timed business to overrun.

■ **If you are asked to do the minutes of a meeting, or to chair a meeting, find out how to do it well.** The difference between a good minute-taker or chair and a poor one is often about whether the people involved understand their roles and have had relevant training about how best to approach the roles.

■ **Take all your relevant paperwork with you.** You are likely to need class lists, for example, at exam boards, together with exam regulations, papers, copies of coursework mark schemes, and so on. Don't be embarrassed by having insufficient material to answer searching questions.

7. Managing your paperwork

Information overload (seemingly encouraged by the availability of computers) is a fact of college life. Usually the information is one-way – onto your desk! This paperwork may also appear to be not directly related to your own course and student responsibilities. The following suggestions can help you to take care of this general paperwork:

- **Perform a crude sorting task on the paperwork.** Most of the paperwork can be safely filed. Some requires action on your part, either in creating your own paperwork or as an item for action.

- **Prioritize your responses.** Deal quickly with financial and budget-related paperwork. Student records and assessment returns can have funding implications so should be dealt with as soon as possible.

- **Employ time-management techniques.** Speed reading, scanning and review techniques are useful for dealing with copious paperwork. Setting aside a time each day to attack the paperwork can also help.

- **Use your secretarial /clerical support staff.** Their job-roles make them likely to be better able than you to process standard paperwork efficiently. They will be aware of any college protocols about official stationery, house styles etc. There is also, because of quality monitoring and a growing interest in litigation, likely to be a requirement that all external and student (or student's sponsor) communications be centrally generated and a file-copy held.

- **Use your photocopier.** Important but straightforward replies can be scribbled on the original, copied and returned.

- **Keep files, not piles!** Handle each piece of paper as few times as possible. Try to avoid the situation of repeatedly sifting through piles of papers, looking for the particular documents you need. Piles seem to 'lose' the document you want! If you think how long you have spent on occasions looking for a particular piece of paper, you will know in your heart that spending just some of that time organizing a good filing system would have been well worthwhile.

- **Learn to love your wastepaper bin and shredder!** How often have you kept something to read later, knowing full well that you would never actually look at it again – except to remind yourself that you didn't want to look at it? Allow a decent period of time to elapse and then feel free to 'weed' the files.

- **Label your paperwork with post-its.** These stand out easily from the papers themselves, and you can write on them short messages to remind you exactly what you are going to do with each of the papers, and save you having to read them all again trying to work this out again. You can make your own colour codes with the post-its, maybe to remind you of the 'urgent', or the 'important' as opposed to the 'routine'.

- **Use plastic wallets.** These are invaluable for making sure that all the papers that need to be kept together stay together. How often have you spent ages searching for that last sheet which has somehow escaped from a set of papers – or (worse) the first sheet?!

- **Get yourself a nine-part organizer.** These are indexed filing wallets, which contain nine sections, and are invaluable for collecting together the sets of papers that you're going to use in the immediate future. For example, one of these can contain the paperwork for each of the meetings you have in the next week or so, and it's much handier just to have to pick up one item to carry around with you rather than search for each meeting's paperwork in turn.

- **Use alternatives to paper**. Would a telephone call be a sufficient response? Can you use e-mail? Electronic communication is quicker, less protocol-bound, avoids paper and saves photocopy costs.

- **Save paper**. Use notice boards for things you want everyone in your department or section to see. For non-urgent dissemination, circulate a single copy of a document with a 'pass on to ...' list, rather than sending everyone a copy – people who want their own copy can spend their own time making one! Make sure that the single copy is destined to end up in a sensible place at the end of its circulation, either back to you, or preferably in the departmental office for filing there.

- **Take your paperwork with you.** Paperwork can often be done in odd moments between other tasks, and if you have it with you it is possible to make good use of such opportunities. But don't carry too much around with you; don't carry home more than you could reasonably expect to be able to do overnight or over a weekend. How often have you only had time to look at a fraction of the pile you carried home?

- **Pass things on.** It's too easy simply to file (or junk) things that aren't actually relevant to us. Keep in mind that they may be of use to a colleague. Put such things straight into the internal mail system, with a post-it saying who they are for, from whom, and the date, and a cryptic message such as 'For inf.' or 'Thought you'd like this' and so on.

- **Keep *your* paperwork output to a minimum!** You will earn the gratitude of your colleagues if you don't add to the pile in their in-tray: Use e-mail or the telephone. Keep any written work short and make it clear what you want them to do with it.

8. Working as a part-time lecturer

Many colleges rely on part-time staff to present a diversified population of academics, as well as to build into curriculum delivery strategies a degree of flexibility. These suggestions aim to help part-time lecturers keep a level head while all around are losing theirs!

- **Learn to live with uncertainty.** The advantage to the college of part-time staff is that you are flexible and cheap. You are likely to be asked to step in at short notice to fill gaps, and you are unlikely to know what is expected of you until the last minute in many colleges. Accepting this and learning to work in a permanently changing context will make for an easier life, and will bring its own benefits to you in terms of variety.

- **Develop a range of flexible activities.** Whatever your subject matter, it is usually possible to devise a series of tasks and exercises to give to students when you are called upon at short notice. Such tasks give you a breathing space in which to plan your programme of curriculum delivery more strategically.

- **Find your way around the college systems.** You will probably have to find out for yourself how to get photocopying done, how to use internal and external communications systems, and what to do to get paid. Make a checklist of questions to ask on your first day, and keep pestering people until you get the answers you need to help you do a good job.

- **Network with other part-timers.** These are the people who are likely to have a lot of the information you need, as they are in the same boat very often. They can also provide you with good support when the going gets tough.

- **Find yourself a full-time mentor.** This may be the person that you report to, or it may be another full-time member of staff working in your area who will be able to keep you updated on important college information. Such a person can also act as your champion in meetings you cannot attend, and ensure that the part-time tutor's perspective does not get forgotten.

- **Help colleagues keep in contact with you.** Make sure that your home phone, fax and e-mail details (if available) are listed, and if possible clearly displayed on a staff room notice board so you can be contacted when needed urgently. Check internal post systems and pigeon holes regularly, and ask a colleague to post mail home to you over non-teaching periods. It is easy for part-timers to get missed out if they are difficult to contact.

- **Fight for the right to file!** Everyone needs space to keep records, store students' work and file teaching materials. Part-timers often consider themselves lucky to have access to a desk and part of a filing cabinet, but you should argue for what you need to help you to do your job well.

- **Bring your own mug.** Tempers get heated when part-timers inadvertently use other people's kitchen equipment, especially if they leave it dirty. It's also a good idea to bring your own tea/coffee/milk and so on, unless you are able to buy into a collective tea fund that doesn't disadvantage people who aren't there all the time. Encouraging you to look after such things may seem a little isolationist, but you may find you need to make an appropriate choice between collegiality and survival!

- **Set reasonable boundaries.** Part-time lecturers often find themselves called upon to work almost full-time for significantly less money than their fully contracted peers. It is especially common for part-timers to be pressurized into coming in for meetings outside their normal hours. You will need to balance a natural desire to be helpful, flexible (and employable), while at the same time not allowing people to take advantage of you. You may also need to check what your contract may say about meetings.

- **Let people know what else you do.** Many people work part-time because they have other work or responsibilities. Artists, for example, often teach part-time to support their studio work, and many part-timers have caring responsibilities or other jobs. By informing people about your other lives, you will help them not to make unreasonable demands in your non-contracted time.

9. Preparing for appraisal

It is now a well-established quality assurance measure to involve all staff in a periodic appraisal process. This enables staff, in discussion with their line managers, to appraise the effectiveness of their performance and to consider how best to undertake further personal development. Ideally, this process is a positive experience, with an opportunity for a confidential, open dialogue that will lead to appropriate action planning for both you and your line manager. These tips are designed to help you to get the most from the personal development and appraisal system:

- **Work through the documentation provided by your college.** This should give you a series of pro-formas or headings under which you look back at what you have achieved since your last appraisal plus any problems or barriers that you encountered. It will probably ask you in some form or other to self-evaluate your performance, both as a lecturer and as a colleague. It should also encourage you to reflect on the performance of your line manager. Focus on your own activities and on things that are directly relevant to the effectiveness and efficiency of your work. Don't dwell too much at this stage on broader issues of college policy or on the action (or inaction) of third parties.

- **Agree the agenda for the appraisal.** You and your line manager (who will normally be your appraiser) should discuss the nature of evidence you will be examining during your appraisal, including, where relevant, the outcomes of observations made of your teaching. Try to ensure that your appraiser allocates ample time to your appraisal, and that the venue agreed will be private and interruption-free.

- **Use the appraisal process positively.** Contribute assertively to the discussion by stressing what you want to get out of the appraisal. Prepare a shopping list of what you would like to be the agreed outcomes, but be prepared to negotiate this. Clearly identify any new areas of work in which you'd like to be involved. Be prepared to talk positively about any professional support, resources and development you will need in order to do your job more effectively and efficiently.

- **An appraisal of your past performance need not be a negative or unproductive activity.** Avoid seeing your appraisal as raking over old ground or digging up past errors and mistakes. Use it as a chance to reflect and to learn from what went wrong or did not work. Do not use this part of your appraisal to criticize other colleagues or dwell on things over which you (or your manager) have little control (particularly a lack of resources).

- **Remember that it is *your* appraisal**. Don't allow it to become a one-way process, with your appraiser doing most of the talking. Use it as a proactive opportunity to improve your own working life. See your appraisal as the most appropriate occasion to renegotiate your job description and make it more interesting or rewarding. If you regard the staff appraisal process as a 'tokenistic' activity in which your manager is simply going through the motions, then that is what it is likely to become.

- **Bring evidence of your achievements to the appraisal.** For example, you might bring along student feedback data; printouts of your students' achievements; examples of your effective organizational and administrative skills; and letters and memos from internal and external colleagues who have acknowledged your efforts. As well as 'blowing your own trumpet', such evidence will most likely fill in the gaps in your appraiser's own knowledge about you, your strengths and your contribution.

- **Use a part of your appraisal to discuss local and college-wide issues that concern you.** These might include equal opportunity matters, health and safety issues, or your concerns about teaching, learning and assessment. The appraisal process provides a rare chance for you to have the undivided attention of your line manager.

- **Use your appraisal as an opportunity to discuss your needs and wants.** You may be able to negotiate time or resources for professional training of various kinds. You might wish to gain approval for your participation in local or national activities relevant to your work. Remember that professional development need not involve high expenditure. Opportunities may exist for you to undertake personal development through work-shadowing, self-instruction or the use of staff development resource materials without large outlays of cash.

- **Finish your appraisal with an agreement as to what will happen next.** Normally this will involve a confidential written record of the appraisal, together with an agreed action plan that includes deadlines and responsibilities for both you and your line manager. Make sure that you know who is doing what before the end of the meeting. Make notes in your diary so you can follow up agreed actions in due course. Contact your appraiser if you don't feel an agreed activity has actually been set in train or had any outcome.

- **Review the appraisal process.** If you feel that you have been short-changed by your appraiser because you felt rushed, not listened to, or not taken seriously, say so and do not countersign the formal record of the appraisal or action plan. If you are happy with the way things have been done, make this clear too so that your appraiser, in turn, can use your satisfaction as evidence in his or her own appraisal.

10. Building your teaching portfolio

A teaching portfolio is one of the most successful ways of demonstrating the quality and range of your teaching. Building one could be regarded as the start of something to continue throughout your university career. It can also provide a useful compendium of information to have available for a variety of occasions, including appraisal, formal 'Subject Review' inspections, and applications for promotion or for posts elsewhere. Having a well-filed collection of evidence of the quality of your teaching is a good start towards assembling your actual teaching portfolio. The danger is that putting it all together seems like an enormous task, and tends not to get started! The following suggestions should help you go about building up a representative portfolio of your work:

- **Remind yourself *why* you want to build a teaching portfolio.** It is best that you *want* to build one, rather than simply that you are required to build one by your institution's staff development programme.

- **Check carefully any specific format suggested for your teaching portfolio.** It helps to keep it firmly in mind both while collecting evidence, and annotating it with your own reflective commentaries.

- **If your portfolio will be assessed, keep the assessment framework in sight.** While you can put anything *else* that you think is relevant into your portfolio if you want to, you *need* to include evidence that relates to the assessment framework.

- **Decide what sorts of evidence you will need.** The exact nature of your own evidence will depend upon the kinds of work you do with students in your job. Make a list of the main things that you do in your job, and alongside each of these write down a few words about the sort of evidence you could collect to prove that you do it well.

- **Start collecting evidence straightaway.** Much of the content of your teaching portfolio will come from your everyday work with students. The most efficient way of starting off a teaching portfolio is to start collecting examples of this evidence as a normal part of your everyday work.

- **Collect evidence of your curriculum design work.** This can include examples of a syllabus area you have planned, intended learning outcomes or objectives you have formulated or adapted, and plans for how you structure your delivery of a syllabus area. You can also include changes you make to existing programmes, with your rationale and justification for such changes.

- **Collect evidence of your teaching itself.** This can include examples of lesson plans, course plans, and examples (not too many!) of the materials that you use in your teaching, such as handout materials, overhead transparencies, and other learning resources that you devise or adapt.

■ **Make sure that you have enough evidence of peer feedback.** Make good use of any observation checklists you are provided with. You can also include examples of video-recordings of actual teaching sessions, ranging from large-group lectures, small-group sessions, and one-to-one encounters with students. Remember to be highly selective! A good teaching portfolio includes many *kinds* of evidence, but only a few examples of each kind.

■ **Collect evidence of student feedback on your teaching.** This can include examples of feedback questionnaires completed by students, along with your own analysis of the overall findings from the feedback. Include in your portfolio reflective comments about changes that you have made, or will make, as a result of feedback from students.

■ **Collect evidence of your assessment work.** This can include examples of tests and exercises that you set students, and a breakdown of how each test performed in practice. It is useful to link the content of each of the tests and exercises to the intended learning outcomes as expressed in the syllabus areas within which you are working.

■ **Collect evidence of your feedback *to* students.** This can include photocopies of typical assessed work, showing how you give students feedback on their written work. You can also include assignment return sheets that you have devised, copies of e-mails you send to students, and an account of other ways that you ensure that students receive feedback on their progress and performance.

■ **Collect evidence of your collegiality.** Such evidence can arise from your participation in course teams, committees and assessment boards. You can also include evidence relating to work you undertake jointly with other staff, showing how well you can work with colleagues.

■ **File your evidence systematically.** Don't put it all in a file or a drawer! Sort it first, according to the particular sections of your portfolio into which the evidence will go. It is worth starting up a number of parallel files, to make sure you make it easy to decide where each element of your evidence should be stored.

■ **Decide on the physical form of your portfolio.** For example, you may decide to use a ring binder for your main evidence (your reflections, peer-observation details and other important evidence) and lever-arch file for your appendices (examples of handouts, overheads, assessment tasks, feedback to students, and so on). Such formats make it much easier to adjust the contents of your portfolio, or to rearrange the order in which you present sections. They also allow you to use punched, plastic wallets to collect together samples of papers such as feedback questionnaires, marked student work, and so on.

■ **Don't use plastic wallets for things that need to be easy to read (or assess!).** While it's fine to use such wallets to keep together sets of similar papers in appendices (such as handouts, overheads, questionnaire responses, and so on), it is very frustrating for a reader (or assessor) to have to take out individual primary evidence sheets to read them.

■ **Make a draft index.** Decide in which order you wish to present evidence of the quality of your teaching. There is no 'right' order for headings and subheadings, even when the overall structure of the sections of the portfolio is laid down. The order of your headings and subheadings will depend on the nature of your work, and the range of evidence you wish to present for the quality of your work. It is, however, very useful to have this order sorted out in your mind before you start to put together the 'front-end' of your portfolio, in other words, your reflections and commentaries *about* your evidence.

■ **Think of your target audience.** Who is going to read your portfolio? More importantly, who will perhaps make judgements on it? The people who are most likely to look at it in detail are those whose responsibility includes teaching quality, and appraisal.

■ **Don't write the introduction too soon!** The introduction to a portfolio is extremely important. There is no second chance to make a good first impression! You can only write a really good introduction when you know exactly what you're introducing, so leave the introduction till you've more or less finished everything else in your portfolio. You can, of course, write a *draft* introduction, but this is probably best as a bullet-point list, or a mind-map sketch.

■ **Get other people to give you feedback about your portfolio.** Another pair of eyes is always useful. Show bits of your portfolio to your mentor, colleagues, friends, and even contacts in your field in other institutions if you can. Ask them to scribble liberally over anything where it could be worth you having second thoughts, or further explanations. Ask them also not to hesitate in pointing out typographical or grammatical errors: it is always easier for someone else to find them than for us to spot our own!

Chapter 8

Getting Published

Getting started

Selling your idea

Writing and rewriting

Our final chapter, like its predecessor, is designed to help *you*. Many lecturers are under quite intense pressure to balance research and teaching, and the main indicator of research effort is taken to be successful publication. It is beyond the scope of this book to provide suggestions on designing and executing research, as the strategies for successful research vary significantly from one discipline to another, and there exists good literature coverage of appropriate research methodologies in most disciplines. The common factor, however, is getting your research findings into print. Therefore, in this chapter we hope that we have included some suggestions that will help you to be successful in achieving the publications profile you need. Our suggestions here may also help you to train your own students towards their own publication futures.

The chapter leads you through the stages of **getting started**, **selling your idea** to a journal or publisher, and **writing and rewriting**.

Finally, the chapter looks at **electronic publishing**. Electronic publishing, or e-publishing, is not just replicating the forms of traditional publishing – it is creating new ones too. Many thousands of e-journals exist, on every imaginable subject. Some are published by individuals, while others are backed by commercial or institutional publishers. Many are only available on the Internet, while others are electronic versions of paper-based publications. Sometimes you are published electronically by default – sometimes you have a choice. Here we offer some tips on why and how you might expand from traditional models of publishing into something virtually different.

1. Why do you want to publish?

Love, fame, fortune … what is it that will drive you to put hours, weeks, months or even years of time and energy into your publishing effort? Knowing this can help you remain motivated, and will also help you shape your work for the right purpose and audience. Most authors find it hard to articulate just what their reasons are – but maybe the following ideas will prompt you, especially if you're an academic doing research:

■ **Take time to allow yourself to dream up as many motives as possible.** There is no right or wrong motive, only the one that appeals to you the most. Set yourself a little time to spend alone testing your motive against some of those below.

- **Is it a driving ambition to be widely recognized for your research?** Nothing wrong with that – ego and the desire for recognition drive most human beings much of the time. If this is your prime motive, you may have to set yourself a long-term goal. Publishing is a slow process, but can eventually bring acclaim and notoriety.

- **You believe that you really have something new to say?** Or perhaps you've finally taken the hint from your department head or supervisor? That's fine, too. These are the very people paid to promote the careers of other academics besides themselves. But, having appreciated the not-so-subtle nudge towards action, you'll need strong personal reasons to embark on this process.

- **To publish or to perish?** A good publishing record enhances your value as a researcher and academic. It demonstrates two important attributes of your role: your ability to conduct worthwhile research and your ability to focus your effort sufficiently to turn that research into a published paper.

- **Your institution's recognition (and funding!) increases with the number of its staff who publish.** Your published work therefore benefits your university or research centre and, in turn, that benefits you. It fuels the funds for further research and the likelihood of increased international collaboration amongst academics worldwide.

- **Trying to publish for the first time invites rejection.** That's an excellent reason to do it. Rejection by a good journal is usually accompanied by clear guidance about why your paper wasn't suitable, and often includes direction about how to do it better next time. Where else can you receive such eminent free advice?

- **Offers to present conference papers usually go to those who are already published.** Just getting yourself on the conference circuit will not only enhance your reputation but will bring you into contact with peers interested in your work. Many life-long professional associations are formed at these events.

- **People may actually read what you have written!** Understandably, you may feel that the published paper is the end of the process, but more often it is only a beginning, People interested in your work will sometimes contact you just to offer feedback, make a suggestion or ask a question.

- **You may even read what you've written!** Most prolific authors say that the writing process is helpful primarily to force their own thinking and clarity of expression. The very act of summarizing and explaining your work makes it clearer in your own mind.

- **Self-confidence.** You wouldn't be reading this section unless you had a need to publish – for any or more than the above reasons. Having done it, you'll feel that you have fulfilled an ambition. And that feeling will make the next paper that much easier.

2. Deciding what to write

Once your momentum as a writer is going, this just isn't a problem. The problem becomes deciding what to get on with writing, and what to leave on the back burner. Here are some suggestions that have helped some people who wanted to write or needed to write, but had no idea what topic to start writing about:

■ **Don't make 'not knowing what to write' become your writing-avoidance strategy.** Thousands of people have already done this, but they aren't too well known as a result of this! Many people are perfectly capable of writing, and have a lot to tell the world, but they have never got down to choosing a topic to write about *and* actually making a start on it as suggested below. Left to themselves, they probably never will start – at least until someone confronts them with their work-avoidance strategy.

■ **Have something to help you not to forget your ideas.** Once the ideas start flowing, they can occur to you at any time and in any place. Have some way of getting them down on paper, where you won't lose them. A small notebook that will fit into a pocket, briefcase or handbag is useful. Loose bits of paper too easily get lost or mis-filed, but are better than nothing if an idea strikes when you haven't got your book with you.

■ **Brainstorm a range of draft working titles.** Review your reasons for wanting to get published, and for each of these jot down a few draft working titles which could become the start of some writing. Don't worry at this stage about whether you feel able to actually write on these titles. Build up a collection of things you may some day *want* to write, or *need* to write, or simply *be in a position* to write. Don't ever feel that there is anything you won't some day be able to write about if you want to. Add to your list anything you're writing anyway, such as a project proposal or a report, which may turn out later to be a good start towards something publishable for a wider audience.

■ **Think creatively.** All of your draft working titles don't have to be sensible! In fact, it's often the rather way-out ideas that turn out to be most interesting to write up, and there's more chance that you may have something original if it's rather unusual. Include topic ideas that you know quite a lot about, but also topics that you may simply want to find out about.

■ **Do an importance-rating for each of your ideas.** It is worth doing this regularly from time to time. For example, rate each idea on a scale 'H', 'M' and 'L' for 'high, medium and low' against a range of factors, such as importance in the context of your job, importance to your boss or manager, fun, relevance to solving a problem or need, having something you really want to share, being already well set up with relevant data or information, and so on. You could then award an 'H' three points, an 'M' two points, and an 'L' one point, and work out which of your draft ideas has the highest score at that moment in time. This may be a reason for starting with that idea, or equally a reason for exercising your right to start with exactly the idea you feel like starting with!

- **Shortlist no more than half-a-dozen possibilities.** You can still go back and revisit other ideas on your backup list. With each of your short-listed ideas, write the draft working title in an oval in the middle of a blank page in your little notebook. Maybe then add a few further ideas about how to make the titles more interesting or punchy. You don't have to choose the actual title for a long time yet.

- **Start fleshing out your working titles with ideas.** Draw spokes radiating from the titles, and add at the end of each spoke questions, keywords, and other very brief reminders of your thoughts (no more than a few words to remind you of each thought). These questions could be the things you would need to research as a basis for your writing. The keywords could remind you of things you already know which you could include in your writing.

- **Regard all of your fleshing out as changeable.** You don't have to stick with any of your original ideas about detail when better or more-interesting ones come along. You can change the questions that your writing will address when more important ones occur to you, or when you find that you don't want to, or can't, address some of your first thoughts.

- **Review your identified possibilities.** They will by now give you quite a lot of help regarding where to make a start. The draft working title with most detail may well be the best place to start writing. On the other hand, sometimes you will have found that for some working titles, you now know enough about it to make an informed decision that you *don't* really want to get started on it, or at least not yet. Don't throw away any ideas, their time may come later, even years hence.

- **Start getting feedback on your draft ideas.** Talk to anyone you can who may be able to help you find out more about your own working titles, and about things you haven't yet thought of about them. Get a friend or colleague to interview you about your ideas. Jot down questions that they ask you that would be worth including the answers to in your writing. Jot down any of their ideas that you may want to use. Keep a careful note of whose ideas you may use, so that you can acknowledge them in your final writing.

3. Collecting your source material

Some people seem to manage to collect source material all of their lives, yet never get round to getting their material published. Since you are now reading this section, you are not likely to be one of these people! The following suggestions will include things of value to you in your own quest to get your act together ready for the process of getting your work published:

- **Polish your information retrieval skills.** Using online library catalogues, consulting the catalogues of publishers with a strong list in your subject, and checking recent issues of key journals, all help to ensure that you minimize the chance of missing a key publication to which you need to refer. You can do a lot of similar research by making effective use of the World Wide Web.

- **Work outwards from the centre of the web.** It's usually productive to work out who are the key authors in the field in which you are going to publish, and see whose work they most commonly cite. This is often more efficient than just relying on database keyword searches.

- **Make good use of citation indexes.** These allow you to start from a key paper or source, and to work forwards in time to find articles that have cited it. The chances are that these more recent papers will also be relevant to your search.

- **Aim for a 'read once' approach for each item of material.** Try to make a decision whether or not you're going to collect or discard an item, rather than put it aside to consider again later. You can have a 'perhaps' file for those pieces that really do need further consideration, but your aim should be to avoid wasting time over rereading the same things.

- **Keep good records of who wrote what.** Card indexes or computerized databases of relevant books, papers and articles are invaluable to an author. It saves a great deal of time when you can get the exact bibliographic details you need to be able to refer to any of your sources. Collect these details in the format that is used in journals that you may intend to publish in yourself, so that when you are making a list of references, your task is made easy.

- **Annotate your list of source materials.** It's easy to forget just who said exactly what about what! As you read others' writing, make your own notes of particularly important ideas that you may wish to refer to in your own work. It can be particularly useful to select phrases or sentences you may wish to use as direct (acknowledged, of course) quotations.

- **Be meticulous in your attributions.** All important ideas and arguments that are not your own must be acknowledged and referenced.

- **Make your own 'importance ratings'.** Work out your own code along the lines **** for a source which is really relevant, authoritative and important, down to * for a source which may deserve a passing mention.

- **Don't throw anything useful away.** The key word here is 'useful', of course. In turn, this means that you need to have an idea about what you may want to publish, so that you can start to collect and store relevant nuggets. Don't, however, just accumulate heaps of potential material. It is really important to be focused and systematic about your data right from the outset.

- **Start to organize your collection of source materials.** It can be useful to collect together materials in labelled folders or wallets, so that you have all the bits and pieces that you'll need for writing a particular chapter or section in one place. Writing a short list of the contents on the front of the folder, and keeping it up to date, can save time when you're looking for exactly where you've stored a particular source.

■ **Work within the copyright laws.** Be especially careful not to exceed 'fair use' limitations on the amount of material that you can quote from another source without permission. It is almost invariably the author's responsibility to obtain such permission, but your publisher may have ideas on how you should ask for this when necessary.

■ **Criticize carefully.** If you need to comment negatively on another's work, do it sensitively. Avoid anything that could be interpreted as libellous, or that could give rise to a possible lawsuit.

■ **It's never too early to write draft paragraphs.** When working through your source materials, whenever you have an idea of the gist of something you may want to write yourself about the source or its content, sketch out your key thoughts in a sentence or two, which may later be turned into a paragraph somewhere in your own writing.

■ **Don't plan to start at the beginning!** Starting off your masterpiece is a crucial task, but one which is best done when you know what you have actually written! It's best to stitch together ideas in the middle of your proposed writing, and gradually work both backwards to where you will begin, and forwards to your ending.

4. Improve your word processing

Almost everybody can benefit from some knowledge and experience of word processing. Word processing is a very useful skill to have as it makes the production of high-quality documents a possibility for anyone. Improving your word processing can help speed up the tasks of preparing and revising handouts for students, as well as in getting yourself published. You may already know most of what follows – but if there's one time-saving suggestion below, it could be worthwhile:

■ **Practise with the different options for selecting text.** The mouse is very useful for selecting text; for example to move, copy or delete it. Other techniques, such as double clicking, clicking in margins and dragging are very useful and less well known. They can make selecting and modifying text much faster.

■ **See for yourself how text can be deleted accidentally.** A common problem that beginners have is that they select some text, then type something. The selected text is then replaced by what they have typed. This can be useful, but beginners often have trouble with work 'disappearing' because of this. Remind yourself how this works and how to 'undo' it to reclaim your work.

■ **Try showing the non-printing characters.** Most word processors allow you to show characters such as spaces and carriage returns that aren't printed and don't normally show on the screen. Making these visible can help you understand why the computer is behaving the way that it is. When something strange is happening to your document, looking at these characters often helps you to find out why.

- **Develop familiarity with Cut, Copy and Paste.** By selecting text and then cutting it, copying it or pasting it into another place, documents can be modified easily. These techniques are also useful for entering text repeatedly. It is often possible to use keyboard commands for these functions and this can be faster than using the mouse to access menus.

- **Learn how to define and use styles**. If you are producing a long, report-type document, it is hard to be consistent about the style (font, size, alignment) of all the different headings, sub-headings and the body of the text. Most word processors allow you to define 'styles' that you can apply to these so that they will automatically be consistent. This is also very useful for producing documents that conform to a 'house' style.

- **Make use of your word processor's outliner.** Many word processors allow you to see your text in an 'outline' view. This makes it easy to set up headings and sub-headings that are automatically formatted. You can promote and demote headings or change the order of headings and the relevant text will move with the headings.

- **Practise the use of headers and footers.** These add information automatically to all the pages in documents. The information can include page numbers and the date as well as any text of the user's choice.

- **Show how numbering and bulleting can help clarify some documents.** It is easy to add numbers or bullets to lists. Paragraphs can even be numbered or bulleted automatically as they are typed and it is even possible to label sub-sections automatically.

- **Make sure the tab key is used for indenting text.** Most fonts used on word processors are proportional. This means that if spaces are used to indent text, correct alignment may be impossible. Even if indenting looks correct on the screen, it may print out incorrectly. Find out how to use tabs and how to set them to the spacing that you want.

- **Explore how to use borders around paragraphs.** Borders are very good for separating sections of text. Find out how they are created and how the lines can be modified and turned on and off.

- **Discover the benefits and dangers of spell checkers.** Spell checkers are very useful for finding errors, but they have major limitations. They only check that words are in their dictionary: they can't check for missing or wrong words.

- **Try some safe global editing.** Take a floppy disk with a copy of one of your word-processed document files on it, and global-edit selected words, such as 'was' to 'is', 'were' to 'are', 'double-quotes' to 'single-quotes', and so on. Also play with the layout of the document, for example by changing all multiple spaces to single spaces between words and sentences. It can also be very useful to global-edit changing each 'manual line-break' to a space, for example when inserting some scanned-in text into an existing document.

■ **Make good use of the 'Find… Replace' command.** This can be useful when you remember making a mistake, but have forgotten where it was in the document. It is also useful to dump something unusual (xxx, &&, ppp, and so on) at points in a long document that you may want to return to quickly, and just use the 'Find' command to return immediately to such points. It is best that such anomalous oddities are such that they would be picked up by the spell-checker facilities later, if they happened to be forgotten!

■ **Try the 'AutoCorrect' function to enter repeated terms quickly.** AutoCorrect is designed to correct frequent typing errors (such as 'teh' instead of 'the'). You can enter your own corrections and this can be used to enter long words quickly. As an example, imagine that you are typing the word 'substantiate' frequently in a document. If you tell AutoCorrect to replace s with substantiate, every time you type s, the full word will appear. You can even do this for complete phrases, such as 'ict' becoming 'information and communications technologies'. It is important, of course, to make sure that you don't end up with a nonsense phrase creeping into ordinary language. The 'Undo' facility can be used to undo single instances of an AutoCorrect modification, such as if you really want say 'ict'.

■ **Try inserting pictures, diagrams and charts.** Most word processors allow you to insert objects into the text. You can then place text around them. Some packages include simple drawing facilities and it is easy to find 'clip art' to use for simple illustrations.

■ **Check options for using symbols and 'foreign' characters.** If you regularly use a foreign language, or scientific symbols, it is worth investigating how to do this. Most word processors can produce a much wider range of characters than are available directly from the keyboard. There are fonts available designed to allow you to put symbols into your text. You can view a table showing you the symbols available in any font. You may be able to access more by using an extra key (such as the alt key). Some machines allow you to use a menu at any time to check what symbols are available with each key.

■ **Use tables effectively.** Defining a table can be much easier than using the tab key to arrange text in tabular format. Don't forget that you may need to allow a row or column for headings (you can usually add them later anyway). Adding borders to a table can make it look very tidy.

■ **It is often easy to use a word processor to produce Web pages.** Many word processors allow you to produce documents in a suitable form for publishing on the World Wide Web. This means that you won't have to learn a new package to develop your Web materials.

■ **Take care when you exchange word processor files with other people.** If you send a file on disk (or by e-mail attachment) to somebody who uses different word processing software, they may not be able to open it. Check with them before you send it to make sure. Your word processor probably allows you to save documents in several different formats, so this problem can usually be overcome. Rich Text Format is widely used and saves most of the layout of a document. As a last resort, Plain Text format is virtually universal, but almost all of the document's layout will be lost.

■ **Don't go into unnecessary complications.** For example, most word processing packages can perform 'Mail Merge' operations, suitable for adding names and address details to letters to a list of different people. However, the number of word processor users who actually *use* this facility tends to be much lower than the people who have met it on a training programme!

5. Ordering and structuring material

There's an old saying people quote about making presentations: tell them what you're going to say, then tell them, and finally tell them what you told them. Written work follows the same format, with a beginning, a middle and an end. Here are some suggestions which we hope will help you plan what goes at the beginning, in the middle, and at the end:

■ **Wrap it all up into 20 words or less.** Before plotting the detail of your structure, make sure you are clear about the purpose of your work. You may assume you know this, but unless you can write it in a clear, simple, statement, you do not yet have the clarity so essential to guide you.

■ **Begin with what interests the reader.** Pieces that begin with your name or the name of your college or company are not reader-oriented. For example, it won't interest the reader to hear that 'Company X is completing research on a new drug to help people with migraine headaches' as much as it will to read 'People who suffer with migraine headaches may soon be helped by a new drug being researched by Company X'.

■ **Tell them where they're going.** The introduction is designed to let your reader know your purpose, why it's important and to whom, and what they will gain by reading your material. For longer articles or books, the introduction should contain an overview of how the material is structured.

■ **Establish credibility.** Before developing the main body of the work, tell the reader why it has any validity. If it's a research paper, who did it? If you're quoting other sources, who are they and why should anyone care?

■ **Create your case.** As you approach the main argument, theory, proposal or findings, tell the readers how or why you, or your sources, arrived at it. Readers need to be reassured that the methods used were sufficiently robust or generally acceptable to support the case being presented.

■ **Summarize regularly.** At frequent intervals, tell the reader where you've got to. This will reinforce the points you are making and help readers maintain concentration. A confused reader who needs to ask 'What on earth are they saying now?' is not going to appreciate your work, or even finish reading it.

■ **Follow AIDA.** A tool used by many professional authors reminds us of this simple order: A for Attention (get the readers'); I for Interest (pique the readers'), D for Desire (make the reader want to know more); A for Action (tell them what they can do about it).

■ **Don't neglect the implications.** Following the main body of your book or paper, you must do more than summarize what you've told your readers. You need to spell out exactly what it means to them, answering the 'so what?' question that lurks in their minds. So, how will all this affect a scientist/manager/teacher/researcher? And what can they do about it?

■ **Always check for the six key questions.** Who, what, where, when, why and sometimes how. If your work covers these questions, you've probably said just about everything important. Work out what is the best order in which to cover these questions in the context of your own writing.

■ **When in doubt, leave it out.** Writing with economy means you must be prepared to edit your work and have it edited for you. Ensure that your salient points are just those, and you don't bore or confuse your reader with tangential or supplementary information. It's really worth having that 20-word summary that we mentioned at the beginning of this set of suggestions, to help you decide what to leave out.

6. Tackling the blank page

Writers are often pictured at their desks in a state of feverish activity, sweat dripping from the brow, seized by inspiration and guided by an almost supernatural energy. Yes, writers have flashes of inspiration, just as do teachers, bank managers and checkout operators. But most of the time they do their work professionally and with discipline. Here are some suggestions about how to handle that moment when the blank page or grey screen taunts you:

■ **Remember, there's no such thing as writer's block.** There is only planner's block. No one, not even the most practised writer, can feel comfortable looking at a blank page if he or she doesn't know what to say. Our tips on 'Preparing to get started' should make sure you have something definite in mind for that blank page.

■ **Writing is not an out-of-body experience.** No one will get those words onto paper except you. There is no muse sitting on your shoulder whispering your lines. Accept that it is your professionalism that will get the job done, not an other-world gift of inspiration or creativity.

■ **Review your plan.** Before you begin to write, you need to have a clear sense of what you want to say and how you will say it. Those thoughts should all be noted against your outline or overview. Refresh your memory.

■ **Don't start writing until you know what you want to say right then.** You will be disappointed and frustrated if you think that at any moment you can simply switch on your computer or pick up your notepad and watch the writing flow. Choose one part of your plans, and get going just on that bit, at least to start with.

■ **Create an objective for each session.** Before turning on the computer, decide which section you are going to write. You should have already planned the time available, so decide now how you are going to use it best.

■ **Expand your notes for your selected section.** Before starting to write, detail key points that you want to cover and the order in which you intend to cover them. Don't worry about getting every word right, but make sure you have your ideas sorted out.

■ **Take one line at a time.** Even if you have created a well-structured outline, the task of writing for an hour might still seem onerous. The journey of a thousand words starts with a single sentence! Allow yourself to gain a sense of achievement; however much you write in a single session, it is still progress.

■ **Take one page at a time.** Try to concentrate only on the specific section you are writing in the time you have allotted yourself. It's confusing to race ahead to further chapters or sections when you haven't finished the few paragraphs that face you.

■ **Make notes for further sections, but don't write them in full.** As you try to concentrate on the page in hand, jot down notes on a separate piece of paper if they come to you and leave them for later. It's easier to get the ideas off your mind and onto a different page to review later.

■ **Remind yourself why they invented word processors.** Part of the supposed 'writer's block' is the anxiety we feel about not getting it right. Don't worry about it. Whatever you write first is only your first draft. No one will see it but you. What have you got to lose?

7. Conference proceedings

Presenting a conference paper is an ideal way to ensure that your research will be written up and offered to the right target audience. The conference may be refereed or not, but either way the definition of an end-point, the need to focus on the audience, and the feedback you will receive on the spot will help your paper's route to successful publication:

■ **Understand the 'Call for Papers'.** These notices are well-considered, finely tuned communications to be closely read and analysed. Conference organizers are specialists in their field, knowing exactly who should come and what they want to find out. If they want papers about new teamwork practices in hospitals, don't bother them with your research about new financial management techniques for hospital accountants.

■ **Set your objectives.** Why do you want to write the paper and present it in person? Apart from the attraction of travel, most people agree that a conference allows them a unique opportunity to meet colleagues and peers. The questions you will be asked and subsequent discussions about your research will enrich it considerably.

■ **Respond with your abstract.** Preliminary notices give clear outlines about what they want at an early stage – usually an abstract of the paper and some information about yourself. Pay attention to: the purpose, the argument and the implications.

■ **Negotiate the terms.** You will never part with the intellectual ownership of your work, but you need to make sure who will assume responsibility for the paper's publication. Most conferences will insist that the paper be included in the conference proceedings and others will offer inclusion in a special issue of a journal. You may want to reserve the right to amend your paper and publish it elsewhere after the conference.

■ **Imagine who will be listening.** Conference papers are presented in person in front of a group of other people. This may seem obvious, but it eludes many presenters who think it's sufficient to stand at a podium and monotonously read their five thousand words to a weary audience. Picture your people as you write your paper.

■ **Stick to the structure.** Every successful presentation follows the same simple adage: tell them what you're going to tell them; tell them; tell them what you told them.

■ **Choose only a few key points.** Looking back at your abstract, construct your paper to cover clear and chronologically the purpose of your paper, the salient points of the argument and the implications. You will never be able to do justice to all of your material in one conference paper and presentation, so ensure you focus on only the key points of most relevance to your audience.

■ **Use your key points as slides.** Rather than show a slide filled with words, create only a few slides of only a few key points at a time. This will help your audience focus and help you remain on track during your presentation.

■ **Use strong visual aids.** The paper may include detailed tables and diagrams, but rarely will these be suitable for projection at a conference. Tables can be broken down into separate tables and diagrams should be presented with as few graphic embellishments as possible.

■ **Leave time for questions.** If you find yourself running short of time, end your presentation early rather than risk not having time for questions or feedback. This is the most useful benefit you'll receive from the conference, so don't sell yourself short.

■ **Apply what you've learned.** Although your conference paper may already be published in the proceedings, the questions and insights you'll take home with you should help you take your thinking one stage further. Revise your paper accordingly and consider submitting it to a journal.

8. Journal articles

Journals are the right publication to target for specific purposes of dissemination to an academic or professional audience. Their standards are specific and rigorous, and the benefits are not commercial but prestigious. Deciding to follow a journals route requires a thorough evaluation of the process and pitfalls. Here are some points that may help you establish your criteria:

■ **Think quality not quantity.** A journal has a lower circulation than a magazine or newspaper. Your article might indeed be read by the 'right' people, but don't expect widespread popularity. You can, of course, decide to write your research up for a further, wider target audience as well.

■ **Speed is not of the essence.** Full-length papers may take anywhere from three months to two years to be published. Cultivate patience rather than expect early results. If it is important that your work gets published quickly, for example if you know of some competing research that is hot on your tail, you may wish to rethink whether a top journal is your target.

■ **Impact values count.** Depending on your speciality, you may be restricted in your choice of the 'top journals'. While we encourage you to widen your potential sources, there may be pressure from your institution or sponsors to appear only in the most notable publications. And that's a crowded space!

■ **Personal creativity is discouraged.** Journals exist to disseminate knowledge to a learned audience and are therefore obliged to set and maintain standards. Your personal preference for style or approach will not be as important as your ability to adhere to guidelines.

■ **Academics are inefficient publishers.** Get used to experiencing delays in communication and longer lead times than you would have thought possible. Many authors despair at the bureaucracy and inefficient nature of academic publishing – but that tends to be its nature. See the second point above!

■ **Yes, there is an 'old-boy network'.** While you would be incorrect in assuming that papers get published because authors are friends of the editor, academe is a tightly knit and well-established community of researchers and reviewers. Relationships won't determine success or failure, but they count.

■ **Change happens slowly.** If your work challenges the established thinking of the journal, you must be prepared to have every detail and phrase examined microscopically. Some journals go out of their way to develop counter-intuitive perspectives, but others may tend to reinforce the status quo.

■ **Feedback is patchy.** It's encouraging for an author to receive constructive feedback, even if a paper is rejected, but many journal editors and reviewers simply don't have the time. It can be disheartening to receive a curt 'no' after waiting for months for a response.

■ **Publication means recognition.** Despite the sometimes irksome nature of academic publishing, having your paper published will lend great weight to your work and to your institution. Although the community may be fairly closed, publication can open many new doors.

■ **Practise makes perfect.** By the time you have endured the difficult and sometimes frustrating process of paper preparation, review and publication you will find it much easier to do it all again next time. The experience will help you to perfect some very useful disciplines.

9. Proposals to publishers

If you are ever to get the chance to get your book published, then it is essential that you write a really good proposal. Even if you have completed the entire manuscript, a publisher will usually request that only a proposal be sent initially. View the proposal as a sales vehicle for your masterpiece and try to include a mention of all its key features:

■ **Follow the publishers guidelines.** If you received any notes from your chosen publisher on the proposed proposal format, then stick to them. Provide information on each of the areas listed in the guidelines and don't leave any out.

■ **Give information on all the areas listed in the Guidelines on Proposals Contents section.** If you are not following specific guidelines, make sure you cover everything that is needed fully and use the broad areas indicated as sub-headings for your proposal.

■ **Use the proposal as a sales tool for your book.** This is the vehicle that will help you to secure a contract for your book, so you need to really polish it. Emphasize its unique and key selling points strongly and make sure that the proposal sounds interesting enough to make the editor feel it will make a good book.

■ **Research your targeted publisher's lists.** Get catalogues from the publishers you plan to target and research which series, if any, your book might fit into. Publishers tend to group the books they publish into lists or series that they can market together. There's no point trying to publish with a publisher who doesn't normally market books in your area of work.

■ **Indicate where your book would fit on your publisher's list.** State in your synopsis which list (or specific series) you see accommodating your book. Explain why you see it sitting alongside other books in the series and how your book would complement them.

■ **Keep the proposal brief.** A proposal should normally be fairly concise, running to up to four sheets of A4 paper or so typed in single spacing. Of course it will take more pages if it is attractively laid out using headings and sub-headings for emphasis.

■ **Get feedback on your proposal.** Once your proposal is drafted, ask one or two people to read it over. These need not be experts in your discipline as their function is to give comments on the overall shape of the proposal. They may also spot typographical and other errors that you have missed, which would otherwise give a poor impression of your work. They can also confirm that it is crystal clear to someone reading it with a fresh eye. If they identify queries or problems, these can be reviewed and resolved before your actual submission.

■ **Submit a clear, clean document.** Make sure that the proposal is printed out freshly, is well laid out and is a clean copy. Leave generous margins around the edges so it doesn't look cramped. If you spot an error or make a last-minute amendment, correct it on the disk and make another copy. Remember that a scruffy, badly presented proposal bodes ill for a good working relationship with a publisher.

■ **Put the title and your name as a footer or header clearly on each sheet.** Number pages clearly and make sure that each sheet is identifiable in case of a mix-up when your publisher photocopies it.

■ **Write a letter to accompany the proposal.** A good letter is important. It is worth finding out the name of the commissioning editor and writing a personalized letter to a named person explaining why you have sent it there. Use the letter to sell your proposal and to outline the general subject area on which your proposal focuses. Also, let the publisher know if you have sent out copies of the proposal simultaneously to other publishing houses. In any case, limit the mail-out to only a handful of the most likely publishers.

10. How editors select papers for publication

An editor's role is to ensure that all papers published in his or her publication reflect the editorial objectives of the publication and therefore the needs of its readers. We're assuming that the publication's objectives are clear and available to prospective authors. The editor must also take responsibility for the final version of the paper, and will often work with authors on revisions. Here are the stages in the selection process most editors go through:

■ **Can this paper survive the five-minute test?** Editors may receive hundreds of papers each week. It wouldn't be possible to read and fully understand each paper just to make a judgement about its suitability for the publication. A fast, foolproof method is required. A quick five-minute scan should reveal whether the paper meets the necessary criteria.

■ **Is the purpose clear?** Has the author clearly stated the purpose within the first few paragraphs? Can you be sure what the purpose is in less than a minute of reading time? If not, it is unlikely the author has the clarity of thinking necessary to carry the paper along.

■ **Does the author's purpose match the purpose of the publication?** Someone may submit a fascinating theoretical paper on quantum physics, but if your publication exists to show young people how to conduct useful experiments at home, you won't be interested.

■ **Can you identify key points quickly?** You should be able to tell in just a few moments what the paper is about. A well-structured paper has sub-headings, which help the reader follow the flow, and summarizes at key intervals to help reinforce understanding.

■ **Do the key points support the purpose?** Can the author retain focus, or does the paper drift off onto interesting but irrelevant tangents? Some authors may be trying to pare down a weighty work into just a few pages – do they demonstrate the skill of being able to work within those limitations?

■ **Do you know why the paper is important?** The author shouldn't be leaving you guessing about the paper's significance. The implications, or 'so what' values of the paper should strike you clearly. If an author hasn't done this, chances are he or she hasn't really thought it through – or maybe the paper isn't important.

■ **Is it readable?** Has it been difficult for you to understand what the author means? If you, who are accustomed to reading hundreds of papers, can't understand it, how will your readers? You may choose to confer with the author about his or her literacy, but it would be easier to wait for a better writer to come along and tackle the same subject.

■ **Does it follow your house style?** Authors who present papers in a style which doesn't match your publication's are not serious about publishing with you. They are the kinds of authors who send their papers to different publications at random – and you may be the last on their list. Unless you're desperate, work with authors who show they are keen to work with you.

■ **Will it make a lot of work for you?** If you feel you may need to do a great deal of editorial work on a paper, you may need to question whether it is worth your time and effort. Is the proposed contribution so unique, so authoritative and so relevant that you must take it seriously?

■ **Will the authors deliver?** It's more dependable to work with experienced authors, but newcomers deserve a chance, too. Before pinning all your hopes on a revised paper coming back to you in the right shape and on time, ask the author to respond much earlier than you really need. Most experienced editors will tell you – 10 promises equals one paper.

11. Targeting the right journal

Editors reject papers mostly because they are not suited to the journal. As many as half of all papers submitted to a journal never enter the review process. The journal may be fundamentally theoretical, yet an author submits a paper based on practice – or vice versa. The paper may be overtly international in scope, yet a proposed paper pays no attention to anything outside the home country. The following suggestions will help you target the right journal:

- **Broaden your scope.** Everyone in their respective fields wants to get published in the most highly rated journal. That's why those journals have rejection rates in the high nineties. Inexperienced authors may break through immediately, but it's unlikely. Commit to widening your prospects from the one or two most famous journals to the ten that are highly respectable.

- **Ask respected colleagues.** You'll find out more about publishing possibilities by talking with those who are already widely published. Talk to them – to your supervisor, department head, counterparts in other institutions. Find out where they first became published and what journals they read apart from the most obvious.

- **Conduct a citation search.** Trace the publication records of those authors whom you respect. You may have read them most recently in the top journal, but where did they publish five or ten years ago?

- **Check directories.** Every university library will have at least one major directory listing journals, their editors, their objectives and their addresses. You will be surprised at the number of possibilities that exist in your field.

- **Study copies of your prospective journals.** Again, this may seem obvious, yet many editors report that papers they receive have been written without regard to the journal's objectives and style. If your own library doesn't have the journals you want to review, source them by inter-library loan or ask the publisher to send you samples. Many paper-based journals now have Web-sites with editorial direction and selected articles.

- **Study key issues of each journal.** Journal editors and advisers often comment importantly on the direction of their journals at strategic times of the year. In the last issue of the journal, editors will often summarize the high points of the year and describe what they found to be the most useful or insightful papers. In the first issue of a new year or volume, the editor may describe the kinds of papers being sought in the future.

- **Obtain Notes for Authors.** The editorial team has painstakingly devised clear instructions for authors to follow. Their advisory notes detail everything from the editorial objectives to the preferred style of referencing. These are usually found in each issue of the journal, or at least in the first of each volume.

- **Get into the minds of your audience.** Who exactly is the editor and what does he or she like? Read the editorials and anything the editor has written recently. Editors are not in the business of keeping secrets from prospective authors. Seek to understand what excites, annoys and bores the editor.

- **Trace the evolution of thinking.** Many authors publish frequently in the same journal and refer to their earlier work and the work of fellow authors. How will your work fit in? Can you see how you can contribute to a particular journal's progress in becoming or maintaining a leading-edge position?

- **Solicit early advice.** While most journal editors say they prefer to receive a manuscript rather than a query, few can resist a carefully targeted letter designed to assess their interest. Something like 'Your encouraging comment in No. 1 Vol. 8 about the value of a multidisciplinary approach prompted me to send you the attached abstract of my forthcoming paper' will often capture an editor's attention.

12. Making your research publishable

What is your paper about? Why should anyone read it? You may think the answers to those questions are implicit in your work, and you may be right. But if you don't make them explicit, your paper will never be published in a respectable journal. In this chapter we will explore the key variables that make your research publishable:

- **What is the purpose of your paper?** Many papers are rejected simply because the editor and review board can't figure out what they're supposed to be saying. We suspect that's because the research is still seen by the author as an end in itself. Now is the time to consider the outcome rather than the process.

- **Write it in 20 words or less.** Draw yourself out of the role of researcher into the role of communicator. Take your years of effort and summarize all of it in 20 words or less. 'The purpose of this paper is to …' Demonstrate a new technique? Refute an old theory? Answer a puzzling question?

- **Don't lose your nerve.** The reason many papers lack a clearly stated purpose is not so much because the author doesn't know what it is, but because the author doesn't want to say it so boldly. It can be a salutary moment: 'Am I really going to nail my ideas down and tell the world exactly what I've done and why they should listen?'

- **Purpose leads to practice.** Once you are clear and confident about your purpose, review your research to develop its real implications. These could be for immediate application or for further research – but sometime soon you will have to say – 'so what?'.

- **Write why it matters.** Our research into acceptance criteria revealed that, all other criteria being met, the most common reason for rejection was that the implications of the paper were not clear. 'So what?' reviewers would ask. Take your research and write two clear sentences (20 words or less!) explaining exactly why your research is important and what the reader should do about it.

- **Define your scope.** A barrier to focus sometimes arises when we fear that readers' will challenge us on why we centred on some aspects of our research and not on others. You may by now have taken your scope for granted. Try to summarize it in one short paragraph to help clarify your thinking.

- **Articulate its limitations.** Time, money, resources, challenges of data gathering – all of these have imposed constraints upon your research. Again, we sometimes fear that others will challenge us about these. Now is the time to review and summarize the limitations that affected your work.

- **Accept your imperfections.** As one doctoral supervisor notably said: 'There are only two types of articles; those that are perfect and never get published, and those that are good enough and do.' There will always be another question, always another, better way to have approached your research. Recognize that and carry on. Accepting your imperfections isn't called failure, it's called learning.

- **Draft your structure.** This will not define your final treatment, but now that you know what you are saying and why, review your research under the following headings: purpose, implications, methodology, analysis, conclusion.

- **Give it a rest.** The above process is lengthy and time-consuming, but it will quite probably be the determining factor in whether or not your paper ever gets written, let alone published. Allow the effort to settle down and resist the temptation to think it's an end in itself. Next, you will take your draft structure and begin to relate it to the needs of different groups of readers.

13. Manuscript appeal

When you're submitting your writing for publication it is well worth trying to make the best of first impressions, particularly those on editors and reviewers. The following suggestions may serve as a checklist:

- **Make it look professional.** This is easy to ask, and much harder to pin down. Professional-looking writing is about the right tone and style for the target audience, and also about avoiding obvious things like misspellings, typographical errors, and punctuation anomalies.

- **Make it look really relevant to the readership of the journal.** This is a key criterion in the minds of journal editors. It is easy for them to reject anything that could be argued to be tangential to the areas covered by the journal, or remote from the interests of the majority of its readers.

- **Highlight the timeliness of your contribution.** 'Why should this be published *now*?' is a good question to bear in mind when choosing how you introduce your writing. While taking care not to write in a way that will cause your article to become dated quickly, draw out the relevance of your writing to ongoing trends and any important new developments in your field.

- **Make it look new and important.** Something that obviously seems to be a new treatment of a subject, or a novel approach to an old problem, is more likely to appeal to publishers and editors. A unique contribution is always of more interest than a piece that goes back over well-trodden territory. An article that can be seen as a clear advancement of knowledge or understanding in a field is more likely to be looked on favourably.

- **Make it appear thorough.** It is important that your writing is taken as credible, even if you're not yet an established writer in the field. Check that your work refers to well-known and respected authorities in the field, and that such references appear quite early.

- **Make your illustrations good.** Where you use tables, diagrams, charts and other visual illustrations, make sure that they look good, and that they are well checked, accurate and relevant.

- **Be up-front about seminal research.** If your article reflects something that could be followed up readily by others working in the field, make it clear that there are still many issues to be explored. In such cases include in your writing the unanswered questions and the challenges, rather than trying to make your work look finished and rounded.

- **Make any controversy overt.** If your article is arguing against accepted views on a topic, let this be seen to be the case from the outset, rather than saving the controversy for your conclusions. Editors will want to be able to decide whether the controversy is a strong reason for publishing your work.

- **Follow the author guidelines to the letter.** If you're asked to supply three copies, double-spaced and with a wide right-hand margin, do so. When most of the submissions that editors consider are correctly 'in format', any that are not stand out at once.

- **Make it readable.** Clarity is probably the most important attribute of tone and style of writing. For your work to be accepted for publication, it is not enough that the editor or referee can understand what you're saying. They probably can understand it, as they're likely to be well versed in the field, but they are working on behalf of readers who may not know the field backwards.

- **Make it relevant.** Writing that goes off on tangents (however interesting) appeals less to most editors than writing that sticks closely to the agenda spelled out by the title and abstract at the beginning. Those looking at manuscripts can become irritated quite quickly if they feel they are being led on a wild goose chase.

- **Make the title self-explanatory and interesting.** A good title should whet the appetite of prospective readers. It should indicate not just what the piece is about, but should also hint at why it will be worth reading. The combination of title and sub-title can be an effective way of invoking interest, and adding that first bit of rationale.

- **Get the abstract perfect!** When your work is in the final stages of being considered for publication, your abstract will be read much more deeply than anything else. Make sure that your article lives up to the promise of its abstract. It is worth rewriting the abstract as many times as may be needed to make sure that it really does summarize the main thrust of your writing and your findings.

14. Improving your 'hit rate'

The previous sections in this chapter have outlined the most important steps to help you achieve your publishing goals. If you take them slowly, step by step, you will greatly improve your chances of becoming published. Here's our summary of how you will get there:

- **Clear your mind before you clear your desk.** Don't distract yourself with the thousand seemingly important tasks – like organizing your paper clips or buying new pencils – that will blur your focus. Start by concentrating on summarizing the value of your research until you can say it in a simple sentence in your sleep.

- **Decide who will be interested.** Your research now is sharply focused. That being so, you will limit your potential audience. That improves your chances of becoming published. Make a list of the two or three target groups with whom you want to communicate.

- **Confer with trusted colleagues.** Take the time now to share your focus and ideas about your audience with others in your field. Solicit and accept their constructive feedback. The more often you open your work to those who represent your particular reference group, the more likely it is they will help you refine your approach.

- **Choose your potential journals carefully.** Properly focused research and its eventual publication will only interest a handful of journals. Read them, understand them, and make sure you have their notes of guidance to potential authors. Most papers are rejected simply because they do not match the editorial objectives of the journal.

- **Quality is what the customer says it is.** The quality of your research and paper is judged by those who intend to benefit by it. They are the ones – the editors, reviewers and readers – who will determine the quality criteria upon which your paper is assessed. Find out what those criteria are.

- **Make it interesting.** Most published papers are never read in their entirety. This is partly because the research findings need only be glanced at to determine their value for the reader, but it's also because many academic papers are tedious and boring. Improve your hit rate by making your work vivid and exciting.

- **Make sure you know why it matters.** Another common reason for rejection is the 'so what?' clause. Reviewers often can't figure out why your paper is supposedly important – mainly because you're not telling them! Draw out implications throughout – of your research question, of your methodology, of the literature, of your findings.

- **Make it readable.** Turgid, vague, verbose papers are no fun to read. The reviewer may be forced through professional duty to read it, but if it's a struggle then the likelihood is it will be rejected or returned for revision.

- **Follow your instructions.** If an editor or reviewer makes a condition or even a strong suggestion, follow it. These are the people who exist to help you transform your research into a masterful piece of fascinating prose. Work with them, not against them.

- **Remain above reproach.** By adhering to house style guidelines, reviewers' comments and deadlines you will make everyone's life easier. People prefer to work with those who make their lives easier, not more difficult.

- **Only submit to one journal at a time.** Editors' schedules are ruined by authors who submit to more than one journal. Journals want to have original, new material. Although this means you must wait until you hear from each editor in turn, it certainly prevents you from being blacklisted by weary editors.

- **And just keep doing it!** The more you write, the better a writer you become. The more often you submit papers, the more likely you are to be accepted. The more often your papers are accepted, the more likely it is future papers will be accepted. And so on!

15. Responding to referees' feedback

Let's say you have reached the stage in the publication process when you receive feedback from the review panel. What do you do? When do you do it? How do you do it? We wouldn't be posing these questions unless we assumed that many authors don't manage this stage well. And they don't. Some ignore the feedback entirely, while others respond in a way that endears them to the reviewer and the editor. Let's see how they do it:

■ **Choose to respond.** There are two black holes in the publishing process. This is when the editor feels he or she has lost control and is at the mercy of outside forces. The first occurs when a reviewer doesn't send back comments in time, and the second occurs when the author doesn't respond. Decide now that if you are entering the process you will honour the implicit assumption of participation.

■ **Acknowledge the editor.** Comments are normally sent to an author via the editor or the editorial staff. You are invited to consider the reviewers' remarks and make the suggested alterations, usually by a given date. Immediately, acknowledge that you have received the letter and will be complying by the deadline. This makes it possible for your paper to be tentatively scheduled in a future issue.

■ **Accept the feedback with good grace.** As you have by now committed to the process, part of the deal is that you will accept that peer review is the benchmark by which you will be judged. Given that you have, we hope, targeted the journal carefully, you should now assume that the review panel has made the correct judgement. Some of their comments may grate a little, but such is the pain that comes with learning.

■ **Confer with colleagues.** The reviewers' feedback may only amount to a few paragraphs or sentences. While most reviewers take time to ensure that their meaning is clear, it is wise at this stage to ask other people to help you interpret the suggestions. Your co-authors, supervisor and other close associates should be sent copies of the comments and asked to discuss them with you.

■ **Reread the journal.** Remember that the people reviewing your paper are busy reviewing other papers for the same journal. If the reviewer seems particularly interested in certain aspects, say your description of your instruments or your lack of guidance for further researchers, read other articles which attend to those points. This will help you deepen your understanding of what the reviewer is exploring.

■ **What if you can't?** Perhaps a review comment concerns you because it attacks something you feel reveals a basic flaw in your original research or its design. You can't go back and do that piece all over again, although in the future you might decide to do it differently. We recommend that you don't arrive at any conclusion before discussing the comments with respected colleagues. It might be that the reviewer is asking for more explanation rather than suggesting your method or design was wrong.

■ **What if you still can't?** If you finally conclude that the reviewer has illuminated something that can't be fixed, admit it. Don't ignore it or try to write something other than what you've been asked to do. You might instead choose to suggest to the editor that the paper be revised, taking that very problem as its starting point: 'How not to do research by this method', and might therefore contribute to the work of other researchers about to make the same mistake.

■ **Revise as requested.** All being well, you will be able to make the amendments according to the suggestions and the deadline. Keep in mind that when you submit your revised paper, your amendments will be checked against the reviewers' original comments. This is no time for lip service.

■ | **Return your paper on time.** Whatever other commitments you have at the moment, this one takes priority. The editor and reviewers have all invested their time and wisdom in your paper – don't insult them now by saying you had something better to do.

■ | **Say 'thank you'.** It won't ensure that your paper is published, but it will reinforce in your own mind and heart that this is one of the best exercises in receiving free advice and support that you've ever been given.

16. Dealing with rejections

Even for well-published authors, there is a feeling of suspense when opening the letter from a publisher or editor that contains the verdict on a piece of your work. When this letter (or fax or phone call) is a bringer of bad news, the following suggestions may provide both comfort and support:

■ | **Don't be surprised.** Whether it was a book proposal or an article submitted to a journal, there are many more letters of rejection written to authors than letters of unconditional acceptance. If you get a rejection, remind yourself that you're now in really distinguished company. We know of no significant author who has not had such letters.

■ | **Don't be surprised even if you're a well-published author.** If your writing is already respected, it can come as a bit of a shock if your latest piece is being rejected. However, there can be many sensible reasons for rejecting it, including that it may not be the most wonderful piece that you've ever written!

■ | **Watch out for your ego.** It's all too easy to become defensive, and to become hostile to the people who have dared not to accept your masterpiece. Resist the temptation to put pen to paper to defend the validity and importance of your work. It's worth putting the piece and letter away for a week or more, and returning to it later when emotions have subsided.

■ | **If rejection hurts, question your motives.** Are you more interested in being vindicated than in getting your work published? It helps to regard getting your work accepted as a game with many variables, where you're constantly trying to make adjustments to your strategy on the basis of experience, and where there is still a considerable element of chance involved.

■ | **Don't stop writing.** When one piece of your work has been rejected by one target publisher or journal, this does not mean that all of your work will be rejected by the whole world. It can be very healthy to redirect your energies, for a while at least, into something else that you're already working on.

■ **Check out whether your piece has really been rejected.** Some rejections are definite and without any statement of reasons or suggestions. However, many rejections are accompanied by explanations, which could be very useful to you in your next piece of writing. Furthermore, rejections are often conditional, and give suggestions regarding ways you could recompose your writing to make it more acceptable to the targeted publisher or journal.

■ **If it's just a matter of 'length', change it.** Publishers and editors normally work to tight page limits, particularly regarding journal articles or book chapters. If your submission is too long, swallow that pride and get cutting! Decide which are the most important parts of the ideas you wish to communicate, and prune out some of the rest. Most articles are all the better for being two-thirds of the original length!

■ **Remember that there are many good reasons for rejecting a good article or proposal.** If your publisher just does not want another book in an area that is well represented in their catalogue, or if your article is just not tuned in to the needs and interests of the readership of a particular journal, it does not mean that there's anything wrong with your writing. One of the factors leading to successful publication is getting the material to the right place at the right time, and there is no shame in not managing to do this very often.

■ **If your referees or reviewers have made suggestions, take heed of them.** It takes no longer to follow up most of these suggestions than it would to write an eloquent exposition regarding how the suggestions are not at all appropriate in the context of your work. Even if you find yourself including discussions that you would rather not have brought into your work, the fact that you have had such topics suggested to you indicates that some readers at least will wish to see such discussions.

■ **If you're going to make changes and have another go, move fast.** Publishers and editors have tight windows, and if you miss your time slot they will not be able to consider your work further. In any case, it often takes no longer to get started on the business of making some changes than to sit putting off the actual moment of starting.

■ **If there's nothing you can do with your rejected piece, don't throw it away in disgust.** You may never be able to publish it in the form that it is in at present, but future circumstances may turn it into a good starting point from which to write something else. Also, it's worth keeping your mistakes to remind you not to make the same ones again.

■ **Rejection of your writing is not rejection of you as a worthwhile person!** Be bold and talk about the rejection, positively, with your friends. They will still be friends.

17. Using the literature search effectively

Few sections of a research paper are more enervating than a mundane literature review. That's because many researchers don't so much review the literature as summarize and faithfully report on it. It's time to go well beyond an undergraduate description of who said what when, and on to an analytical exposition of who said what when and why it was important (or not) and what you think should be done about it:

- **Plan to reveal, not just review.** You have amassed hundreds of papers and read scores of books. All of your reading impacted on your research – but not all of it is directly relevant to a single paper about your research. Decide at the outset that you will use only what is necessary to inform your reader.

- **We've seen it all before.** Remember, the editor and review board knows the broad field better than you do. They won't be impressed by three pages of irrelevant references, all of which could have simply been lifted from another book or database.

- **Review your scope.** The effort you spent describing your scope will be of real benefit here. The literature you describe and analyse will be that which reflects your chosen scope, not necessarily all aspects of the field.

- **Review your beginning and end.** The literature needs to follow the purpose and support or be refuted by your implications. Now that you have articulated your purpose and implications, selecting the emphasis for your literature section will follow naturally.

- **Summarize the relevant literature.** As a first step, draw together the key contributors who impact on your field and, in particular, on your specific research and its scope. Of all those you have read, you will want to describe most fully the work of those with the most impact on your implications.

- **Synthesize the work of key contributors.** Summarizing the relevant literature is where many people stop, but you need to go further. This is where you will make sense of your predecessors' work. You can synthesize along chronological lines, showing how our understanding has arisen systematically from one person's idea to the next, or according to key themes or questions.

- **Analyse the work so far.** Now that you have summarized and made sense of your predecessors, here's your opportunity to comment upon it, revealing their strengths and weaknesses, brilliance and failings. This is a most useful and interesting part of any literature review and shows your ability to critically evaluate the work of others.

- **Put your stamp on it – authorize.** This is where authors make the vital connection between what the body of knowledge has offered so far, and what their contribution now is. This is where you ask the burning question foremost in your reviewers' minds: 'so what?'. How is your research going to support or challenge the existing thinking? What will other people learn from what you've done?

■ **Edit without mercy.** Having done all of the above, your literature review will still be too long and unwieldy. It's terribly difficult to resist the opportunity to show off our erudition, and name-dropping is the most convenient way to do it. Go back over your review and cut away all but what is essential, forcing yourself to be concise, analytical and conclusive.

■ **Don't over-refer to your own publications.** Too many references to your own work (however relevant you feel it may be) can make you seem boastful. It is easy to be tempted to include all of your own references whether they are relevant or not, especially as you are likely to have accurate details to hand!

18. Finding the right voice

How we hear an author speak is known as a 'voice'. Authors speak through writing, of course, not the spoken word, but the tone of voice in an article can be as clear as if we were hearing human speech. Just as we interpret someone's meaning partly through their tone of voice when they speak, so we interpret meaning through the voice of the written word. Here we present some suggestions about finding and articulating the right voice:

■ **Read, read, read.** Have you ever wondered why you sometimes know that a sentence doesn't 'sound right' – or that it does? Your mind and inner hearing are attuned to certain rhythms and resonances embedded in grammatical convention. You nurtured that sense through reading. Read selected journals regularly and you will begin to condition yourself to their tone.

■ **Any voice might do.** There isn't an absolute right or wrong about voice. Some journals like articles that begin with snappy sentences in journalistic style, while others prefer a more formal academic tone. Find out what your selected journals want by studying their editorial guidelines and reading them regularly.

■ **Prefer the positive to the negative.** A pompous tone evolves as we use certain structures. One of the most obvious is expressing something in a negative tone. 'This research is not unlike that which' is a negative expression of 'This research is similar to'.

■ **Prefer the active to the passive.** Even academic formal writing is brightened by reducing the number of passive sentences. Rather than saying 'authors have frequently been troubled by rejection' try 'rejection frequently troubles authors'. Check your word-processing package for the grammar-check function and use it to highlight your passive sentences.

■ **Seek to express, not impress.** Using long, obscure words shrouds your writing with an aura of mystery that you may mistake for erudition. It is neither clever nor interesting to force your reader to check a dictionary every few paragraphs, and only increases your tone of pomposity.

■ **Invite your reader into your world.** Dispensing with jargon altogether will improve the inviting tone of your voice. The more often your reader must pause to work out what you mean by a curious phrase or abbreviation (and shame on the editor who let these pass!), the less inviting your voice sounds.

■ **Vary your sentence length.** Long sentences are more difficult to follow, even if they are grammatically pristine. Now and then they can be useful and even engaging, but strung together they add a sombre note to your work which makes your voice sound heavy. Intersperse them with short sentences to vary the pace and brighten the tone.

■ **Eliminate personal asides.** The tone of most academic journals is formal, to greater or lesser degrees, but strikingly different from a short magazine piece. One of the distinctions is that of familiarity. Academic researchers should be distancing themselves from the reader sufficiently to allow a more objective review of the work.

■ **Pass your paper around.** This is one occasion where no previous experience is necessary. Ask your friends, family, colleagues and acquaintances to read portions of your writing and tell you how they hear your voice. Amend where you must until it matches the voice of the journal you aspire to. (Oh, yes, not ending a sentence with a preposition is a rule made to be broken if it matches your voice!)

■ **Develop your own range of voices.** The more you write, the more comfortable you are likely to be writing in different voices for different audiences. Aim to write as naturally as you can in whatever voice you've chosen for each particular purpose, and you will soon develop the knack of making your work come across well to quite different audiences.

19. Style points

Style is that sometimes indefinable quality which gives a certain personality or character to someone or something. But style doesn't happen by accident. Components of style are often not unique; a black hat and a pair of black gloves will not alone create a stylish outfit, but the combination will. Creating personal style requires paying attention to the components of your writing and the way you put them all together. We review here some common characteristics of stylish writing:

■ **Whose style is it?** Every publication has its own 'house style' to govern such variations as headings, footnotes, reference systems and so on. These are the mechanics that will help make your paper easy for the publisher to process. Whatever variations on the themes of style you may choose, house style is not an option.

- **Take care of the basics.** Papers which are ugly to look at and hard to read may not receive the attention they deserve. Your adherence to points of commonly accepted style plus the journal's house style demonstrates that you have a good grasp of the language. Make sure you get these right before attempting to impose your own personal idiosyncrasies.

- **Economy is the best value.** Always err on the side of brevity. If you can't summarize your research and implications in a few short sentences, you may not have the clear focus so necessary for clear writing. Once you start writing, continue to edit and shorten rather than expand and lengthen.

- **Throw away your thesaurus.** A short word is always better than a longer substitute. Most of the time we know the right word but try to find a longer one because we think it's more impressive. It's not. What impresses reviewers and readers is your ability to communicate simply and clearly.

- **Double-check for meaning.** It's sometimes surprising how often academics will choose the wrong words to express an idea – confusing their infers and implies, illusions and allusions, effects and affects. The number one rule of writing figures here: when in doubt, check it out. Don't let the bad habits you may have developed take over when a quick glance at a dictionary would set you right.

- **Check spelling.** No points here for trying to position yourself as a world-leading academic when you haven't bothered to check your spelling. No one is a perfect speller, which is why software includes the spell-check function. Of course, it's not infallible and won't correct your its and theirs, but activating it should be an automatic gesture before saving any file.

- **Punctuation should enhance understanding.** The reason we have commas, full stops (periods), semi-colons and parentheses is because they help the reader grasp our meaning. If you don't know the difference between a colon and semi-colon, either find out or don't use them. The punctuation check deserves the time of an experienced copy-editor.

- **Metaphors are a slippery slope to hoe.** Most of the time, we use metaphors because we can't be bothered to say what we really mean. We choose, instead, to allude to a picture. Pictures can be vibrant, but most aren't. Most metaphors are so hackneyed that the reader glosses over them without gaining anything new. Think carefully before using metaphors, and when you do, make sure you don't mix them up.

- **Ask other people specifically about your style.** This is actually rather harder to do than to ask people for feedback on your content, as style is somewhat more personal, and you may find it harder to view critical comments objectively. Check your style out with a friend. A second opinion often helps you to see your work anew.

■ **Work on it.** Writing is a craft, and like any craft it needs to be mastered through understanding and practice. Your library and bookshop have shelves of books devoted to the finer points of style. Now that you've decided to be a writer as well as an academic, you should take the time to develop the skill, just as you took the time to develop your knowledge of your speciality.

20. Diagrams, drawings and tables

Whether you use visual components such as these will depend on your discipline and on the sort of book or article you are writing. If words alone are all you need, count yourself fortunate to have one less area to worry about, and skip this section! However, if diagrams, charts, tables, drawings, graphs, pictures, or any other visual means of communicating data or ideas are relevant to your writing, it's best to set out to use them well from the outset of your writing. The following suggestions will help you avoid the most frustrating pitfalls:

■ **Think about the value of making your writing visual, and not just textual.** For readers, a double-page spread of unbroken text tends to be less attractive than something that is broken up by headings, sub-headings, and (above all) *figures*. Not numbers of course, but graphs, diagrams, pictures, tables, charts, flowcharts, sketches, even cartoons. Adding this kind of visual variety to your work can keep your readers engaged.

■ **Read your publishers guidelines carefully.** Most publishers offer detailed suggestions to authors regarding how best to incorporate visual material into their writing.

■ **Make the quality of your figures suitable for reproduction by your publisher.** The perceived quality of a book is often linked to the clarity and relevance of its illustrations. Many publishers prefer to have masters of figures supplied separately from the text, and in a format that they can reduce (such as an A4 diagram to be reduced to A5, or further, in the actual book). Most publishers insist on original photographs, printouts or drawings, rather than photocopies.

■ **Don't number your figures from 1 to 97.** It is best to code your numbering by chapter. It is easier to alter the number of the figures from Fig. 3.4 onwards, when you decide to insert a *new* Fig. 3.4 into Chapter 3, than to have to go right through all the following chapters as well.

■ **Check that your figures are correctly referred to in your text.** This is particularly important when you've inserted a new one or deleted one, changing the numbers. It's one of the hardest things for an author to spot, as we all tend to read what we meant to say, rather than what we actually said, and it's even worse with numbers than with words!

■ **Take particular care with figures you may be using from other people's work.** It is not just a matter of acknowledging them, and seeking and getting permission to use them (and probably paying for this). It may well be necessary for you to redraw a figure to bring it up to the standard that your publisher needs from you to be able to produce it from your manuscript.

■ **Make your captions full and self-explanatory.** It should be possible for readers to get a fairly full impression of what any figure is about even before looking in the text for what you actually say about it.

■ **Try to ensure that your figures will be visible when readers are reading about them.** Few things are more irritating to readers than to have to flip backwards or forwards to look at a figure while reading your description or discussion of it. Publishers usually ask authors to indicate approximately where in the text a figure should appear, such as by inserting:

Figure 3 about here

■ **Decide whether you need to include a list of figures.** If your illustrations are particularly important, readers may find it useful to be able to return to a specific figure easily, and such a list helps them do so.

■ **Triple-check your figures at proof stage.** Some of the most common errors in proofs relate to the wrong caption being placed with a figure, figures themselves being transposed, figures occasionally being missed out altogether, and figures being wrongly referenced in the text. Then there are all the possibilities of there being something wrong with the figures themselves. It is worth doing a completely separate check through all of your figures, captions and numbers at proof stage. Once you find one mistake, look even more carefully for others. All this is worth the trouble, compared to the possibility of incorrect figures being on your public record.

21. Making a good finish

Making a good last impression is almost as crucial as making a good first one. This applies not only to many of your readers, but also to most reviewers, who tend to take a close look at how you conclude your writing. This is not least so that they can find out what your main conclusions are, and whether they really want to find out all about it by going through your work in detail. The following suggestions may help you reach your conclusions in a robust way:

■ **Decide quite early on what your main conclusions are going to be.** This is best done at the planning stage of your writing. You may feel that you have a wide range of things that are important enough to qualify as main conclusions, but any book, paper or article has its last 100 words.

■ **Work out what you wish your conclusions to achieve.** There are many possibilities, including summarizing a case you have made, or pointing your readers further to possible future developments in the field, or summing up the questions which further research may follow up.

■ **Decide which one impression you would like your readers to go away with.** Ask yourself 'If there's only one thing they will remember, what do I want it to be?'. This is likely to be the most suitable basis for your final words.

■ **Take particular care with the wording of your conclusions.** These are the parts of your work that may be most likely to be quoted by others, and you need to protect yourself from the position of having to live with words that you would prefer to have been different.

■ **Keep your conclusions quite short.** Whether you plan your ending as a final climax, or a twist in the tail, or a drawing together of related elements, don't take too long over it, or too many readers may miss the significance you are trying to communicate.

■ **Don't just conclude your piece as a whole.** With books, it is worth reaching a robust concluding section at the end of every chapter, and even in an academic paper or article it's often worth making summaries at the end of each major section.

■ **Don't repeat yourself too obviously.** Readers normally don't like to feel that they are reading something that they have already read. It is possible to reiterate main points in ways that are different. For example, the gist of several conclusions can be gathered together as a bullet-point list.

■ **Don't introduce new material into your conclusions.** The conclusions should be the punch-lines that review for your readers where your book has taken them, and summarizes the main arguments as a finale.

■ **Flag your conclusions well.** The heading 'Conclusions' is probably over-used. It does no harm to use a heading that reminds your readers exactly what your conclusions are about. Question-headings are useful here, such as 'What causes destabilization? A summary'.

■ **Pilot your conclusions.** Ask as many people as you can to look over your last page or two, and to give you their feedback. Check whether the messages you're trying to deliver are getting across. Ask whether the wording is clear enough. Ask whether it reads interestingly. Also ask particularly for feedback on anything that is not correct, or badly phrased, or ambiguous.

■ **Check that your conclusions are visible in the contents pages.** This helps readers who have not much time to see at least some of the context leading up to your conclusions, and also allows them to locate and read intermediate conclusions or summing-up sections in your work.

22. Get your references right!

This can seem boring! It is hard work. Sooner or later, however, you will need to develop your skills to refer to other people's work in the ways that publishers require. A poorly referenced piece of work has every chance of being rejected altogether by a publisher. The suggestions below should help you to do so before you're told to put your references right by your publisher!

- **Check the format that your publisher normally uses for references.** The main two types are books, and papers in journals. Guidance is normally provided in 'Guidelines for Authors', and such guidelines are particularly crucial for chapters in edited collections, and for articles in journals. A common format for referencing books is as follows:

  Brown, S and Race, P (1995) *Assess your own Teaching Quality* Kogan Page, London.

- **Get the punctuation right!** You may think that this is unimportant, but it is important that in books, edited collections, and particularly in journals, *all* authors provide references in an agreed format. Major publishers normally prefer this to be as simple a format as possible, without quotation marks for titles, and without colons, semi-colons or anything other than a comma between author's family names and forenames or initials.

- **Find out which system is used for including references in the text.** The most common system is the Harvard one, such as 'Jones (1998) suggests that …'. If there is more than one work published in one year by an author, you may need to use 'Jones (1998a) suggests that …'.

- **Keep all the necessary details of your sources as you write your book.** Whether you use a card indexing system, or create a database on your computer, you will need such details as author's family name, author(s)' initials or forenames, the exact title of your source, the date of publication, the publisher's name and location(s). For edited collections, you will also need details of the editor(s), and the title of the collection. For journal articles, you will need the volume number, and page numbers of the articles.

- **Remember that your list of references may be the first part of your book or article that referees or reviewers look at.** The quality with which you refer to the available relevant literature is often taken as a measure of the quality of your own work. A good bibliography shows that your work is up to date and well researched.

- **Don't miss out references to important work that you happen not to like!** Some authors seem to wish to pretend that other views on their pet subjects don't exist. It is better to be seen to be taking such work into account (even critically) than to ignore it.

- **Hesitate to cite anything that is not generally available.** However crucial or relevant the reference may seem to be, few readers take delight in seeing you refer to 'Jones (1997) *Unpublished Report: Factors to Consider in Quality Assessment*'. Even less liked are 'unpublished correspondence', 'conference handout', or even 'PhD Thesis, University of Poppleton'! It is best if readers of your work, wherever they are in the world, have a reasonable chance of being able to track down your sources should they wish to do so.

■ **Prepare yourself to make accurate quotations.** When you quote verbatim any extract from a source, it is important that it is clearly seen as a quotation, and is fully acknowledged. It is preferable to quote exactly which page(s) the material comes from, taking care to mention which edition of a book the material may have been drawn from in your reference.

■ **Check your references really carefully at proof stage.** If you have supplied your work on disk, and if you got your references right in the first place, this should be a straightforward task. If, however, someone else has keyed in your references, there will be far more mistakes here than in any other part of your work, not least because the names of your sources will not be familiar to the typist. Also, it is particularly easy to mis-key numbers or dates, or to miss out volume numbers.

■ **If you fall short on any of the suggestions made above, watch out for your author queries!** Publisher's readers and copy editors are hot on referencing, and will normally list your deficiencies in this aspect at length. Sooner or later, you'll be required to make a good job of it by any reputable publisher, so you may as well learn to do it all correctly at the outset.

23. Getting feedback on your drafts

When you're writing something, the most important way to improve it is to get feedback from people. It's not just that authors are the last people to spot their own typographical or grammatical errors, though this level of feedback is invaluable in its own right. What you also want is feedback on how the piece of writing serves the purpose for which you are writing it, and that's where your pilot reviewers come in. The following suggestions can help you to make a useful pilot version of your work, and use it to make the final product much better:

■ **Don't wait till it's perfect.** It never will be! It's far better to get your book, article or chapter 80 per cent or so right and then print it out several times, so that you're able to pass drafts on to other people who will give you feedback.

■ **Decide whom to ask for feedback.** There are three main things to think about here: punctuality, quality of feedback, and authoritativeness. The best people to ask for feedback are those who've already given you really useful feedback on your past writings! However, if you're starting from scratch, cast your net quite widely, and regard it as research into whom you're going to ask for feedback on your *next* effort. Excellent feedback is no good if it comes too late, and similar comments from more than one person usually means good-quality feedback.

- **Don't just drop it on them!** It's well worth ringing up the people from whom you would like feedback, and asking them if they will be so kind. Promise them something reasonable, such as a copy of your final submission, or even a copy of the finished product if you can afford this. Be wary of people who expect to be paid for the time they may spend giving feedback; they're not usually as good as those who are willing to read your writing out of interest, collegiality or friendship.

- **Give a firm date by which you want your feedback.** Don't make the time-scale too long. If you give people months, they will put it on the shelf for later, and probably forget about it. Make your firm date about two weeks before you *really* want to start adjusting your material using all the feedback you receive.

- **Encourage robust feedback.** It's much better to get critical feedback before your work is published, than in adverse reviews. Ask your chosen people direct questions about your draft. These can be along the lines of 'What have I missed out?', 'What have I said too much about?', 'What's the most interesting bit?', 'What's the most opaque bit?', 'Who *else* should I have referred to in the references?' and so on.

- **Check up that your feedback is on its way.** Drop a note, send an e-mail, ring up, anything just to gently remind your pilot reviewers that you're looking forward to receiving their feedback. Sometimes they'll hedge somewhat (having not yet started) then get down quickly to the task having been reminded.

- **Thank people *immediately*.** As soon as you get your marked-up drafts, pass on your thanks by phone, note or e-mail. It's worth doing this even before you're in a position to weigh up exactly how valuable the feedback turns out to be. When it's really useful, don't hesitate to thank people again, this time explaining what you really appreciate in their feedback, and how you're going to take heed of it.

- **Don't argue with your pilot reviewers.** Tempting as it is to defend yourself whenever someone criticizes your masterpiece, you don't have to act on every piece of feedback you receive. If only one or two pilot reviewers find a particular fault or weakness, and if everyone else really likes the section concerned, make your own decision about whether it needs adjusting or not. Hold your judgement about what is good feedback and what isn't until you know the whole picture.

- **Remember to acknowledge the people who give you feedback.** Create your acknowledgements paragraph at the same time as editing your material with their ideas. Don't risk the embarrassment of forgetting who gave you feedback about what, or missing out the name of someone whose feedback was really useful. Thank particular people for particular things as you write your acknowledgements, so that you don't end up thanking the wrong person for a particular idea. Don't forget to acknowledge the people who gave you feedback that you didn't like, or that you decided to ignore; they too have tried to help you.

■ **Remember to keep your promises.** Send your pilot reviewers that finished version you said you would send. If you promised free copies of the published product, make sure that you honour your promise. Being good to your pilot reviewers is not just professional, but it also helps these people to be more willing to give you useful feedback on a future occasion.

24. Checking your proofs

Most authors hate proof-checking. It is much more fun to be creative than to do the tidying-up and housekeeping. However, think ahead to the day of publication. Imagine reading your work, full of pride and satisfaction, then getting that sinking feeling as you see in print errors, missed words, unfinished sentences, wrong captions on diagrams, and such like. These will now be on public record at least until your next edition! The following suggestions may help you to prevent such nightmares becoming a reality for you:

■ **Find out when your proofs are expected to be ready.** It is worth liaising with your editor in the weeks leading up to this stage, so that you can make available enough time to check them thoroughly. Turn-round times for proofs are frequently measured in days, or two weeks at best.

■ **Set aside some time to check your proofs.** Once you know when your proofs will be delivered, confirm with your editor that you will have a specific time window when you will give them your attention.

■ **Make sure you know how, when and where your proofs will be delivered.** If they are to be left at your work address, make sure that the people who handle incoming mail are expecting them. We know of some proofs that were sent by air-mail right round the world, only to be returned with 'not known at this address!' from the institution where the author was waiting for them!

■ **Read your publisher's instructions carefully.** Check exactly how you are to mark up your proofs. Normally there are strict guidelines, such as 'correct errors in red', 'indicate corrections in the margin as well as in the text', or 'make minor changes and additions that are not corrections in blue (and remember you may have to pay for these out of your royalties!)'. Some publishers will send you a sheet of terminology and codes to use in marking up proofs; these can be somewhat daunting at first sight, but in practice you will probably only need to use a small cross-section of the mark-up language.

■ **Don't just read your proofs!** The biggest danger with reading what you've written is that you see what you *meant*, and don't always see what is actually printed there. Reading proofs is an activity that has to be done much more slowly and deliberately than normal reading. It can be worth getting someone to read out aloud your manuscript version, and check up that everything is there. Having said this, expect to find all sorts of minor adjustments to your language and style, which may have been done by your publisher's copy editors. With such adjustments, always check that the points you were intending to make are still coming through.

- **Resist the temptation of second thoughts.** When it is really important to make changes other than corrections at proof stage, it can still be done. However, it can be an expensive business, especially if it may alter the page numbers (and therefore the index, glossary, contents list, and so on). Only make changes if they are absolutely necessary (such as when a major development has happened since the book was written, and needs to be mentioned in the body of the text rather than in a 'postscript' added on at the end of the book).

- **Take particular care with corrections that could affect subsequent pagination.** If, for example, a paragraph has been missed out accidentally, inserting it could alter all the pages that follow, and have knock-on effects on the index, contents pages, and so on. In such circumstances, it may be advisable to try to make the correction without affecting the page structure. This could mean editing down some other parts of the page concerned.

- **Check danger areas particularly well.** The places where errors are most likely include parts that may have not have been transcribed directly from your manuscript (or disk), such as contents pages, alterations that you made on the basis of Author Queries, and any other changes made since the first submission of your manuscript. Double-check photographs, figures and captions: Are they in the right place? Does the caption match the figure? Are the figures correctly referenced in the text? It is all too easy just to read through the proofs without ever noticing serious errors that can happen in these areas.

- **Watch out for 'Friday afternoon sections'!** When you find two or more mistakes close together, it could be that the copy editor or type-setter was having an off moment, so look even harder for other mistakes. They tend to come in clusters.

- **Meet or exceed the publisher's deadline.** It is probable that the publication window for your book will be critically dependent on the proofs being received by the due date. If your book misses this window, it could be some time before it will be processed.

- **Make copies of pages containing important alterations.** It is not often that a set of marked-up proofs goes missing in the post, but we know of occasions when it has happened. It takes far longer to do all the alterations again than to make some copies. Also, it is an indescribably frustrating experience going again through proofs trying to remember where the corrections and adjustments were needed.

- **Parcel the marked-up proofs securely.** Address the package clearly, for example 'for the attention of Ms Jones at …'. Also mark the package 'marked-up proofs'; publishers know how important these particular packages are.

- **Check that your proofs have actually been received.** It's worth telling your editor that you have sent them off, and which delivery service you have used. Telephoning to confirm that they have arrived is well worth the trouble for the peace of mind that it brings.

25. Electronic publishing: why and how?

■ **Review your objectives.** E-publishing isn't for everyone. As we explore in a later section, there are distinct advantages and disadvantages involved. Make sure you know why the electronic medium interests you. You will be targeting this channel just as you would any other publisher, so make sure it's right for you.

■ **Create your own homepage.** Many Internet providers offer advice and good financial deals to help you set up your own site. This will help people find you by entering the appropriate key words when they access a search engine.

■ **Create virtual communities.** Your interest area can be represented by a conference, a site, a journal, a discussion group, a list of e-mail addresses – the possibilities are only confined by your imagination.

■ **Invent ways to collaborate (e-mail forum groups).** You can join a discussion group in your interest area, or even start your own! All you need is an e-mail address, and the e-mails of some people you would like to share ideas with. Follow the instructions on your e-mail software to set up a discussion group to share ideas.

■ **Invent new ways to review papers.** You can post papers for general discussion and feedback from whomever, or you can offer papers for general reading but feedback from only a select few, or you can offer papers electronically to only your reviewers – or a combination of these and other methods. The draw of virtual publishing is often the wider access and dissemination it allows.

■ **Review your deadlines.** Potential collaborators and reviewers are usually busy people, so the fact that we are now operating electronically is only one factor that may influence the speed of response. Electronics impact mostly on our ability to capture multi-source feedback almost simultaneously.

■ **Update your material.** Consider your material a live source of knowledge. If you publish a paper on the Internet, work with the publisher to agree an updating schedule. This means you can periodically add to your paper as your research continues. Otherwise, you might as well put it on a shelf in the library.

■ **Become a publisher.** Through your own site you can attract potential authors and create your own e-journal. The cost of promoting and publishing on the Internet is much less than traditional methods. You will still have to establish a reputation.

■ **Validate your work by other sources.** The Internet is comparatively young, and therefore people are still enthusiastic and willing to learn about the medium. Consider linking your own, new, site to other, more mature, sites with established reputations.

■ **Use electronic publishing as a way to build your networks.** It can give you a rapid way of getting to know at least some of the people working in your field. You can then use these contacts you make to help you publish in traditional ways as well as electronically.

■ **Whose work is it, anyway?** Being published electronically may not be what you have in mind, but it may happen anyway. When you publish in a paper-based publication, check the contract. Many publishers assume the rights for electronic publication when they publish on paper.

■ **Should you object to being published electronically?** Authors who resist the kind of blanket copyright clauses described above usually do so on principle. The intellectual ownership of one's work is already established, but the choice to distribute it in any particular way is initially the author's. There are many advantages to electronic publishing, and you may not feel in a position to argue anyway. It is, however, important that you check it out and reach your own conclusion.

■ **Target your journals.** As with paper-based journals, authors must select the journal appropriate to the subject and audience. There will be as many or more choices available electronically as on paper.

■ **But is it respectable?** Some members of the academic community resist electronic publishing because they think it is without standards, reputation and form. They're right, of course, and they're wrong. Respectability varies according to the journal and how its business is conducted, not the medium.

■ **Establish its standards.** There's no reason in theory that an e-journal should be any less rigorous than a paper-based journal. The problem really lies with those who support it. You can find out who reviews and editorially guides the journal by accessing its site.

■ **Read it regularly.** Just as with a paper-based journal, e-journals exist to fulfil a need and meet an editorial objective. Log onto the site and read not only the notes to contributors, but the articles as well.

■ **Offer comment.** Many e-journals have different levels of review – one for open access and another for a selected review board. Take the opportunity to offer comment when you're capable. The feedback you give may generate useful discussion that will impact on your potential paper.

■ **Adhere to submission guidelines.** Like any journal, e-journals have specific house style and other requirements that need to be met. Before submitting a paper, ensure you download and understand all the submission requirements.

■ **Encourage updating.** A unique feature of electronic publishing is the possibility of continuous improvement. E-journals should be encouraged to offer mechanisms for regular updates by authors and incorporation of readers' comments.

■ **Understand copyright issues.** Depending on the journal, your work may be available for certain periods of time, to certain other sites, to readers to download and even for conversion to paper-based text. You may or may not object to any of these, but avoid future misunderstandings by agreeing it all at the outset.

26. Using electronic means to support traditional publishing

The Internet has brought profound changes to the publishing industry. In this section we look at some of the ways electronics can help you get published, how you can use the Internet to find information on people and ideas, and what electronics mean to you as an author:

■ **Search for collaborators.** The world is getting smaller and more accessible daily as more people and organizations get e-mail addresses and Internet sites. If you are interested in finding one or more collaborators, try running a search on topic areas you are interested in, and follow the links.

■ **Join a discussion group.** Many interest areas sponsor discussion groups and welcome new members. All you need to do is follow their joining instructions and watch how the dialogue unfolds. Soon, you'll feel confident enough to contribute.

■ **Be specific in your searches.** The Internet has several million sites, and a search for a very common keyword like 'quality' will bring up many thousands of references. Look to narrow your search to find what you need! If you are researching tourism in Iran, ask your search engine for 'tourism in Iran' rather than just 'tourism'.

■ **Search for references.** Do you remember the name or author of a book, but don't have a record of the publication details? Try online bookshops such as amazon.com which have comprehensive search engines for books both in and out of print.

■ **See who else is publishing in your field.** However obscure your area of interest, it is likely that there will be, somewhere in the world, an electronic journal (e-journal) related to it, and a discussion forum (newsgroup) where people share ideas. Use the Deja News search engine to search newsgroups.

■ **E-mail potential collaborators.** Don't be shy! One of the greatest values of the Internet and e-mail is the way it opens access worldwide to people and institutions. If you see someone's e-mail address and you're interested in exchanging views or ideas, just drop a line.

■ **Ask for help.** Try sending a proposal or the outline of a paper to a select group of individuals. Even people you've never met may be willing to look at your work and respond.

■ | **Use electronic means to help you to get a worldwide view.** You may be surprised to find out about work going on in countries that you just had no idea about as being part of the research community in your subject. Getting feedback from colleagues internationally can help you to get a wider perspective, and may well point you to new directions you can take in your own research.

■ | **Consider using electronic communication to help you undertake research.** When you are able to use electronic means to target appropriate constituencies, such as by asking people to fill in questionnaires electronically, or to respond to open questions, you may be able to gain lots of useful data for your research.

■ | **The medium doesn't change the message.** Just because we do things electronically doesn't mean we do them totally differently. Don't expect everyone to volunteer to speak openly on an electronic conference when they wouldn't in a live setting. Be patient.

Index

In a book of this length, covering a very wide range of aspects of learning, teaching, and assessment, a full index would be too long to be useful! I have, therefore, provided in this index only the *principal* pages where important topics are introduced.